T0182015

Lecture Notes of the Institute
for Computer Sciences, Social Informatics
and Telecommunications Engineering   351

More information about this series at http://www.springer.com/series/8197

Sanjay Goel · Pavel Gladyshev ·
Daryl Johnson · Makan Pourzandi ·
Suryadipta Majumdar (Eds.)

Digital Forensics and Cyber Crime

11th EAI International Conference, ICDF2C 2020
Boston, MA, USA, October 15–16, 2020
Proceedings

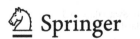 Springer

Editors
Sanjay Goel
State University of New York
University at Albany
Albany, NY, USA

Pavel Gladyshev
School of Computer Science
University College Dublin
Dublin, Ireland

Daryl Johnson
Rochester Institute of Technology
Rochester, NY, USA

Makan Pourzandi
Ericsson Security Research
Montréal, QC, Canada

Suryadipta Majumdar ⓘ
CIISE
Concordia University
Montréal, QC, Canada

ISSN 1867-8211   ISSN 1867-822X (electronic)
Lecture Notes of the Institute for Computer Sciences, Social Informatics
and Telecommunications Engineering
ISBN 978-3-030-68733-5   ISBN 978-3-030-68734-2 (eBook)
https://doi.org/10.1007/978-3-030-68734-2

This Springer imprint is published by the registered company Springer Nature Switzerland AG
The registered company address is: Gewerbestrasse 11, 6330 Cham, Switzerland

Preface

We are happy to publish the proceedings of the eleventh edition of the European Alliance for Innovation (EAI) International Conference on Digital Forensics & Cyber Crime (ICDF2C 2020). This conference is a platform for researchers, developers, and practitioners around the world to present and discuss a wide range of topics on digital forensics and cyber crime. The focus of ICDF2C 2020 was "various applications of digital evidence and forensics beyond "traditional" cybercrime investigations and litigation such as information security analytics, incident response, risk management, business and military intelligence, etc."

The technical program of ICDF2C 2020 consisted of 12 full papers. The conference program was organized in five different sessions as follows: Session 1 – Digital Forensics; Session 2 – Cyber-physical System Forensics; Session 3 – Event Reconstruction in Digital Forensics; Session 4 – Emerging Topics in Forensics; and Session 5 – Cybersecurity and Digital Forensics. In addition to top-quality presentations by the accepted paper authors, the conference program also included one keynote speech by Dr. Nicole Beebe from The University of Texas at San Antonio.

The coordination with the steering chair, Imrich Chlamtac, was essential for the success of the conference. We sincerely appreciate his constant support and guidance. It was also a great pleasure to work with such an excellent organizing committee team for their hard work in organizing and supporting the conference. In particular, the Technical Program Committee, led by our TPC Co-Chairs, Dr. Pavel Gladyshev, Dr. Daryl Johnson, and Dr. Makan Pourzandi, managed the review process of submitted full papers and poster papers and organized a high-quality program. We also want to thank Dr. Suryadipta Majumdar, publications chair, for coordinating with the authors to get the final camera ready papers. In addition, we are grateful to the Conference Manager, Natasha Onofrei, for her great support. Finally and most importantly, we are thankful to all the authors who submitted their papers to the ICDF2C 2020 conference.

We strongly believe that the ICDF2C conference provides a good platform for all researchers, developers, and practitioners to discuss various research topics on digital forensics and cyber crime. We also expect that future versions of the ICDF2C conference will continue its success and contribution in the field of digital forensics.

Sanjay Goel

Conference Organization

Steering Committee

Imrich Chlamtac   Bruno Kessler Professor University of Trento, Italy

Organizing Committee

General Chair

Sanjay Goel   University at Albany, SUNY, USA

TPC Chair and Co-chairs

Pavel Gladyshev   University College Dublin, Ireland
Daryl Johnson   Rochester Institute of Technology, USA
Makan Pourzandi   GTFL ER Security, Canada

Sponsorship Chair

Deborah Snyder   University at Albany, SUNY, USA

Workshops Chair

Devipsita Bhattacharya   University at Albany, SUNY, USA
Paulo Nunes   Federal University of Espírito Santo, Brazil

Publicity and Social Media Chairs

Deborah Snyder   University at Albany, SUNY, USA
Lee Spitzley   University at Albany, SUNY, USA
Suryadipta Majumdar   Concordia University, Canada

Publications Chair

Suryadipta Majumdar   Concordia University, Canada

Web Chair

Cristian Balan   SUNY Plattsburgh, USA

Tutorials Chairs

Babak Habibnia   University College Dublin, Ireland
Fabio Auffant   University at Albany, SUNY, USA

Conference Manager

Natasha Onofrei   EAI

Technical Program Committe

Ahmed Shosha	Microsoft
Alexey Chilikov	Bauman Moscow State Technical University
Anca Delia Jurcut	University College Dublin
Andreas Wespi	IBM Research Zurich
Aniello Castiglione	University of Naples Parthenope
Babak Habibnia	University College Dublin
Bo Chen	Michigan Technological University
Brian Nussbaum	University at Albany, SUNY
Corey Schou	Idaho State University
David Lillis	University College Dublin
Ding Wang	Nankai University
Farkhund Iqbal	Zayed University
Gary C. Kessler	Embry-Riddle Aeronautical University
George Markowsky	Missouri University of Science and Technology
Glenn Dardick	Embry-Riddle Aeronautical University
John Sheppard	Waterford Institute of Technology
Joshua I. James	Hallym University
Leon Reznik	Rochester Institute of Technology
Liliana Pasquale	University College Dublin
M. Fahim Ferdous Khan	Toyo University
M. P. Gupta	Indian Institute of Technology Delhi
Mark Scanlon	University College Dublin
Martin Loeb	University of Maryland
Martin Olivier	University of Pretoria
Mengjun Xie	University of Tennessee at Chattanooga
Michael Oehler	Government Mitigations
Mohan Kankanhalli	National University of Singapore
Nhien An Le Khac	University College Dublin
Omid Mirzaei	Northeastern University
Paulo Nunes	Federal University of Espírito Santo
Pradeep K. Atrey	University at Albany, SUNY
Prakash G.	Amrita Vishwa Vidyapeetham
P. Vinod Bhattathiripad	Hon. Advisor (IT) to the Director General of Police, Kerala, India
Raghu Santanam	Arizona State University
Sai Mounika Errapotu	University of Texas at El Paso
Sanjay Goel	University at Albany, SUNY
Shaikh Akib Shahriyar	Rochester Institute of Technology
Spiridon Bakiras	Hamad Bin Khalifa University
Stig F. Mjølsnes	Norwegian University for Science and Technology
Syed Shah	University of New South Wales

Vivienne Mee   VM Group
Umit Karabiyik   Purdue University
Xianzhi Wang   University of Technology Sydney
Xiaochun Cheng   Middlesex University London
Yuan Hong   Illinois Institute of Technology

Contents

On Reliability of JA3 Hashes
for Fingerprinting Mobile Applications

Petr Matoušek[1]([✉]), Ivana Burgetová[1], Ondřej Ryšavý[1], and Malombe Victor[2]

[1] Brno University of Technology, Brno, Czech Republic
{matousp,burgetova,rysavy}@fit.vutbr.cz
[2] Strathmore University, Nairobi, Kenya
vmalombe@strathmore.edu

Abstract. In recent years, mobile communication has become more secure due to TLS encapsulation. TLS enhances user security by encrypting transmitted data, on the other hand it limits network monitoring and data capturing which is important for digital forensics. When observing mobile traffic today most transmissions are encapsulated by TLS. Encrypted packets causes traditional methods to be obsolete for device fingerprinting that require visibility of protocol headers of HTTP, IMAP, SMTP, IM, etc. As a reaction to data encryption, new methods like TLS fingerprinting have been researched. These methods observe TLS parameters which are exchanged in an open form before the establishment of a secure channel. TLS parameters can be used for identification of a sending application. Nevertheless, with the constant evolution of TLS protocol suites, it is not easy to create a unique and stable TLS fingerprint for forensic purposes. This paper presents experiments with JA3 hashes on mobile apps. We focus especially on the stability, reliability and uniqueness of JA3 fingerprints for digital forensics.

Keywords: Mobile application · TLS fingerprinting · Network forensics · JA3 hash · Encrypted communication

1 Introduction

With the disclosure of millions of private documents on Wikileaks in 2015, users and companies massively started to improve the security of transmitted data, especially against the interception. A high demand for security of transmitted data led to the adoption of encrypted techniques by many network protocols. Today, the majority of network applications and services support only encrypted communication encapsulated by Transport Layer Security (TLS) [10,26].

Encryption was also adopted by many mobile app vendors. Table 1 shows the structure of network protocols involved in mobile communication. Datasets 1 to 4 created by the authors of this study in 2018 show that the ratio of encrypted communication to unencrypted varies from 51,7 to 91,7%. You may notice a

© ICST Institute for Computer Sciences, Social Informatics and Telecommunications Engineering 2021
Published by Springer Nature Switzerland AG 2021. All Rights Reserved
S. Goel et al. (Eds.): ICDF2C 2020, LNICST 351, pp. 1–22, 2021.
https://doi.org/10.1007/978-3-030-68734-2_1

Table 1. Encrypted and unencrypted mobile communication in 2018 and 2019

	2018				2019
	Dataset1	Dataset2	Dataset3	Dataset4	Dataset5
Time	70 min	12 min	37 min	21 min	96 min
Size	452 MB	35 MB	423 MB	18 MB	610 MB
Packets	542.725	44.699	424.922	25.525	597.097
Protocol	**Encrypted Traffic**				
SSL/TLS	44,26%	86,03%	30,52%	80,10%	98,06%
UDP over 443					1,12%
IMAPS	0,65%	1,67%			
FB Zero	0,65%	0,12%	0,01%	0,13%	
QUIC	6,15%	3,90%	4,74%	8,07%	
OpenVPN			54,94%		
Total	*51,71%*	*91,72%*	*90,21%*	*88,30%*	*99,18%*
Protocol	**Unencrypted Traffic**				
HTTP	41,47%	1,65%	7,55%	2,12%	0,32%
DNS, mDNS	0,93%	1,78%	0,64%	2,41%	0,31%
DHCP	0,05%	0,13%	0,04%	0,26%	0,01%
ICMP/IGMP	0,36%	0,53%	0,14%	0,60%	0,07%
ARP	2,11%	1,01%	1,62%	3,17%	0,06%
Total	*44,92%*	*5,10%*	*9,99%*	*8,56%*	*0,77%*

presence of non-encrypted HTTP traffic. Especially HTTP headers, e.g., *User-Agent, Accept-Language, Accept-Charset*, have been largely used as an important data source for various fingerprinting techniques [11,17].

A year after our first experiments, we noticed that the ratio of encrypted communication increased to 99% which prevented the further use of traditional fingerprinting methods. As seen in Fig. 1, besides the encrypted TLS traffic transmitted over port 443, only Domain Name System (DNS) data remained open. It is a question for how long because of various attempts to encrypt DNS traffic using DNS over TLS (DoT) or DNS over HTTP (DoH) [15,16].

As a reaction to the encryption, researchers focused their activity on analysing behavior of encrypted communication in order to obtain meta data about the encrypted traffic. One research direction is focused on statistical analysis of the encrypted transmissions [9,29], the other direction deals with the features obtained from a TLS handshake that form the so called *TLS fingerprint* [3,6,18,24]. A popular implementation of TLS fingerprinting called *JA3 fingerprinting* was proposed by John B. Althouse, Jeff Atkinson and Josh Atkins in 2015[1]. This method is incorporated into multiple network monitoring and intrusion detection systems (IDS) like Flowmon, Bro, or Suricata, where it serves for the malware detection [4], identification of network applications [19], or black listing[2].

In our research, we focus on mobile devices, especially on the detection of mobile apps in network traffic. One of the features of mobile apps is that they regularly communicate over the Internet without explicit user interaction because of software updates, data synchronization, or checking on the remote status [24].

---

[1] See https://github.com/salesforce/ja3 [April 2020].
[2] See SSLBL project at https://sslbl.abuse.ch/ [April 2020].

This makes it possible to identify a mobile device based on a characteristic set of applications installed on the device [20]. Mobile apps can be identified from the captured TLS traffic using JA3 hashes (retrieved from the client's side of communication) or JA3S hashes (the server's side of communication).

However, there are important questions related to digital forensics: *Are these fingerprints reliable enough to identify a specific application? How stable are they? How can we create a unique fingerprint database of a mobile app?* The goal of this paper is to study the reliability of JA3 fingerprints on selected mobile apps, to demonstrate how unique fingerprints can be generated and to discuss the application of JA3 fingerprinting to the digital forensics.

1.1 Contribution

This work analyses the utilization of JA3 fingerprints for mobile apps identification. We primarily focus on the reliability and stability of JA3 fingerprints. Based on our experiments we found out that JA3 hashes alone are not sufficient for mobile app identification due to the high number of JA3 hashes common to multiple apps. By introducing additional TLS features like the JA3S server hash and Server Name Indication (SNI) extension, more accurate identification becomes possible. One of the contributions is a procedure describing the generation of unambiguous fingerprints for a given app. We also show the advantages and limits of the proposed technique. The second contribution is the generation of datasets with the captured traffic of mobile apps that contain the full TLS communication useful for further experiments with TLS fingerprinting. The third contribution includes a discussion of the stability and reliability of JA3 fingerprints which is important for digital forensics and mobile app identification.

1.2 Structure of the Text

The paper is structured as follows. Section 2 overviews recent works related to TLS fingerprinting and mobile apps identification. Section 3 gives the background of JA3 fingerprinting method and discusses its reliability for mobile apps identification. The main part of the paper is in Sect. 4 which describes how extended JA3 fingerprints of mobile apps are created and used for identification. Section 5 brings the results of our experiments and the evaluation of the proposed technique on the datasets. Section 6 discusses the application of TLS fingerprinting to digital forensics. The last section concludes our findings.

2 Related Work

TLS fingerprinting is not a new technique and its development is connected with the security research of Ivan Ristić who developed in 2008 an Apache module that passively fingerprinted connected clients based on cipher suites. Using this technique he created a signature base that identified many browsers and operating systems [1]. This technique was later applied on the identification of

HTTP clients [18] and implemented in IDS systems Bro and Surikata for passive detection.

Blake Anderson et al. in [4] studied millions of TLS encrypted flows and introduced a set of observable data features from TLS client and server hello messages like TLS version, TLS ciphers suites and TLS extensions that they used for malware detection. They also observed the server's certificate and the client's public key length, sequence of record lengths, times and types of TLS sessions. They identified cipher suites and extensions that were present in malware traffic and missing in normal traffic. The authors defined the TLS client configurations for the 18 malicious families. Similarly, they identified the TLS server configurations most visited by the 18 malicious families. They applied TLS features together with other features (flow data, inter-arrival times, byte distribution) to malware classification and achieved an accuracy from 96.7% to 98.2%. As demonstrated by their study, omitting TLS features led to a significantly worse performance.

Kotzias et al. [19] passively monitored the TLS and SSL connections from 2012 to 2015 and observed changes in TLS cipher suites and extensions offered by clients and accepted by servers. They also used client TLS fingerprinting with features similar to JA3 fingerprinting. From handshakes they omitted GREASE values. Using the captured data, they observed 7.3% fingerprint collisions in the TLS fingerprints. They also mapped fingerprints to a program or library and the version. One of their main results was the observation of the TLS fingerprints stability. They noticed that the maximum duration of a fingerprint seen in their databases was 1.235 days (3 years, 4 months). However, the median of duration 1 day and the mean was 158.8 days. They noticed some fingerprints that were seen very briefly and did not reappear later. They found out that 1,203 fingerprints of the 69,874 fingerprints were responsible for 21.75% of connections. Further, they analysed the vulnerability of TLS against various attacks which is a different direction comparing to our research. Their results related to the stability and collisions of TLS fingerprints was also observed in our experiments.

Another interesting approach published by Anderson and McGrew [3] combines the end host data with the network data in order to understand application behavior. This approach, however, requires an access to both the end hosts and the network. Their fingerprint database represented the real traffic generated by 24,000 hosts and having 471 million benign and millions of malware connections[3]. Using the end point data, the authors were able to associate the destination information with the end point data like the timestamp, endpoint ID, operating system and process name. They also observed that while GREASE values are generated randomly, their position is deterministic. Thus, instead of removing GREASE values, they set them to a fixed string 0a0a. They also studied the similarity of TLS fingerprints using Levenshtein distance. Two TLS fingerprints were similar if their distance was less than or equal to 10% of the number of cipher suites, the extension types, and the extension values. The authors stated that the Levenshtein distance was an intuitive method for identifying close fingerprints. Especially TLS libraries often make minor adjustments

---

[3] Data capturing tools are available at https://github.com/cisco/mercury [April 2020].

to the default cipher suites or extensions between the minor version releases and more drastic changes between the major version releases. They also noticed that some TLS libraries change their default parameters to better suit the platform on which they are running. Another interesting point is the prevalence of application categories in the dataset where 37.1% connections belong to browsers, 19.3% to email applications, 17,2% to communication tools, 9% to the system, etc. Longevity of fingerprints like system libraries, tools osquery and DropBox, and browsers was 6 months or greater.

The above mentioned approaches worked mostly with common network traffic and network application. Another work closer to ours deals with TLS usage in Android Apps [24]. The authors analyzed the behavior of TLS in mobile platforms. They developed an Android app Lumen that was installed on a mobile device where it intercepted the TLS connections and gathered statistics about the traffic. Using Lumen, the authors observed how 7.258 apps use TLS. They analyzed handshakes with respect to the TLS API and the library that the app used. Their work was focused on apps security and TLS vulnerabilities. They showed that TLS libraries and OS API modified supported cipher suites across versions which caused changes in the TLS fingerprints. They also showed that each TLS library and OS version had a unique cipher suite lists. They built a database of fingerprints paired with corresponding OSes and libraries where they observed the influence of major and minor revisions of OS or TLS libraries on the fingerprint. Unfortunately, Lumen was not able to captured TLS handshakes which would have been useful to our research. Thus, we used an additional approach of how to obtain reliable TLS fingerprints of mobile apps.

The mobile application fingerprinting using characteristic traffic was considered by Stöber et al. [28]. They created a classifier that identified communicating applications based on the analysis of side-channel information such as timing and data volume. Mobile application fingerprinting has been tackled by machine learning techniques using timing and size of packets [31], which improved previous work presented in [30] that observed the traffic that was common among more than one apps. The method is applicable to encrypted traffic, which is used by most smartphone applications and relies only on information available from the side channel. The fingerprinting system was trained and tested on 110 most popular Android applications. The training was done automatically using the implemented application AppScanner. The significant feature of the method was that it analyzed the traffic represented as bursts. A burst was defined as a group of packets within TCP flow representing an interaction for a typical smartphone application that communicated using HTTPS protocol. Statistical features were then extracted for bursts and used for training random forests classifier. The method did not rely on any other source of information, e.g., DNS, TLS, IP addresses, etc. The achieved accuracy as presented by the authors was between 73 to 96% for the selected set of applications. Recently, the work was extended by [12] that used a semi-supervised method for both app recognition and detection of previously unseen apps.

Another line of research that considered mobile device identification is represented by Govindaraj, Verma and Gupta [14]. They proposed a methodology for extracting and analyzing ads on mobile devices to retrieve user-specific information, reconstruct a user profile, and predict user identity. As the published results showed it was possible to identify a user in various settings even if he/she used multiple devices or different networks. Their work stemmed from the study by Castelluccia, Kafar and Tran [7] who demonstrated the possibility to infer user interests from targeted ads.

Our work uses previously published results and focuses on passive identification of mobile apps using JA3 fingerprints. It also observes traffic that is common to multiple apps and that should be excluded from fingerprinting. Based on the app, we employ JA3, JA3S, and Server Name Indication (SNI) features to accurately identify the unknown traffic that was sent by a mobile app. We are able to detect only apps that were previously learnt and stored in the fingerprinting database. Unlike some of the above mentioned approaches, our technique for mobile app detection is simple, fast and reliable. Its accuracy depends on the quality of learnt fingerprints.

3   How JA3 Fingerprinting Works

In this section we give a brief overview of principles of TLS communication and JA3 hashing that is necessary for understanding the proposed method.

Transport Layer Security (TLS) [10,26] is a transmission protocol that works on top of TCP where it provides privacy and data integrity for communicating applications. The protocol is composed of two parts: TLS Handshake Protocol and TLS Record Protocol. TLS Handshake Protocol negotiates the security parameters, e.g., version, methods for key exchange, encryption, authentication, and data integrity, secure channel options, etc. TLS handshake communication is not encrypted. The TLS Record Protocol encapsulates high-level protocol data and transmits encrypted packets. An example of TLS handshake is in Fig. 1.

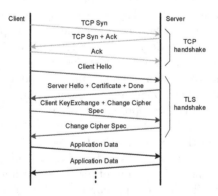

Fig. 1. Establishing TLS connection.

After opening a TCP connection by a three-way handshake, the TLS negotiates security parameters using TLS Client and Server Hello packets. The client application offers a set of supported encryption and authentication methods using the TLS Client Hello. The TLS server processes these options and sends back options that are supported on the server side. The server can also include a server certificate to authenticate itself. After all security parameters are agreed on, the application data encapsulated by TLS Record Protocol are exchanged.

Most of TLS fingerprinting methods use the first packet sent by the client: the *Client Hello*. The Client Hello contains an imprint of TLS configuration of the client application that depends on the used TLS library and operating system. In this paper we study *JA3 fingerprint* that is computed as an MD5 hash from five TLS handshake fields: TLS Handshake version, Cipher suites, Extensions, Supported Groups (former Elliptic Curve), and Elliptic Curve point format, see Fig. 2. Some TLS fingerprinting implementations use different TLS fields, e.g., Kotzias et al. [19] omit the TLS version.

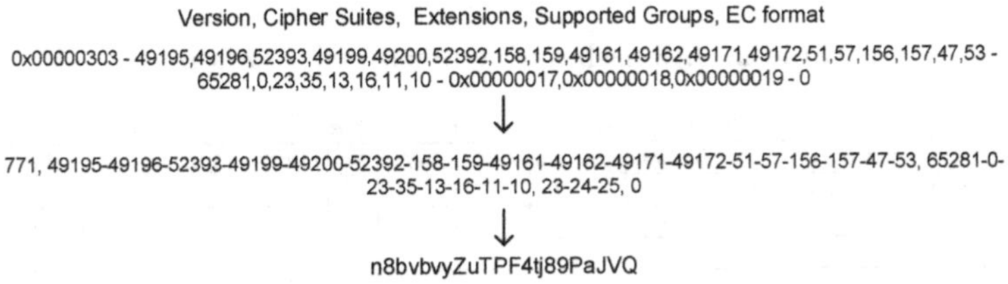

Version, Cipher Suites, Extensions, Supported Groups, EC format

0x00000303 - 49195,49196,52393,49199,49200,52392,158,159,49161,49162,49171,49172,51,57,156,157,47,53 -
65281,0,23,35,13,16,11,10 - 0x00000017,0x00000018,0x00000019 - 0

$\downarrow$

771, 49195-49196-52393-49199-49200-52392-158-159-49161-49162-49171-49172-51-57-156-157-47-53, 65281-0-
23-35-13-16-11-10, 23-24-25, 0

$\downarrow$

n8bvbvyZuTPF4tj89PaJVQ

Fig. 2. Computing JA3 hash

The computation of JA3 fingerprint includes (i) the extraction of selected fields from TLS Hello packet, (ii) concatenation of extracted data in decimal format into one string, and (iii) application of MD5 hash algorithm on the string. The result is a 32-bit string in hexadecimal format. There are open implementations of JA3 fingerprinting available[4]. Unlike nmap or web browser fingerprinting methods which actively request the source device or application, JA3 fingerprinting uses a passive approach. The process of creating TLS fingerprints is fast because it only works with a TLS header. Common network monitoring and IDS tools implement the extraction of TLS parameters for analysis of the encrypted network traffic.

The application of TLS fingerprints to the identification of network apps requires TLS fingerprint values to be unique, accurate and stable. The following subsections describe aspects that limits the reliability of TLS fingerprints.

3.1   Impact of TLS Library on JA3 Hashes

A TLS fingerprint of a mobile app depends on the TLS library that was used during its implementation. There are plenty of TLS libraries available to developers, e.g., GnuTLS, Oracle JSSE, BSD LibreSSL, OpenSSL, or Mozilla NSS.

---

[4] See https://github.com/salesforce/ja3 or https://ja3er.com/ [April 2020].

When two applications are implemented using the same TLS library, their TLS fingerprints are usually the same. TLS fingerprints can also change with a new version of the app, TLS library, or operating system. This change can be caused by adding strong ciphers or removing weak ciphers, changing default parameters that better suit the running platform, or by adopting a new standard.

Table 2 shows JA3 hashes for popular web browsers: Mozilla Firefox v.73, Chrome v.80, and Opera v.66 under four operating systems: Linux Ubuntu, Windows 10, Kali Linux and Mac OS. We can see that Firefox has four unique JA3 fingerprints. Two of them are present in all tested operating systems. In case of Chrome and Opera, one JA3 fingerprint value corresponds to both browsers under all operating systems. These browsers were possibly compiled with the same TLS library. This experiment proves that TLS fingerprints change with the version and operating system. A similar experiment over a larger dataset was carried out by Razaghpanak et al. [24].

Table 2. JA3 hashes of common Web browsers

JA3 hash	Firefox				Chrome				Opera			
	Ubuntu	Win	Kali	MacOS	Ubuntu	Win	Kali	MacOS	Ubuntu	Win	Kali	MacOS
0e6f3c8f2b18f3011f1d6cbbdcfcbd65						x				x		
1344ed2e9d7d8e3e84e6ab655047ba32	x	x	x	x								
1f3c530fc35e41300422550c3c980e85						x	x		x	x	x	x
4863015f73b8332cf91cfa3a14a4893d		x										
5a291b49748c50adf1da70f8142d4cc4					x				x			
756094f51da8214018fbfba93211d59f	x	x	x	x								
a839cfeed30d55439b09de5f1b47fa3a					x	x	x	x	x	x	x	x
d889531a0389787425d5638caf6d84b3					x	x	x	x	x	x	x	
d90d517f72e9b8af9a8c1e2fe1fb2da8	x			x								

3.2 Randomized Values in TLS Extensions

In 2016, Google started to Generate Random Extensions And Sustain Extensibility (GREASE) values to TLS. This technique was adopted by IETF in January 2020 as RFC 8701 [5]. GREASE values are randomly generated numbers of cipher suites, extensions and supported groups present in TLS Hello packets. They prevent extensibility failures in TLS ecosystem. During TLS handshake, the responding side must ignore unknown values. Peers that do not ignore unknown values fail to inter-operate which means a bug in the implementation. Therefore, RFC 8701 adds GREASE values as a part of the list of cipher suites, extensions and supported groups to detect the invalid implementations.

When experimenting with Opera browser under Win 10 we noticed that the browser generates 155 unique JA3 fingerprints out of 207 TLS handshakes. By excluding GREASE values, the number of unique JA3 fingerprints decreased to four. The high number of JA3 fingerprints was caused by random GREASE values in TLS handshakes. Table 3 shows six JA3 fingerprints of Opera browser under Ubuntu with all extracted TLS values (the upper six lines). The last six lines presents TLS values without GREASE values. The brown values in the upper table represent GREASE values as defined in [5]. When ignoring these values, the last four lines in the upper table would have the same JA3 hashes.

Table 3. JA3 hashes with and without GREASE values

List of Cipher Suites	List of Extensions	Supported Group	JA3 hash
49199-49200-49195-49196-52392-52393-49171-49161-49172-49162-156-157-47-53-49170-10	13172-0-5-10-11-13-65281-16-18	29-23-24-25	839868ad711dc55bde0d37a87f14740d
49199-49200-49195-49196-52392-52393-49171-49161-49172-49162-156-157-47-53-49170-10	13172-0-5-10-11-13-65281-16-18	29-23-24-25	839868ad711dc55bde0d37a87f14740d
56026-4865-4866-4867-49195-49199-49196-49200-52393-52392-49171-49172-156-157-47-53-10	60138-0-23-65281-10-11-35-16-5-13-18-51-45-43-27-19018-21	35466-29-23-24	ee972d7d47ec01a9cb9b04efb7946e32
60138-4865-4866-4867-49195-49199-49196-49200-52393-52392-49171-49172-156-157-47-53-10	39578-0-23-65281-10-11-35-16-5-13-18-51-45-43-27-56026-21	23130-29-23-24	cb4415a180704432d2e3f70f8dca5783
31354-4865-4866-4867-49195-49199-49196-49200-52393-52392-49171-49172-156-157-47-53-10	47802-0-23-65281-10-11-35-16-5-13-18-51-45-43-27-51914	43690-29-23-24	74a57a5f55ce2c9fe637b1f4567308b4
14906-4865-4866-4867-49195-49199-49196-49200-52393-52392-49171-49172-156-157-47-53-10	31354-0-23-65281-10-11-35-16-5-13-18-51-45-43-27-43690	58026-29-23-24	a10f93ffdc89d383db0f4437a0530569
49199-49200-49195-49196-52392-52393-49171-49161-49172-49162-156-157-47-53-49170-10	13172-0-5-10-11-13-16-18	29-23-24-25	5a291b49748c50adf1da70f8142d4cc4
49199-49200-49195-49196-52392-52393-49171-49161-49172-49162-156-157-47-53-49170-10	13172-0-5-10-11-13-16-18	29-23-24-25	5a291b49748c50adf1da70f8142d4cc4
4865-4866-4867-49195-49199-49196-49200-52393-52392-49171-49172-156-157-47-53-10	0-23-10-11-35-16-5-13-18-51-45-43-27	29-23-24	a839cfeed30d55439b09de5f1b47fa3a
4865-4866-4867-49195-49199-49196-49200-52393-52392-49171-49172-156-157-47-53-10	0-23-10-11-35-16-5-13-18-51-45-43-27	29-23-24	a839cfeed30d55439b09de5f1b47fa3a
4865-4866-4867-49195-49199-49196-49200-52393-52392-49171-49172-156-157-47-53-10	0-23-10-11-35-16-5-13-18-51-45-43-27	29-23-24	a839cfeed30d55439b09de5f1b47fa3a
4865-4866-4867-49195-49199-49196-49200-52393-52392-49171-49172-156-157-47-53-10	0-23-10-11-35-16-5-13-18-51-45-43-27	29-23-24	a839cfeed30d55439b09de5f1b47fa3a

In addition to GREASE values, it is also good to omit extension value 65281 from TLS fingerprinting. This value represents renegotiation option in TLS handshake [27], see red numbers in the list of extensions. Additionally, TLS Client Hello Padding Extension defined by RFC 7685 [23] can be omitted. The padding extension (value 21, depicted by green value in the table) is added by a client to make sure that the packet is of a desired size.

The above mentioned values can be added by a TLS client or server based on the local setting of a network connection which means they produce volatility of JA3 fingerprints. By removing these values we can increase the stability of JA3 fingerprints. Most of the JA3 implementations already ignore GREASE values.

3.3 Ads and Tracking Services in TLS Traffic

By observing TLS handshakes of mobile apps, we noticed that an app does not open the connection to its application server only, but it communicates with various sides without explicit user activity. These connections include ad servers, tracking services, or web analytic servers. This is typical especially for free apps that receive funding from ads providers. The destinations of these services are usually dynamic which means that each time the application is launched, it connects to a different site with a different TLS fingerprint. This causes problem for finding ground-truth communication for learning TLS fingerprints.

Dynamic behavior of ad connections is caused by mobile advertising auctions that redirect the app from the ad server to the content provider based on the results of an auction [21]. Since different mobile apps include the same ad, tracking or analytic plugins, the captured traffic of these apps contain the same TLS fingerprints. This extra traffic is called *a communication noise* or *ambiguous traffic* [31]. Table 4 shows TLS fingerprints obtained from Gmail app communication. There are five different JA3 fingerprints computed from captured TLS handshakes that were invoked by the Gmail app. Using the Server Name Indication (SNI) extension we can recognize the noise traffic directed to Google API (www.googleapis.com) and Google user content (googleusercontent.com). This traffic is not directly related to the app and can be found in communication of other apps. The remaining fingerprint with SNI mail.google.com uniquely characterizes the Gmail app. Thus, it is important to exclude ad, tracking and analytic traffic from TLS fingerprinting. One solution how to remove the noise traffic is using available black lists of ad and tracking servers[5]. By comparing server names in SNI field of TLS handshake with names of ad servers in the black lists, we can partially clean up the captured TLS communication from the noise during the learning phase. Table 5 shows a percentage of the noise for selected mobile apps. Especially free apps include ad plugins producing such noise.

Table 4. JA3 hashes of Gmail App

SrcIP	DstIP	Server Name Indication	JA3 Fingerprint
10.0.2.15	172.217.23.193	ci5.googleusercontent.com	d5dcde95b8fa38b5062a128f7eff0737
10.0.2.15	172.217.23.225	ci3.googleusercontent.com	d5dcde95b8fa38b5062a128f7eff0737
10.0.2.15	172.217.23.229	mail.google.com	81d2604dcc31ff39cdddb6079692b0b0
10.0.2.15	216.58.201.106	www.googleapis.com	193c522402283ed9e84b8bb38137829f
10.0.2.15	216.58.201.106	www.googleapis.com	3d9a16cdc1b2a98f6046af1c833054b8
10.0.2.15	216.58.201.74	android.googleapis.com	ca75d9d90e40897206fa2a08d9100df0
10.0.2.15	216.58.201.97	ci4.googleusercontent.com	d5dcde95b8fa38b5062a128f7eff0737

3.4 Time Stability of JA3 Hashes

A very important issue related to the mobile apps fingerprinting is the stability of TLS fingerprints over time. We demonstrated, that a TLS fingerprint depends on TLS library and operating system, see Sect. 3.1. An update of the TLS library, adding new or excluding weaker ciphers can change the fingerprint. The longitudinal study of TLS fingerprints of Kotzias et al. [19] shows that the maximum duration of TLS fingerprints is 3 years and 4 months (median is 1 day, mean 158,8 days). If the app is not updated, it keeps its original TLS fingerprint.

Table 5. The number of TLS connections to Ad servers for selected Apps

App	All TLS handshakes	AD servers	Percentage
Accuweather	520	232	45%
BoomPlay Music	361	53	15%
Gmail	60	6	10%
Tor Browser	9	0	0%
Reddit	1892	840	44%
Muj vlak	451	195	43%
Viber	12	6	50%
Discord	24	0	0%
TitTok	203	20	10%
WhatsApp	243	30	12%
NextBike	444	39	9%
Facebook	178	13	7%
EquaBank	387	14	4%

---

[5] E.g., https://hosts-file.net/ad_servers.txt, https://pgl.yoyo.org/adservers/, or https://gitlab.com/ookangzheng/dbl-oisd-nl [April 2020].

The time instability means that for successful identification of mobile apps based on TLS fingerprints, we need to update the fingerprint database whenever a new version is released, otherwise the app will not be correctly identified. Nevertheless, our experiments show that the variability of TLS fingerprints is not so large and fingerprints stay the same even when an OS is updated.

4 Identification of Mobile Apps Using TLS Fingerprinting

This section describes how TLS fingerprints are created (learning phase) and used for mobile apps identification (detection phase).

4.1 Learning TLS Fingerprints

As mentioned above, the crucial task for mobile apps identification using TLS fingerprints is to create a reliable fingerprint database with unambiguous entries. Even if an app is running in the controlled environment like the Android Virtual Studio, the captured traffic contains a mixture of app traffic with communication of OS, pre-installed apps and plugins that are common to multiple apps. Here, we introduced a technique, how to clean up the captured traffic in order to receive only TLS handshake related to the given app, see Fig. 3.

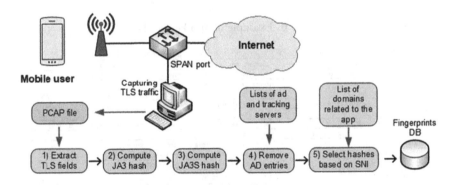

Fig. 3. Creating TLS fingerprints

First, we need to launch an app communication on the mobile device. We made experiments both with virtual devices running on the Android Virtual Studio (datasets MA2, MA3) and on real devices (datasets MA1, MA4). When using the virtual environment, we can capture network traffic on the interface connected to the virtual environment. However, there can also be communication of virtual OS and other applications installed on the system. When using real smart phones, we can create a WiFi connection only for this device and capture traffic on the WiFi interface. Fingerprint creation include the following steps:

1. Extract TLS Client Hello packets where `tls.handshake.type==1` and obtain the following data: source and destination IP address, source and destination port, TLS handshake type (client or server hello), SNI, a list of TLS cipher suites, extensions, supported groups, and EC point format. Exclude GREASE values, padding and renegotiation options, see Sect. 3.

2. Compute JA3 hash using TLS values in TLS Client Hello packet as explained in Sect. 3. Apply MD5 hash function on TLS version, a list of cipher suites, list of extensions, supported groups and EC point format. JA3 hash uses MD5 function with 32-bit output in hexadecimal format.

3. Compute JA3S hash using TLS values in a Server Hello packet. Link the JA3S hash with the JA3 hash using IP addresses and ports. The JA3S hash is a MD5 digest of the TLS version, cipher suite and extensions only.

4. Based on the list of ad servers and tracking servers, remove TLS fingerprints where SNI matches any domain name present in these lists.

5. From candidate TLS fingerprints select only those fingerprints that are related to the app based on matching SNI field with keywords related to the app. Keywords can be obtained manually or using the tools Lumen or AppVersion that show information about the app like domain names. An example of keywords that match the app SNI names is listed in Table 6. In most cases, keywords also include the app name. Formally, the keyword is the maximum common substring of all SNI names related to the app.

Table 6. Example of app keywords

Application	Keyword (s)	SNI
BoomPlay Music	boomplaymusic	source.boomplaymusic.com, android.boomplaymusic.com
Accuweather	accuweather, accu-weather	api.accuweather.com, cms.accuweather.com, vortex.accuweather.com
Viber	viber	content.cdn.viber.com
Discord	discord	best.discord.media, discordapp.com, dl.discordapp.net, gateway.discord.gg, ...
Mobilni Banka	mojebanka.cz, mobilnibanka.cz	www.mojebanka.cz, wa.mojebanka
KB klic	kb.cz	login.kb.cz, www.kb.cz
Nextbike	nextbike.net	api.nextbike.net, maps.nextbike.net, my.nextbike.net, static.nextbike.net, ...
EquaBank CZ	equa.cz, equamobile.cz	acs.equa.cz, ma.equamobile.cz
TitTok	tiktok	abtest-va-tiktok.byteoversea.com, mon.tiktokv.com
Duolingo	duolingo	android-api.duolingo.com, duolingo-leaderboard-prod.duolingo.com, ...
Youtube	youtube	www.youtube.com, youtubei.googleapis.com
Google Calendar	calendarsync	calendarsync-pa.googleapis.com
WhatsApp	whatsapp	media-prgl-l.cdn.whatsapp.net, pps.whatsapp.net, static.whatsapp.net
Gmail	mail.google.com, inbox.google.com	mail.google.com, inbox.google.com
Muj vlak	timetable.cz	ipws2.timetable.cz

This procedure does not guarantee uniqueness of the obtained fingerprints which is essential for successful detection. When analysing JA3 fingerprints learnt from our datasets, we noticed that there were 30 distinct fingerprints, however, many of them belonged to multiple applications. Only 21 JA3 hashes were assigned unambiguously reaching uniqueness of 70%. Thus, we added JA3S fingerprint to a feature set and obtained 122 distinct combinations with 114 unique fingerprints related to only one app. Remember that one app can have a set of unique fingerprints. Combination of JA3+JA3S increased uniqueness to 93,44%

but there were still several JA3+JA3S combinations that belonged to more than one app. After adding SNI to a feature set we received 154 distinct combinations with 153 combinations related to only one app. The results are given in Table 7.

Table 7. Uniqueness of features in the TLS fingerprint

Feature	Distinct items	Unique items	Uniqueness
JA3	30	21	70,00%
JA3+JA3S	122	114	93,44%
JA3+JA3S+SNI	154	153	99,35%

The number of unique fingerprints does not express, how many applications from our MA datasets we can cover with these fingerprints. We further analysed the sets of unique fingerprints to reveal this information. When using JA3 hashes only, we can uniquely identify only 33,33% of apps from our dataset. Remaining apps cannot be identified with JA3 hashes only (66,67%), because there are no unique JA3 hashes for these apps in our datasets. When adding JA3S hashes, we are able to cover 79,17% of apps from our datasets. Adding SNI to a feature set increase the coverage of apps to 91,67%. Using all three features, we were not able to cover 2 of 24 apps - Messenger and Telegram.

It seems that the combination of JA3, JA3S and SNI provides unique and reliable TLS fingerprints of mobile apps. This statements is not always true. It depends on the function of the mobile app. Most mobile apps communicate only with a limited number of servers related to the app. Some apps, for instance web browsers, communicate with an open set of destinations based on user activity. These apps cannot be identified by JA3S and SNI because these features depend on the destination which changes by each connection. Also for applications that connect to servers with random or anonymized domain names, only JA3 hash can be employed for app identification. Interestingly, the JA3 hash of Tor app was unambiguous and sufficient for successful identification. Most of the apps, however, require the full combination of JA3, JA3S and SNI features.

4.2 Detection of Mobile Applications Using TLS Fingerprints

The above written procedure describes a generation of TLS fingerprints from captured TLS traffic. The process includes TLS data pre-processing and refinement that produces a unique TLS fingerprint composed of JA3 hash only, combination of JA3+JA3S or JA3+JA3S+SNI. Having such fingerprints, we can monitor unknown network traffic, retrieve selected values from the TLS Hello packets, and compute JA3 and JA3S hashes. By comparison with the fingerprint database, we can identify an app that initiated this communication.

4.3 Stability and Reliability of TLS Fingerprinting

As mentioned in Sect. 3, the stability of TLS fingerprints of a mobile app depends on an app version, TLS library, and operating system. When using JA3S hashes, it also depends on the server version and its TLS library. This means that we have to update our fingerprint database whenever a new version of the app is released. The fingerprint can be generated using the procedure described in Sect. 4.1. In some cases, a new version may keep the same fingerprint as the previous one. Fingerprint stability is demonstrated on experiments with dataset MA3 where we observed TLS fingerprints of four apps on Android 7.1, 8.1 and 9. The results are presented in Table 8. The first column represents the number of unique values of JA3, JA3S and SNI in the TLS fingerprint of a given mobile app under Android 7. Columns Android 8.1 and 9 show the number of features that were added or missing in comparison to the previous version. We can see that SNI for CP app and Mujvlak are stable across versions. JA3S hash of CP app was changed when migrating from version 7 to 8 but it stayed unchanged to version 9. Adding new values does not negate stability of the fingerprint because the original fingerprint can still identify the app. If there are more additions, it may happen that the fingerprint of the older version would not match newly added features (false negative). However, when updating the fingerprint database by a new fingerprint, the accuracy of the identification is preserved.

Table 8. Stability of TLS fingerprints over OS version

Mobile App	Android 7	Android 8.1		Android 9	
Feature	present	added	missing	added	missing
CP JA3	1	1	1	0	0
CP JA3S	2	2	2	0	0
CP SNI	2	0	0	0	0
Mujvlak JA3	1	1	1	0	0
Mujvlak JA3S	1	0	0	0	0
Mujvlak SNI	1	0	0	0	0
Reddit JA3	1	2	1	0	0
Reddit JA3S	1	2	1	0	0
Reddit SNI	9	3	2	4	0
Seznam CZ JA3	3	3	3	2	1
Seznam CZ JA3S	11	0	0	2	0
Seznam CZ SNI	12	0	1	1	0

5   Experiments

This section describes our experiments with fingerprinting mobile apps. First, we describe our datasets and then achieved results of mobile apps identification.

5.1   Datasets

This section introduces datasets used in the experiments. First we observed available datasets with the mobile traffic. ReCon dataset[6] [25] was created to observe leakage of personal identifiers through mobile communication. The dataset contains HTTP(s) logs of 512 mobile apps. The logs do not contain TLS headers that are important for TLS fingerprinting. However, for a given mobile app, we can

---

[6] See htttps://recon.meddle.mobi/appversions/ [April 2020].

extract a list of sites the app usually connects to. For example, for `accuweather` app, we get fonts.googleapis.com or ssl.google-analytics.com (noise servers), and vortex.accuweather.com or accuwxturbo.accu-weather.com (app related domain names). These domain names can be traced in SNI extension during the TLS analysis which is important for creating unambiguous fingerprints.

An interesting mobile apps dataset is Panoptispy[7] [22] that was created to study media permissions and leaks from Android apps. The dataset consists of network traffic that have instances of media in an HTTP requests body. Besides dumps of HTTP requests, it contains a list of apps with a package name, version, app name and app md5. However, this is not sufficient for TLS fingerprinting.

Andrubis and Cross Platform datasets mentioned in [12] were not located by the authors of this paper. Nevertheless, we explored Mirage dataset[8] [2] which contains mobile app traffic for ground-truth evaluation. The captured traffic is stored in a JSON format and contains the bi-flows with src/dst ports, number of bytes, inter-arrival times, TCP window size, L4 raw data, and various statistics. Since the TLS header is hidden in byte-wise raw L4 payload, it is not easy to extract TLS values that are interesting for our research. However, we plan to use this data for a ground-truth evaluation of our method presented in the paper.

For our experiments we created our own dataset that contains communication of selected mobile apps, see Table 9. We ran the app five to ten times on the same platform in order to receive a representative sample of the traffic. In case of MA3 database we ran each app 10 to 20 times on the three Android's versions with and without cache (after restarting a device) in order to observe the impact on the temporary data saved in the cache. That is why dataset MA3 is larger.

Table 9. Mobile apps communication dataset

Dataset	Apps	Device	OS	PCAP (MB)	Packets	TLS Handshakes	List of Apps
Web browsers (WB)	3	PC	Linux, MacOS, Win 10	193	224.717	2.621	Chrome, Firefox, Opera
Mobile Apps I (MA1)	5	Sony, Huawei	Android 9, 7.0	2	5.700	79	Discord, Messenger, Slack, Telegram, WhatsApp
Mobile Apps II (MA2)	4	Android Studio	Android 6	35	50.820	595	Accuweather, Gmail, Tor, Viber
Mobile Apps III (MA3)	4	Android Studio	Android 7.1, 8,1, 9	827	642.919	3.180.345	Cestovne Poriadky, Mujvlak, Reddit, Seznam
Mobile Apps IV (MA4)	14	Tecno	Android 5.1	446	578.812	5.308	Boomplay Music, Chrome, EquaBank, Facebook, ...
Total	30			1504	1.502.968	3.188.948	

Even if using a small number of apps, our datasets are sufficient for studying typical features of TLS mobile apps fingerprints: uniqueness, stability and reliability, and for training and detection of mobile apps. These datasets are available in PCAP format in github[9] and contain five parts:

Web Browsers (WB). The first dataset consists of TLS communication of web browsers Chrome v80, Firefox 68.2, Firefox 73.0, Firefox 70.0, Opera 66.0 and

---

[7] See https://recon.meddle/mobi/panoptispy [April 2020].

[8] See https://ieee-dataport.org/open-access/mirage-mobile-app-traffic-capture-and-ground-truth-creation [April 2020].

[9] See https://github.com/matousp/ja3s-fingerprinting [July 2020].

Opera 67.0. These browsers were running under four different operating systems: Kali Linux, Mac OS, Windows 10 and Linux Ubuntu. During experiments we requested 10 different URLs. We created TLS fingerprints for all browsers based on TLS handshakes related to requested URLs. The dataset contains 2.621 TLS handshakes. It does not contain mobile traffic. It was used to observe an impact of TLS libraries on JA3 fingerprints, see Sect. 3.1.

Mobile Apps I (MA1). The second dataset includes five mobile applications: Discord v16.3, Messenger v253.0, Slack v20.03, Telegram v6.0 and WhatsApp v2.20. The applications were installed on two mobile devices: Sony Xperia X71 Compact with Android 9 (API level 28) and Huawei P9 with Android 7 and EMUI 5.0.1 (API level 24). Devices were connected to a PC and TLS data captured using `tshark`. To make sure that the packets include initial handshake, the tested application were restarted using ADB commands. The dataset contains 79 TLS handshakes.

Mobile Apps II (MA2). The third dataset includes communication of four mobile applications: Accuweather, Gmail, Tor and Viber. For tests, we used Android Emulator which is a part of Android Studio. In the Android Emulator, we created two virtual devices: Google Pixel C with Android 8.1 and Google Nexus 10 with Android 6.0. Using ADB interface we installed the above mentioned mobile applications on the virtual device and simulated user behavior using the command-line tool *Monkey*. The Monkey emulates user behavior on a given app, thus the captured traffic is initiated by this app only. An example of emulating Viber app on the virtual device is below. The dataset contains 595 TLS handshakes.

```
$adb shell monkey -p viber -v 500  # emulate 500 events on package viber
```

Mobile Apps III (MA3). This dataset includes communication of the following mobile applications: Cestovne Poriadky (Time Table), Muj vlak (My train), Reddit and Seznam. TLS fingerprints of these apps were obtained using Virtual Box where these apps were installed. The apps were tested on Android version 7.1, 8.1 and 9. On each Android system, the app was repeatedly launched and the communication captured. We also observed if the application cache has influence on the communication, so each app was running twenty times without cache and twenty times with cache on each system. Together, we obtained 3.180.245 TLS handshakes.

Mobile Apps IV (MA4). The last dataset was focused on a variety of mobile apps installed on a real device Tecno J8 with Android 6.1. The dataset includes the following apps: BoomPlay Music, Chrome Browser, Equa Bank app, Facebook app, Gmail app, Google calender, KB klic, Messenger, Mobilni Banka app, NextBike, Telegram, TikTok, WhatsApp and Youtube app. Each app was running five times on the restarted device so that the captured communication corresponds to a typical usage. We extracted 5.308 TLS handshakes from the captured traffic.

5.2 Results

We evaluated our TLS fingerprinting method using datasets MA3 and MA4 as they contain multiple runs for each application and can be divided into training and testing sets. In order to get the balanced sets we used reduced dataset MA3 (11 runs per app). We observed communication of 16 apps captured in distinguished time windows. We selected one run of each application for testing and the others we used for training. For training, we used the procedure described in Sect. 4.1. The testing set contained 244 TLS handshakes in total. These handshakes were classified as belonging to some application or unknown traffic.

Table 10. Detection of mobile apps based on JA3 hash

		A	B	C	D	E	F	G	H	I	J	K	L	M	N	O	P	X
									Real values									
Predicted values	A	0	0	0	0	0	0	0	0	0	0	0	0	0	0	0	0	0
	B	0	0	0	0	0	0	0	0	0	0	0	0	0	0	0	0	0
	C	0	0	3	0	0	0	0	0	0	0	0	0	0	0	0	0	14
	D	0	0	0	4	0	0	0	0	0	0	0	0	0	0	0	0	12
	E	0	0	0	0	0	0	0	0	0	0	0	0	0	0	0	0	0
	F	0	0	0	0	0	0	0	0	0	0	0	0	0	0	0	0	0
	G	0	0	0	0	0	0	0	0	0	0	0	0	0	0	0	0	0
	H	0	0	0	0	0	0	0	0	0	0	0	0	0	0	0	0	0
	I	0	0	0	0	0	0	0	0	0	0	0	0	0	0	0	0	0
	J	0	0	0	0	0	0	0	0	0	0	0	0	0	0	0	0	0
	K	0	0	0	0	0	0	0	0	0	0	3	0	0	0	0	0	0
	L	0	0	0	0	0	0	0	0	0	0	0	2	0	0	0	0	13
	M	0	0	0	0	0	0	0	0	0	0	0	0	0	0	0	0	0
	N	0	0	0	0	0	0	0	0	0	0	0	0	0	0	0	0	0
	O	0	0	0	0	0	0	0	0	0	0	0	0	0	0	0	0	0
	P	0	0	0	0	0	0	0	0	0	0	0	0	0	0	0	0	0
	X	5	5	0	0	1	6	1	4	9	1	1	0	13	6	1	1	139

Table 10 shows the confusion matrix of TLS handshakes classification based on JA3 hash only. Letters A to P represent mobile apps as follows: BoomPlay Music (A), EquaBank (B), Facebook (C), Gmail (D), Google Calendar (E), Chrome App (F), KB Klic (G), Mobilni Banka (H), NextBike (I), TikTok (J), WhatsApp (K), Youtube (L), Seznam CZ (M), Reddit (N), Muj vlak (O) and Cestovne Poriadky (P). Letter X describes unknown traffic. The rows contain predicted values, columns represent real values.

We can see the limits of JA3 fingerprinting that works well with apps C (Facebook), D (Gmail), K (WhatsApp) and L (Youtube) but other apps have JA3 hashes same as unknown traffic (X class). By adding JA3S hash to TLS fingerprint, the number of correctly classified apps increases, see Table 11. However, there is still a high number of false positives (column X). Table 12 presents classification results for three features JA3+JAS3+SNI. We can see that the classification is more accurate when using all these features with the exception of apps Chrome (F) and Youtube (L). Table 13 shows the accuracy, precision and recall of classification. JA3 hash is reliable only for specific apps and produces many false negatives (row X). JA3+JA3S classification has the comparable accuracy but better recall. This means that it produces a lot of false positives. The best result shows a combination of JA3+JA3S+SNI. It also places some samples into the X (unknown app) category, however, this can be improved by extending a list of keywords and inserting additional SNIs into the fingerprint database.

Table 11. Detection of mobile apps based JA3+JA3S

	Real values																
	A	B	C	D	E	F	G	H	I	J	K	L	M	N	O	P	X
A	5	0	0	0	0	0	0	0	0	0	0	0	0	0	0	0	0
B	0	3	0	0	0	0	0	0	0	0	0	0	0	0	0	0	0
C	0	0	3	0	0	0	0	0	0	0	0	0	0	0	0	0	13
D	0	0	0	4	0	0	0	0	0	0	0	0	0	0	0	0	18
E	0	0	0	0	0	0	0	0	0	0	0	0	0	0	0	0	0
F	0	0	0	0	0	2	0	0	0	0	0	0	0	0	0	0	4
G	0	0	0	0	0	0	0	0	0	0	0	0	0	0	0	0	0
H	0	0	0	0	0	0	0	1	0	0	0	0	0	0	0	0	0
I	0	0	0	0	0	0	0	0	6	0	0	0	0	0	0	0	0
J	0	0	0	0	0	0	0	0	0	0	0	0	0	0	0	0	0
K	0	0	0	0	0	0	0	0	0	0	2	0	0	0	0	0	0
L	0	0	0	0	0	0	0	0	0	0	0	2	0	0	0	0	10
M	0	0	0	0	0	0	0	0	0	0	0	0	10	0	0	0	2
N	0	0	0	0	0	0	0	0	0	0	0	0	0	6	0	0	0
O	0	0	0	0	0	0	0	0	0	0	0	0	0	0	1	0	0
P	0	0	0	0	0	0	0	0	0	0	0	0	0	0	0	1	0
X	0	2	0	0	1	4	1	3	3	1	2	0	3	0	0	0	131

Table 12. Detection of mobile apps based on JA3+JA3S+SNI

	Real values																
	A	B	C	D	E	F	G	H	I	J	K	L	M	N	O	P	X
A	5	0	0	0	0	0	0	0	0	0	0	0	0	0	0	0	0
B	0	4	0	0	0	0	0	0	0	0	0	0	0	0	0	0	0
C	0	0	3	0	0	0	0	0	0	0	0	0	0	0	0	0	8
D	0	0	0	4	0	0	0	0	0	0	0	0	0	0	0	0	0
E	0	0	0	0	1	0	0	0	0	0	0	0	0	0	0	0	0
F	0	0	0	0	0	0	0	0	0	0	0	0	0	0	0	0	0
G	0	0	0	0	0	0	1	0	0	0	0	0	0	0	0	0	0
H	0	0	0	0	0	0	0	3	0	0	0	0	0	0	0	0	0
I	0	0	0	0	0	0	0	0	7	0	0	0	0	0	0	0	0
J	0	0	0	0	0	0	0	0	0	0	0	0	0	0	0	0	0
K	0	0	0	0	0	0	0	0	0	0	3	0	0	0	0	0	0
L	0	0	0	0	0	0	0	0	0	0	0	1	0	0	0	0	0
M	0	0	0	0	0	0	0	0	0	0	0	0	12	0	0	0	0
N	0	0	0	0	0	0	0	0	0	0	0	0	0	6	0	0	0
O	0	0	0	0	0	0	0	0	0	0	0	0	0	0	1	0	0
P	0	0	0	0	0	0	0	0	0	0	0	0	0	0	0	1	0
X	0	1	0	0	0	6	0	1	2	1	1	1	1	0	0	0	170

Table 13. Evaluation of combination of TLS features

	Total items	Accuracy	Precision	Recall
JA3	244	61,89%	23,53%	18,18%
JA3+JA3S	244	72,54%	49,46%	69,70%
JA3+JA3S+SNI	244	90,98%	86,67%	78,79%

6   Application to Digital Forensics

The identification of smartphone apps can be applied to digital forensics as a complementary method to obtain forensically valuable information. First, the background traffic of installed apps can be analyzed to identify a communicating device [28]. This can distinguish a smartphone model from different vendors based on a pre-installed set of apps [13] and the background traffic. Next, by the identification of communicating applications, we can observe user-specific information, habits and interests as well [8].

Most digital investigations that include mobile device analysis use a logical extraction to access the existing files such as call history, text messages, web browsing history, pictures and other files available on the smartphone. However, logical extraction requires the possession of a device and bypassing the password. With smartphones better protected against the unauthorized access, the passive monitoring of their activities stands for the complementary data source for forensic analysis. The possibility to identify the mobile app, and therefore the device or even the user of the device is applicable in the following scenarios:

- Forensic analysis. LEAs may send a preservation order to the ISP to collect the communication for a specific device. The captured information can be used for learning about the activities of a suspect at different points in time. Creating a profile of the suspect and correlating identified activities with the information obtained from the other sources can bring an important insight to the case being investigated. Even if most of the app traffic is encrypted, the presented method can detect installed applications. The presence and usage of a specific application at a given point of time may reveal the intention of the suspect. Later, after the device is physically available to an investigator the information obtained from the monitoring phase can be corroborated with the findings of the logical acquisition outcomes to support the reliability of the evidence. Criminals aware of secrecy provided by IM apps can use them for communication to protect against traditional call record analysis [32]. However, if we can identify the activity of mobile apps, the traffic generated by the communicating IM hosts can be used to record communication between suspects. Also, posts published under the anonymous social network account can be revealed by comparing the time of the public posts with the time of the actions as inferred by the application usage aiding to hate crime investigations.
- Intelligence operations. The agencies may be able to trace certain individuals on basis of tracking the communication characteristic of the apps installed on their smartphones. To be feasible, the amount of information that needs to be collected and processed has to be limited. For instance, NetFlow-based monitoring is considered as suitable technique for this purpose [33]. The advantage of TLS fingerprinting can be applied at massive scale. Adding TLS fingerprinting to existing NetFlow monitoring requires to include TLS fingerprints to NetFlow records, which many existing monitoring solutions already provide for detection of security threats that use encrypted communication.

The presented cases consider the scenarios when the method is applied as a part of legal investigation done under strict law requirements applied to data collection and analysis. Unfortunately, as for most communication monitoring techniques collecting sensitive information possibly revealing user privacy, also this method can be misused. For instance, the totalitarian states can easily adapt the method to block selected apps and because it is computational inexpensive they can apply it on a large scale. Avoiding this situation requires the modification of TLS parameters of applications to make their JA3 hashes indistinguishable or intractable, e.g., by adding randomly generated parameters in the extension list and avoiding the use of SNI field.

7   Conclusion

Mobile apps fingerprinting can be considered a practical method with potential applications in digital forensics. In this paper, we have presented a study on the reliability of JA3-based methods for mobile apps identification. The advantage of this method is that it only depends on the TLS handshake information that is obtained during the establishment of the secure channel.

We have shown that using JA3 is not sufficient for the accurate identification of mobile apps. More reliable results are obtained by a combination of JA3, JA3S and SNI features that can be easily computed from the TLS handshake messages. We have also considered the issues of TLS fingerprint volatility. Based on our experiments the variability of TLS fingerprints is not so large. Also, when a new major version of the application is released, it is not difficult to obtain a new fingerprint in the virtual environment and update the fingerprint database.

The presented results are valid for existing TLS versions that provide access to the source information necessary for computing the fingerprints. However, ongoing work on TLS protocol suggests an increase of user privacy by hiding some of currently visible fields, e.g., SNI[10], or even the encryption of TLS Hello message. Addressing these emerging challenges is a topic for our future work.

Acknowledgement. This work was supported by project "Integrated platform for analysis of digital data from security incidents", 2017–2020, No. VI20172020062, granted by Ministry of Interior of the Czech Republic. The authors would like to give thanks to students Matej Meluš, Radovan Babic and Alberts Saulitis who participated in the generation of datasets for the research experiments.

References

1. Abel, R.: SSL/TLS fingerprint tampering jumps from thousands to billions. SC Magazine (2019)
2. Aceto, G., Ciuonzo, D., Montieri, A., Persico, V., Pescapé, A.: MIRAGE: mobile-app traffic capture and ground-truth creation. In: 2019 4th International Conference on Computing, Communications and Security (ICCCS), pp. 1–8 (2019)

---

[10] See Internet Draft at https://tools.ietf.org/html/draft-ietf-tls-esni-06 [March 2020].

3. Anderson, B., McGrew, D.: TLS Beyond the browser: combining end host and network data to understand application behavior. In: Proceedings of the Internet Measurement Conference, pp. 379–392 (2019)
4. Anderson, B., Paul, S., McGrew, D.: Deciphering malware's use of TLS (without decryption). J. Comput. Virol. Hacking Tech. (2018)
5. Benjamin, D.: Applying Generate Random Extensions And Sustain Extensibility (GREASE) to TLS Extensibility. IETF RFC 8701, January 2020
6. Böttinger, K., Schuster, D., Eckert, C.: Detecting fingerprinted data in TLS traffic. In: Proceedings of the 10th ACM Symposium on Information, Computer and Communications Security, pp. 633–638. ASIA CCS 2015. Association for Computing Machinery, New York (2015)
7. Castelluccia, C., Kaafar, M.A., Tran, M.D.: Betrayed by your ads!. In: Fischer-Hübner, S., Wright, M. (eds.) Privacy Enhancing Technologies, pp. 1–17. Springer, Heidelberg (2012). https://doi.org/10.1007/978-3-642-31680-7_1
8. Conti, M., Mancini, L.V., Spolaor, R., Verde, N.V.: Can't you hear me knocking: identification of user actions on android apps via traffic analysis. In: Proceedings of the 5th ACM Conference on Data and Application Security and Privacy, CODASPY 2015, pp. 297–304. New York, NY, USA (2015)
9. Danezis, G.: Traffic Analysis of the HTTP Protocol over TLS (2009). https://pdfs.semanticscholar.org/9d75/9184cdc524624fe551b9fc15de9a4cd199fa.pdf
10. Dierks, T., Rescorla, E.: The Transport Layer Security (TLS) Protocol Version 1.2. IETF RFC 5246, August 2008
11. Eckersley, P.: How unique is your web browser? In: Proceedings of the 10th International Conference on Privacy Enhancing Technologies, PETS 2010, pp. 1–18. Springer, Heidelberg (2010). https://doi.org/10.1007/978-3-642-14527-8_1
12. van Ede, T., et al.: FlowPrint: semi-supervised mobile-app fingerprinting on encrypted network traffic. In: NDSS (2020)
13. Gamba, J., Rashed, M., Razaghpanah, A., Tapiador, J., Vallina-Rodriguez, N.: An analysis of pre-installed android software. In: 41st IEEE Symposium on Security and Privacy. IEEE (2020)
14. Govindaraj, J., Verma, R., Gupta, G.: Analyzing mobile device ads to identify users. DigitalForensics 2016. IAICT, vol. 484, pp. 107–126. Springer, Cham (2016). https://doi.org/10.1007/978-3-319-46279-0_6
15. Hoffman, P., McManus, P.: DNS Queries over HTTPS. RFC 8484, October 2018
16. Hu, Z., Zhu, L., Heidemann, J., Mankin, A., Wessels, D., Hoffman, P.: Specification for DNS over Transport Layer Security (TLS). IETF RFC 7858, May 2016
17. Hupperich, T., Maiorca, D., Kührer, M., Holz, T., Giacinto, G.: On the robustness of mobile device fingerprinting: can mobile users escape modern web-tracking mechanisms? In: Proceedings of the 31st ACSAC, pp. 191–200. New York, USA (2015)
18. Husák, M., Čermák, M., Jirsík, T., Čeleda, P.: Https traffic analysis and client identification using passive SSL/TLS fingerprinting. EURASIP J. Inf. Secur. (2016)
19. Kotzias, P., Razaghpanah, A., Amann, J., Paterson, K.G., Vallina-Rodriguez, N., Caballero, J.: Coming of age: a longitudinal study of TLS deployment. In: Proceedings of the Internet Measurement Conference 2018, pp. 415–428 (2018)
20. Kurtz, A., Gascon, H., Becker, T., Rieck, K., Freiling, F.: Fingerprinting mobile devices using personalized configurations. Proc. Privacy Enhancing Technol. 1, 4–19 (2016)
21. Kwakyi, G.: How Do Mobile Advertising Auction Dynamics Work? Incipia Blog (2018). https://incipia.co/post/app-marketing/how-do-mobile-advertising-auction-dynamics-work/

22. Pan, E., Ren, J., Lindorfer, M., Wilson, C., Choffnes, D.: Panoptispy: characterizing audio and video exfiltration from Android applications. Proc. Privacy Enhancing Technol. 33–50 (2018)
23. Benjamin, D.: A Transport Layer Security (TLS) ClientHello Padding Extension. IETF RFC 7685, October 2015
24. Razaghpanah, A., Niaki, A.A., Vallina-Rodriguez, N., Sundaresan, S., Amann, J., Gill, P.: Studying TLS usage in Android apps. In: Proceedings of the 13th Conference on Emerging Networking Experiments and Technologies, pp. 350–362. New York (2017)
25. Ren, J., Rao, A., Lindorfer, M., Legout, A., Choffnes, D.: ReCon: revealing and controlling PII leaks in mobile network traffic. In: Proceedings of the 14th Annual International Conference on Mobile Systems, Applications, and Services, pp. 361–374 (2016)
26. Rescorla, E.: The Transport Layer Security (TLS) Protocol Version 1.3. IETF RFC 8446, August 2018
27. Rescorla, E., Ray, M., Dispensa, S., Oskov, N.: Transport Layer Security (TLS) Renegotiation Indication Extension. IETF RFC 5746, February 2010
28. Stöber, T., Frank, M., Schmitt, J., Martinovic, I.: Who do you sync you are? Smartphone fingerprinting via application behaviour. In: Proceedings of the Sixth ACM Conference on Security and Privacy in Wireless and Mobile Networks, pp. 7–12 (2013)
29. Sun, G., Xue, Y., Dong, Y., Wang, D., Li, C.: An novel hybrid method for effectively classifying encrypted traffic. In: 2010 IEEE Global Telecommunications Conference GLOBECOM 2010, pp. 1–5 (2010)
30. Taylor, V.F., Spolaor, R., Conti, M., Martinovic, I.: Appscanner: automatic fingerprinting of smartphone apps from encrypted network traffic. In: IEEE European Symposium on Security and Privacy (EuroS&P), pp. 439–454 (2016)
31. Taylor, V.F., Spolaor, R., Conti, M., Martinovic, I.: Robust Smartphone App Identification Via Encrypted Network Traffic Analysis. CoRR abs/1704.06099 (2017). http://arxiv.org/abs/1704.06099
32. Tsai, F., Chang, E., Kao, D.: Whatsapp network forensics: discovering the communication payloads behind cybercriminals. In: 2018 20th International Conference on Advanced Communication Technology (ICACT), p. 1 (2018)
33. Verde, N.V., Ateniese, G., Gabrielli, E., Mancini, L.V., Spognardi, A.: No nat'd user left behind: fingerprinting users behind nat from netflow records alone. In: IEEE 34th International Conference on Distributed Computing Systems, pp. 218–227 (2014)

Make Remote Forensic Investigations Forensic Again: Increasing the Evidential Value of Remote Forensic Investigations

Marcel Busch[✉], Florian Nicolai, Fabian Fleischer, Christian Rückert,
Christoph Safferling, and Felix Freiling

Friedrich-Alexander University Erlangen-Nuremberg, Erlangen, Germany
{marcel.busch,florian.nicolai,fabian.fleischer,
christian.rueckert,christoph.safferling,felix.freiling}@fau.de

Abstract. Due to the increasing use of encrypted communication and anonymous services, many countries introduced new regulations that allow law enforcement to perform *remote forensic investigations*. During such investigations, law enforcement agencies secretly obtain remote access to a suspect's computer to search for and collect evidence, including full copies of the (unencrypted) communication data. In this paper, we argue that the evidential value of the acquired evidence can be substantially increased by two technical methods: (1) employing integrity verification techniques offered by secure hardware, and (2) exfiltrating the decryption key of encrypted communication only in order to decrypt communication obtained by lawful interception. To prove the practicality of both methods, we design and implement TEE-BI, a solution for Trusted Execution Environment-based introspection. We deploy TEE-BI on an Android-based hardware platform featuring an ARM Trust-Zone and demonstrate the stealthy extraction of Secure Sockets Layer encryption keys from an Android userland application. We evaluate the effectiveness, performance, and compatibility of our prototype and argue that it provides a much higher level of evidential value than (the known) existing remote forensic software systems.

Keywords: Remote forensic investigation · ARM TrustZone · Principle of proportionality · Evidential value · Translation table introspection · Android

1 Introduction

Due to end-to-end encrypted connections for many Internet services (*i.e.*, web browsing or instant messaging) as well as strong anonymization provided by services like Tor, law enforcement is struggling to prevent "going dark" on cybercrime. One general approach to counter the increasing abilities of cybercriminals is to perform *remote forensic investigations* [55]. In many countries, this term

© ICST Institute for Computer Sciences, Social Informatics and Telecommunications Engineering 2021
Published by Springer Nature Switzerland AG 2021. All Rights Reserved
S. Goel et al. (Eds.): ICDF2C 2020, LNICST 351, pp. 23–43, 2021.
https://doi.org/10.1007/978-3-030-68734-2_2

is used to describe the practice of using hacking techniques to access and install government spyware on the end device of a suspect [22]. Given a government spyware on the target system, most investigative tasks are substantially simplified. For example, by bypassing anonymization services, law enforcement can identify the IP address and, thereby, often the location of a target machine. In a further practice, known as *remote forensic search*, law enforcement uses spyware to covertly search and acquire evidence directly from the system. Moreover, encrypted communication can be intercepted *before* it is encrypted, then stored and exfiltrated to law enforcement. In analogy to remote forensic searches, we call this technique *remote forensic telecommunication surveillance*. While law enforcement agencies do not publicly report a lot about these practices, those cases of government spyware that have been publicized [20,54] confirm the above observations.

There are several downsides with the current practices. Firstly, it is a severe practical problem to get government spyware onto the target device without the device owner noticing. In practice, this is often achieved by social engineering (*i.e.,* tricking the user into installing the spyware under false presumptions) [39] or physical access to the device in combination with a root exploit or knowledge of access credentials [20]. Obviously, both approaches are not generally applicable, especially if the device owner is a cybercriminal fully aware of these tactics. In addition to the practical problems, these methods pose significant risks to the security of the Internet (*i.e.,* reducing the functions of computers by bypassing security techniques or the proliferation of zero-day exploits).

The second downside is a general problem with the evidential value of the data obtained through such remote forensic searches. The legal dangers do not necessarily lie in the expressiveness of the data obtained but rather in the unreliability of the method since a defendant can always claim that law enforcement "manipulated the computer" or "planted" the evidence. This claim is hard to refute since it is difficult to prove which version of the software actually was running on the remote computer at a particular point in time and whether it did exactly what it should have done.

The third problem of remote forensic investigations pertains to using them for surveillance of encrypted communication. Since the current technique of remote forensic telecommunication surveillance described above must acquire the content of the communication *before* it is encrypted, there is a small window of uncertainty of whether and when the encrypted communication is sent over the network. This is especially relevant in countries such as Germany, that have introduced regulations that may use remote forensic software for telecommunication surveillance as long as the police has access to only the content of the communication that is finally sent over the physical wire (often called *source wiretapping* or *source telecommunication surveillance* [23,47]). Given the above uncertainties, government spyware is inclined to overapproximate communication data and thereby fails to comply with legal requirements.

To state it clearly and upfront: This paper does not focus on the first problem, *i.e.,* it is *not* about how to secretly inject spyware onto mobile phones. We simply assume that governments can enforce the addition of some functionality on a mobile device, *e.g.,* by cooperating with the manufacturer of the device. Instead, we are concerned with the second and third problem, *i.e.,* the question of *how to design tools for remote forensic investigations that comply with general legal principles.*

1.1   Contributions

In this paper, we study design variants of methods for remote forensic investigations. As mentioned above, we do *not* focus on how to install the spyware on the phone but rather assume a government/manufacturer collaborative approach for targeted communication interception that inserts government software into the general trusted computing base of mobile devices. Our contributions are as follows:

1. We argue that remote forensic software should be embedded into the trusted computing base of end devices that support guarantees rooted in secure hardware. Such techniques exist in many contexts in the form of *Trusted Execution Environments (TEEs)*, most notably with *ARM TrustZone (TZ)* on many mobile devices. Having a hardware-based root of trust makes it much easier to argue that the software was running as specified.
2. We discuss a novel design variant of remote forensic telecommunication surveillance: The central idea of our solution is to exfiltrate only the minimal amount of information from the end device – the cryptographic key – to open the cryptographic shield "on the wire" and to proceed with (classical) wiretapping. We argue that this technique is legally the least intrusive method for remote forensic telecommunication surveillance of encrypted traffic and therefore is the only method that satisfies general legal principles.
3. We design and implement TEE-BI, a TEE-based introspection framework for Android devices that (1) uses ARM TZ to guarantee and attest the integrity of a software, and that (2) can reliably and stealthily extract encryption keys from running applications to allow data to be decrypted in transit.
4. To show TEE-BI's effectiveness, we evaluate our prototype by extracting SSL crypto material from an SSL encrypted echo server on a real hardware platform using a recent Android version (Android 9). The chosen example is universal since it makes use of the `boringssl` library which is the default crypto library used by applications on the Android platform.

1.2   Roadmap

We begin with a discussion of the legal view on remote forensic investigations in Sect. 2 and give some background on the used technologies in Sect. 3. The design and implementation of our solution are described in Sects. 4 and 5, followed by the evaluation in Sect. 6. We discuss related work in Sect. 7 and then conclude in Sect. 8.

2   Legal Perspective

Like all investigative measures, remote forensic investigations also require regulation. We first give an overview of international legislation regulating the use of government spyware and then discuss the legal requirements that must be met by investigative techniques. We will later use these requirements to evaluate and compare our solution.

2.1   Legislation Allowing Remote Forensic Investigations

Many countries now have established legal provisions to install spyware on end devices of citizens and therefore conduct remote forensic investigations. A recent overview of the European Union [22] on the practices in several countries concludes that many countries, including most member states of the EU, now explicitly permit and regulate "hacking by law enforcement" [22], i.e., remote access to computers by spyware as a criminal investigative measure. In Germany, the Federal Code of Criminal Procedure was amended in this way just recently. [23]. In many other countries, remote forensic investigations are carried out within the bounds of existing laws which can be problematic [18].

For example, in the UK, the "Investigatory Powers Bill" enacted in 2016 allows law enforcement to "interfere" with targeted electronic equipment to retrieve data and communication [22, p. 104], and in the United States an amendment to Rule 41 of the Federal Criminal Procedure Rule offers law enforcement "remote access" to data [22, p. 121]. A new regulation in Germany even distinguishes between two forms of remote forensic investigation: a general "remote forensic search" ("Online-Durchsuchung") and a more specific "remote forensic telecommunication surveillance" ("Quellen-TKÜ") [23, 47]. Roughly speaking, the latter is a restriction of the former case, but only to telecommunication data, *i.e.*, data that could be intercepted via wiretapping if encryption would be turned off.

2.2   Principle of Proportionality (Europe)

The proportionality principle is common to most domestic legal systems in Europe and is indeed a central figure of EU law itself and routinely applied by the European Court of Human Rights [17, p. 10–14] [15]. It is also an integral part of other legal systems like Canada [9] or Hongkong [11]. If authorities infringe upon a citizen's fundamental right, the infringement must not be immoderate in relation to the aim pursued by the government. The *proportionality test* consists of the following steps [4], [17, p. 16–17]: At first, an actual infringement of rights by a governmental act has to be stated, which is given for remote forensic telecommunication surveillance. The infringed right is the right to freedom of telecommunication. It is granted in national law, *e.g.*, Art. 10 Basic Law for the Federal Republic of Germany, but also in supranational law as in Art. 8 ECHR (European Convention of Human Rights) and Art. 7 CFR (Charta of Fundamental Rights of the European Union) [43]. Therein any form of undisclosed communication between natural and legal persons is protected from intervention by any government authority [30]. Subsequently, we have to examine if the intrusion stands in proportion to the governmental interest, in this case the interest in effective criminal investigation and prosecution, which is decided by the following: (1) The governmental aim has to be legitimate, which applies to criminal investigation and prosecution, and therefore to gaining access to telecommunication data (legitimacy). (2) The infringement must be suitable to pursue that legitimate aim (suitability). Remote forensic telecommunication surveillance can help to pursue that aim by gaining information for the investigation through telecommunication data. (3) The chosen measure has to be the least intrusive on individual rights amongst the equally suitable (necessity). We will argue later that due to the above stated smaller infringement, given a widespread possibility of application for our novel TEE-BI technique, the currently used method would be considered as not necessary in the sense of proportionality, and therefore is not justified. (4) Moreover, the infringement must be proportional to the government's gain of advantage for the investigation (proportionality strictu sensu). This is a specific consideration for every individual case, which cannot be generalized. In our case, this step would not be taken, since the current method, given TEE-BI, already fails on the level of step 3, i.e. the infringement is already stated as not legitimate.

2.3 Balancing Test (US)

The American legal system also compares the level of infringement to the importance of the governmental aim, not by applying the principle of proportionality, but by performing the *balancing test*. The balancing test is divided into two steps: After stating the infringement, it is directly examined for being properly balanced to the governmental interest [17, p. 17–18]. The freedom of (digital) communication is guaranteed by the Fourth Amendment [27], which is infringed by remote forensic telecommunication surveillance. This infringement must be in balance to the governmental interest, therefore reasonable. While the Supreme Court stated that being reasonable is not invariably bound to being the least intrusive method [8,48], a more intrusive way of performing investigative actions is not immune to being declared unreasonable, thus unbalanced, in view of a less intrusive method. All of these aspects taken into consideration during the proportionality test, e.g., necessity, can, even if not explicitly named as such, be part of the balancing test [17, p. 17–23]. Thus, the current method of remote forensic telecommunication surveillance is not immune to being regarded as unjustified. In addition, it is, in any case, desirable to apply methods that are less intrusive into fundamental rights such as the Fourth Amendment.

2.4 Requirements for Digital Evidence

The value of evidence in criminal proceedings is determined by a set of general requirements that have been discussed widely in the literature. Such requirements have to be also met for digital evidence to have (stronger) evidential value. We now list the three most important ones for the present work [24]:

- Authenticity: The investigated data must be authentic to be of value for a criminal procedure. That applies to all electronically stored information involved [5]. The analysis, procedure, outcomes, and limitations must be explainable in a way, that the evidential value of the data can be assessed during the trial [40], so it can be assured the data was not altered.
- Reliability: Digital evidence has to be based on accurate and scientifically verified technologies, which have to be reliable themselves to make sure the evidence can be part of the (free) consideration of evidence and, in pre-trial stages, to establish a necessary degree of suspicion (e.g. US: "reasonable suspicion" (Terry vs. Ohio, 392 U.S. 1, 1968); Germany: "sufficient factual indication" (§152 (2) GER-CCP)) [24, p. 5].
- Verifiability: To ensure that the evidence acquisition can be followed up by the parties of the criminal procedure, the measure of collecting the data and information has to be repeatable and reproducible to prevent an extreme decrease of evidential value. With due regard to recommendations of the US National Institute of Standards and Technology (NIST) there were already established further definitions of those criteria and how they can be met [24, 38]

We will use these requirements later in the evaluation to compare TEE-BI's approach to current practices in remote forensic investigations.

3 ARMv8-A TrustZone Preliminaries

ARM chipsets are dominant on modern mobile devices, which usually incorporate the ARMv8 Instruction Set Architecture (ISA) [12] and support for ARM TrustZone [13]. A typical software architecture based on these hardware features consists of the logical components depicted in Fig. 1. This architecture is achieved by partitioning the System-on-Chip (SoC)'s hardware components, especially the CPU and the RAM, and assigning them to either of two states, the Normal World (NW) or the Secure World (SW), as illustrated in Fig. 2.

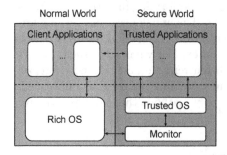

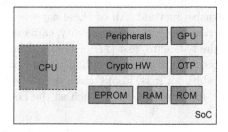

Fig. 1. ARMv8-A systems with ARM TrustZone support split the software architecture into a Normal World and a Secure World execution context.

Fig. 2. ARM TrustZone allows for the partitioning of hardware components into a secure or non-secure state.

Most mobile devices use the NW to host feature-rich software, *i.e.*, a Rich Operating System (RichOS) and Client Applications (CAs), whereas security-critical tasks are carried out in the SW using a Trusted Operating System (TrustedOS) and Trusted Applications (TAs). On Android devices, dependent on the Original Equipment Manufacturer (OEM), we can find different TrustedOSs and TAs, like fingerprint unlock or face identification unlock. Therefore, NW and SW are also referred to as Rich Execution Environment (REE) and TEE, respectively. A context switch between these two execution contexts usually happens by entering the Monitor.

The two operating systems, RichOS and TrustedOS, have their own page tables and, consequently, do not share the same view of their virtual address spaces. As can be seen from this architecture, both contexts can run apps that are isolated from each other and the operating system using the means of virtual memory.

Given these architectural components, it is important to note that the process of initializing such a system is crucial for the security of the entire system. OEMs refer to this process as *Secure Boot* [19] and engineered the boot process to only load correctly signed and verified components forming the Trusted Computing Base (TCB). This TCB usually includes software executed in the SW.

TEE-BI is based on the architectural primitives given by ARMv8-A. Those are the same primitives vendors like Qualcomm, Samsung, or Huawei base their system designs on. Thus, the hardware requirements needed for a system like TEE-BI, are already present on millions of devices used by consumers these days.

4 Design

Trusted Execution Environments (TEEs) have become commonplace on modern mobile devices [10, 35, 42, 44, 45]. They are the foundation for our disk encryption, manage the access to security-sensitive peripherals like the fingerprint sensor, and decrypt our Netflix 4K streams on-thy-fly. More advanced features implemented within TEEs are real-time kernel integrity monitoring [14] and trusted user interfaces [33]. All of these features are available today and part of the mobile devices you can buy at your neighborhood electronics store.

Using this versatile technology, we are capable of performing a vast array of actions from a trusted context. Of course, when talking about this trusted context, we refer to the trust relationship you are committing to by deciding for a certain vendor. In this section, we suggest adding another party to this trusted context, which is *your government*. We propose TEE-BI, a TEE-backed system to exfiltrate only the minimal amount of information from a suspect's end device – the cryptographic key – to open the cryptographic shield "on the wire".

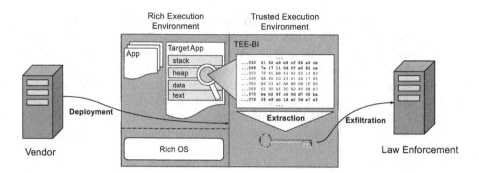

Fig. 3. TEE-BI is capable of stealthily exfiltrating cryptographic material from a target application using TEE-based introspection.

In the following sections, we elaborate on the three steps of TEE-BI. First, we discuss deployment variants of TEE-BI. Second, we explain the process of targeted cryptographic key extraction. Third, we examine different ways of exfiltrating the extracted keys. Figure 3 illustrates these steps and serves as an overview.

4.1 Deployment

The goal of the deployment process is to load TEE-BI reliably into the TEE using the most direct way possible and guarantee its integrity and confidentiality during this process.

For this research, we reviewed major commercially used TEEs and found that the capabilities of dynamically loading code and guaranteeing its integrity are commonly available features. Samsung [45], Qualcomm [42], as well as Huawei [35], use signed executables and a verifying loader to run trusted code in their TEEs exclusively. In addition to the verification of executables, Huawei also employs a decryption step that is based on asymmetric cryptography in order to provide confidentiality guarantees. We assume these capabilities of a "secure loader" to guarantee TEE-BI's integrity and confidentiality since they are already used on millions of devices.

To reliably deliver TEE-BI to the target device, we suggest two different schemes, depending on the capabilities of the TEE. For both schemes, the underlying thought is that every mobile device connects back to update servers or other backends managed by the device vendor, which can be leveraged to deliver TEE-BI to the target device.

In the first scheme, the TEE has direct access to the networking interface of the device. The TEE can temporarily claim exclusive access to the networking interface, which is a technique already used for other peripherals, for instance, to accomplish trusted user interfaces [28,44]. For trusted user interfaces, the framebuffer, as well as the touch screen sensors, are temporarily taken over by the TEE from the REE. In our scenario, this peripheral would be the networking interface.

The second scheme, which is less complex and widely deployed, is the usage of the existing networking software stack of the RichOS. In fact, for this scheme, GlobalPlatform (GP), a standardization body for TEEs, already provides a detailed specification on how to integrate and implement the network access from a TEE context [26].

The deployment of TEE-BI requires vendors to load and execute third-party code in their TEEs. This use case is already part of major TEE platforms. For instance, Widevine [29] is a content protection framework for media that consists of components running inside of the TEEs of major mobile device vendors (*i.e.,* Samsung and Google devices). Considering the fact that all telecommunication providers in almost all countries can be forced to cooperate with law enforcement by regulations, it seems clear that similar regulations should at least in principle be possible in many countries.

4.2 Extraction

The process of data extraction from the TEE context has two steps. First, the target application has to be localized, and second, the relevant information has to be found and extracted. Both of these steps are making use of TEE-based introspection, meaning, TEE-BI leverages its unrestricted access to the main memory in order to reconstruct the virtual address space of the target process running within the REE and applies a set of heuristics to locate the information of interest.

The RichOS (*i.e.,* Android uses the Linux kernel) maintains a list of tasks corresponding to userland processes. This list of tasks is referenced from the RichOS. To get access to this list of tasks, TEE-BI exploits the fact that it has access to the translation tables of the REE and, therefore, can reconstruct the virtual address spaces of the RichOS and its userland applications.

To locate the target application, TEE-BI traverses this list of tasks and looks for indicators identifying the target application. In the simplest case, such an indicator is the name of the target application, which is part of its task list entry.

After finding the target application, TEE-BI takes the base of its first level page table from the task list entry, to identify all memory regions belonging to this application.

Given all the pages of the target app process, TEE-BI can reconstruct its entire virtual address space and extract any data from it. The process of finding the relevant information from a virtual address space of an application is implementation-specific. We use a set of heuristics to identify and extract cryptographic key material from the boringssl library [2], the predominantly used cryptography library on Android systems.

4.3 Exfiltration

As it is the case for the deployment of TEE-BI, we need a reliable way to communicate with a remote party (*e.g.,* law enforcement servers in Fig. 3) for effective exfiltration. This communication can happen by leveraging one of the two schemes described above in Sect. 4.1: (1) temporary take-over of a network interface by the TEE, or (2) leveraging the REE networking software stack. The outgoing connection from the TEE to the law enforcement server must be cryptographically secured. After successful exfiltration of the key material, law enforcement entities can decrypt the traffic that they already captured via established methods [21,37].

5 Implementation

We implemented TEE-BI on a LeMaker HiKey 620 development board, which is one of the reference boards for prototyping Android systems [1]. This board is equipped with a Hisilicon Kirin 620 SoC (Cortex-A53 Octa-core 64-bit) implementing the ARMv8-A ISA. Our REE software stack consists of Android 9, which is based on a 4.14 Linux kernel. In the TEE, we run OP-TEE 3.4.0 [6]. Based on this setup, we implement TEE-BI to perform TZ-based introspection for fine granular data extraction.

5.1 Physical Memory Access

TEE-BI's core is implemented as an Open Portable Trusted Execution Environment (OP-TEE) Pseudo Trusted Application (PTA). PTAs, in contrast to TAs, run in the TrustedOS and, have access to privileged functions (*i.e.,* mapping arbitrary physical memory). Access to these functions is necessary in order to map physical memory used by the REE into the virtual address space of TEE-BI.

OP-TEE offers an interface to map physical memory pages as part of its shared memory implementation. For TEE-BI, we leverage this interface and add auxiliary functions to access physical memory in various ways conveniently. In particular, we add primitives for eight-byte and one-byte reads, as well as for reading null-byte terminated strings. Listing 1.1 shows the interface we use to access the physical memory.

```
uint64_t read_64(paddr_t paddr);
uint8_t read_8(paddr_t paddr);
void read_str(paddr_t paddr, char *buf, size_t buf_size);
```

Listing 1.1. TEE-BI's primitives for physical memory access.

5.2 REE Virtual Address Resolution

TEE-BI needs capabilities to resolve virtual addresses from the REE to physical addresses in order to traverse data structures used by the RichOS and its userland applications. Virtual address translation on ARMv8 is carried out using the interplay between the Memory Management Unit (MMU) and the Translation Table Base Registers (TTBRs) (*e.g.*, `ttbr0_el1` and `ttbr1_el1`).

On Linux, the highest bit of a given virtual address decides which of the two TTBRs is used. Having a memory layout with 4KB pages and a 4 level translation table, virtual userspace addresses reside in the range of

`0x0000000000000000` to `0x0000ffffffffffff`

and the kernel virtual address space is located within

`0xffff000000000000` to `0xffffffffffffffff`.

Therefore, page table walks for userspace are based on `ttbr0_el1`, and page table walks for the kernel are based on `ttbr1_el1`.

For TEE-BI, this means we have to differentiate virtual addresses from the RichOS and its userland to correctly resolve their underlying physical addresses. In order to resolve a userland virtual address, we implemented the four-level page table walk of 4KB pages in software.

Based on these resolution mechanisms, TEE-BI provides the same memory access functions as earlier introduced (see Listing 1.2), just for retrieving data for REE virtual addresses.

```
1  uint64_t read_64_virt(vaddr_t vaddr);
2  uint8_t read_8_virt(vaddr_t vaddr);
3  void read_str_virt(vaddr_t vaddr, char *buf, size_t buf_size)
```

Listing 1.2. TEE-BI's primitives for REE virtual memory access.

5.3   Task List Traversal

As discussed in Sect. 4.2, our entry point to the RichOS's process management is a task list. In the Linux kernel, the entry point to this list is the initial task (`init_task`). TEE-BI performs a task traversal as illustrated in Fig. 4. We traverse the process tree by following children and sibling references until we find our target process. By doing this, we need to translate kernel virtual addresses to physical addresses, as explained above. Our search criterion to identify the target is its `task_struct`'s `comm` field, which contains the name of the process. TEE-BI offers a modular and extendable design to allow developers to implement more advanced heuristics to identify the target process, if necessary.

Task structures within Linux have an `mm_struct` member describing their memory. As part of this struct, we can find the `pgd` member, which is the virtual address of the first level page table (see Fig. 4). Since the layout of `task_struct` and `mm_struct` can change between kernels, TEE-BI provides configuration options for these parameters. Overall we use five different offsets for the traversal:

off_children: Offset of children list pointer in the `task_struct`
off_siblings: Offset of `siblings` member in the `task_struct`
off_comm: Offset of comm member in the `task_struct`
off_mm: Offset of mm member in `task_struct`
off_mm_pgd: Offset of `pgd` member in the `mm_struct`

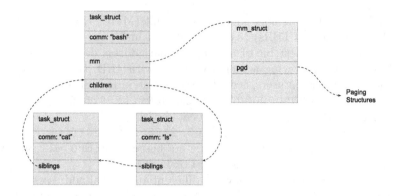

Fig. 4. TEE-BI traverses the process tree to find the target process.

5.4   Page Table Traversal

Having the entry point to the target process' paging structures, it is possible to traverse its virtual address space. Since the page tables hold physical addresses, TEE-BI uses the physical memory access functions for the traversal.

The modular design of TEE-BI allows developers to specify a callback function for each memory page (see Listing 1.3). The callback function allows for modularization and extendability of memory area handling. Using this technique, each use case can have its own callback function. This may be a simple search for strings or regular expressions but could also be a more complex extraction of nested data structures.

```
static uint64_t
    handle_memory_area(paddr_t pgd, vaddr_t vaddr, uint64_t len);
```

Listing 1.3. TEE-BI uses a callback function to handle contigous regions in memory.

5.5   Data Extraction

For the use case of extracting cryptographic key material of ongoing TLS-encrypted connections, we implement a callback function that extracts the Master Secret and the Client Random [7] of a target process that uses the boringssl library. We assume that the data structure layouts used by boringssl are known or can at least be probed before scanning for the cryptographic key material. The two values underlying secure connections for the boringssl library are referenced by the Secure Sockets Layer (SSL)-context data structure. By finding this structure, we can follow the appropriate offsets and memory references to extract the desired information. In particular, we find this data structure by searching for a fingerprint consisting of certain lengths values used for key sizes and cipher ids indicating different ciphers. Additionally, the alignment of the members is considered during the search. Once the structure is identified, we can systematically traverse the memory and retrieve the target information.

5.6 Prototype Limitations

Our TEE-BI prototype is focused on providing a proof of concept for the viability of TEE-based introspection and extraction of cryptographic key material. Therefore, we initiate the extraction right after the process using the `boringssl` library established a secure connection. In a production state, TEE-BI would implement a polling-based mechanism for the extractions step. Since cryptographic keys for TLS connections only temporarily reside in memory, the time frame to extract the keys is limited. TEE-BI cannot rule out the possibility that a key is already wiped from memory, but it can increase the chance of searching at the right point in time by scanning the memory with a higher frequency. Furthermore, a secure timer is needed to trigger and guarantee the execution of the extraction routine without the RichOS being able to interfere with this process.

6 Evaluation

In this section, we evaluate TEE-BI concerning its effectiveness, performance, and compatibility, as well as its compliance with legal requirements.

6.1 Target Application

For testing TEE-BI, we use a client application, which opens an SSL-encrypted connection and transmits data to a remote server. Furthermore, we show the general approach and explain the callback functions used for obtaining the target data. Additionally, we demonstrate how to extract cryptographic key material from the target process. For this purpose, we implement a client and an echo server, which both utilize Transport Layer Security (TLS) encrypted sockets.

To ensure secure communication with the server, the target client uses BoringSSL. After opening a connection, it initiates an SSL-handshake. Next, the client sends data to the server, which the server directly echoes back to the client.

We run the client application as our target in the REE. TEE-BI is able to retrieve the Master Secret and the Client Random from the client application.

6.2 Effectiveness

To show the effectiveness of TEE-BI, we use the target application. The target application running in the REE connects to the server hosted on a remote machine. As mentioned before, the connection between the client and the server is encrypted using SSL (TLS 1.2). We capture the encrypted traffic onto the server machine with `tcpdump` and open it using Wireshark. At this point, it is not yet possible to decrypt the traffic. However, by using TEE-BI, we can now extract the Master Secret and the Client Random that were used for the secure connection. Listing 1.4 depicts the format of the extracted secrets, consisting of three strings on a single line. The first string is the label CLIENT_RANDOM, the second string is the 64-digit Client Random encoded as a hex-string, and the third string is the 96-digit Master Secret al.so encoded in hex.

```
1  CLIENT_RANDOM \
2  f282e8e9873964504ce6f94c8be4d15d\
3        5db4b508de20a61499bad70f0c8ff34c \
4  fc309fdd46cf4f5a6e5754b3c91c6f70\
5        0848991270e4624d771b038c7757136f\
6        a64e33554b713b6bcf751042d29deaf3
```

Listing 1.4. Master Secret and Client Random in correct format for Wireshark.

With the above format in Listing 1.4, Wireshark is able to read the secrets and decrypt the traffic. Since we were able to decrypt the SSL-traffic successfully, TEE-BI is effective in extracting cryptographic key material from a target process running in the REE.

6.3   Performance

We measure the performance of TEE-BI by considering the overall duration for the task list traversal and the extraction of cryptographic secrets. For comparison, we also count the number of pages mapped, and the number of performed page table walks. In order to get reliable results, we execute the task list traversal and the extraction of secrets 1000 times each and take the arithmetic mean of our measurements.

Since TEE-BI needs to map pages for reading their content programmatically, we also need to measure this impact. During the introspection, there were 192 processes running, and 207 pages needed to be traversed for the extraction of the encryption secrets. Table 1 shows the performance measurements. During task list traversal, the virtual address mapping has been changed 2935 times, which includes pages that have been mapped more than one time. In comparison, the virtual address mapping for the extraction was updated 7008 times. Table 1 also shows that for the extraction 48 713 μs of the overall 50 491 μs are necessary for the mapping procedure. Also for the task traversal, the mapping of the pages into the virtual address space of the TEE takes most of the overall duration. Looking at the duration for the page table walk during the extraction of secrets, we can see that most of the time is spent on mapping pages as well. In average, mapping one page takes 48 713 μs/7008 = 6,95 μs. Compared to the overall time for page table walks we can conclude that the page mapping has a strong impact on the performance of TEE-BI.

Table 1. Performance measurements of TEE-BI on the HiKey development board.

	Page table walks	Pages mapped	Overall duration
Task list	-	2 935 pages	
Traversal	0 µs	20 598 µs	21 132 µs
Secrets	25 walks	7 008 pages	
Extraction	441 µs	48 713 µs	50 491 µs

In summary, we can observe that the adjustment of the memory mapping in the TEE has a strong impact on TEE-BI's performance. TEE-BI does not implement sophisticated caching mechanisms yet, which leaves significant room for improvements.

6.4   Compatibility

Since ARM processors hold a large market share, it is important to evaluate the adaptations necessary for porting TEE-BI to other ARM-based systems.

First, we have a look at mobile consumer devices such as smartphones and tablets. The majority of these devices use Android and processors with the ARMv8-A ISA. Therefore, these devices have an MMU and most likely support for ARM TrustZone. These are the same prerequisites we assume for TEE-BI. Given these similarities, using TEE-BI on a mobile consumer device should be straightforward.

Depending on the kernel configuration and the used memory management model, it might be necessary to adjust some parameters, for instance, for the page table walk. These parameters affect the number of paging levels or the granule size of the pages in use [12]. For instance, the kernel on our HiKey development board uses four-level page tables. We designed TEE-BI in a configurable way to enable its portability and, thus, can adjust the number of paging levels and the page size.

Besides mobile consumer devices, ARM processors are used in various embedded devices. Assuming an ARM TrustZone is present on such a device, there is the possibility to implement TEE-based introspection. It might be more complex to adjust the prototype to such a device depending on its memory model. If an MMU is present, the procedure is likely similar to our procedure. In case an MMU is not present, the processor is often used as a microcontroller (ARMv8-M). These processors use a Memory Protection Unit (MPU) instead of an MMU. In this case, the introspection needs to be adjusted to its specific use case. This might be more complex as well, but still possible.

We can summarize that compatibility with architectures commonly used for mobile consumer devices seems given. Also, in the embedded area, our approach could be utilized but requires more adjustments.

6.5   Legal Requirements

As argued by Fröwis et al. [24], digital evidence in criminal proceedings under the rule of law must meet the following requirements: Lawfulness of data processing, authenticity and integrity of data, reliability of the applied methods, qualification of the investigators, verifiability of the evidence and the conclusions, chain of evidence. As we now argue, the method we present in this paper has advantages over traditional methods of remote forensic telecommunication surveillance, especially with regard to the following criteria, which increase the value of evidence for legal proceedings: Authenticity and integrity, reliability and verifiability.

Authenticity and Integrity. Authenticity is given if the data presented as evidence actually originate from the source indicated by the investigating authorities. Integrity can be affirmed if the data has not been altered after their collection [24, p. 5]. The advantage of TEE-BI's method is that after the extraction of the key, the telecommunication data can be obtained from the telecommunication providers in the traditional way as a 1:1 copy following a classical wiretap. The telecommunication provider then guarantees that the data actually resulted from a specific communication event and went "over the network". With TEE-BI, it is, therefore, harder to argue that law enforcement authorities have planted the communication data on purpose on the monitored system. Furthermore, the methods of IT forensics, which have been tried and tested for years, can be used to avoid changes to these data sets [16].

Reliability. The reliability of the investigative method is ensured if it is a precise and scientifically validated method for the respective data processing and if it is used correctly in the individual case [24, p. 5]. The advantage of TEEs, such as TrustZone, lies in the fact that they guarantee that only particular versions of the software get to be executed, namely those that were digitally signed by some trusted party (usually the manufacturer). This means that the remote forensic software must be *signed* before it is able to run. This makes it much harder for law enforcement to deploy arbitrary functionality.

In addition, the installation of the remote forensic software is achieved through methods that the manufacturer explicitly supports. This prevents collateral damage from more "offensive" installation scenarios (e.g., manual or via exploit) that dominate the mobile phone forensics market [20,54] and have problems of their own. TrustZone even provides a technique for *remote attestation*, i.e., the possibility to construct a cryptographic security proof that a particular *version* of software was running on the system at any given point in time. Realizing this would definitely increase the trust in the reliability of the extraction and analysis of the evidence because it not only can be proven that a software package was running at a certain point in time, but also its exact version.

Verifiability. The results of the evaluation of data sets are verifiable if they meet the criteria of repeatability and reproducibility [24,38]. Traditional remote forensic telecommunication surveillance faces the problem here that, by extracting the telecommunication data before or after the sending process, there is no possibility to repeat this process or to show that the data was actually sent later/before. There is also the danger of overapproximating the data that is sent over the network, circumstances which are illegal in Germany [23].

Unfortunately, with TEE-BI, we also cannot repeat the acquisition process at a later time since cryptographic keys are usually eliminated from memory when a connection closes. However, this form of repeatability is also not present in classical forms of source telecommunication surveillance. The fact that the original data comes from the telecommunication provider makes it harder for law enforcement to plant new evidence into a file with network traffic. What, however, can be done is to extract repeatedly the unencrypted communication data from the encrypted network communication that was seized through wiretapping. This replication step clearly has evidential value in criminal cases.

A threat to reproducibility is the introspection element because there is always the chance that data that already resides in memory might be misunderstood or wrongly interpreted by the software. Cryptographic techniques (like authenticated encryption), however, will ensure that decryption does not produce any false positives, i.e., messages that are "valid" decryptions of the plaintext without being actual messages from the producer. Even though scanning for cryptographic keys is heuristic in nature, the decryption backend can always try more than one decryption key. Therefore, if data can be successfully extracted, then the chosen key is correct, and the extracted data was, in fact, the data that was previously encrypted.

7 Related Work

TEE-BI introspects the translation tables of a lower-privileged execution context from the TEE. This idea of introspection originated from the usage of hypervisors for Virtual Machine Introspection (VMI). VMI describes the access and evaluation of a running system and its resources from outside of the system [25]. The concept of VMI primarily applies introspection to main memory, but, more generically, could also include non-volatile background storage and other hardware. VMI is primarily used for secure monitoring of running Operating Systemss (OS'ss) [34]. An approach using the hypervisor extensions of ARM chipsets, instead of AMD's or Intel's technologies, was proposed by Lengyel et al. [36], who evaluated VMI on ARM with the Xen hypervisor. In this context, LibVMI is a promising project to harmonize and simplify the required introspection Application Programming Interface (API) [41].

Other research involving TEE-based translation table introspection was first shown by Azab et al. [14]. Their system is executed within the TEE and ensures the integrity of the running rich OS's. In contrast to Azab et al.'s work, TEE-BI has its focus on the exfiltration of data from userland processes, instead of monitoring the kernel. Furthermore, Guerra et al. [32] introduce the ITZ-library, which generalizes the introspection of NW memory from the TEE. For their research, they use the Genode OS's Framework [3]. Since the ITZ-library is based on Genode, and OP-TEE does not support the Genode Framework, we do not use the ITZ-library but implement the memory access based on the interface provided by OP-TEE.

Moreover, TrustDump [50] is a forensic tool for reliable and trustworthy memory acquisition on smartphones. This tool uses TZ for the generation of physical memory dumps. Instead of generating a memory dump, TEE-BI evaluates the physical memory while the target operating system is still running.

Next, Stüttgen et al. [49] evaluate the possibility of injecting a minimal acquisition module into a running Linux Kernel Module (LKM). This approach reduces the impact on the target system, but still changes the codebase of the targeted OS's significantly. TEE-BI's acquisition is carried out from the isolated context of a TEE and, therefore, naturally has a minimal impact on the integrity of the introspection target.

Further, DroidKex [52] targets Android apps and extracts data from applications' address spaces. DroidKex is a rich OS's module and intercepts calls to the SSL library used by targeted applications. TEE-BI's goal is similar to DroidKex's, but we integrate the extraction of the SSL secrets into the TEE, instead of modifying the REE software stack. With our setup, the monitoring runs stealthily alongside the REE and can barely be detected. Effective hiding techniques are a major challenge for other monitoring tools [46, 51].

For the live analysis of Android applications, Thing et al. [53] developed a tool for the extraction of process memory. The live analysis runs as system service in the Android environment and is able to gather data from user processes such as deleted messages from Instant Messengers (IMs). Thing et al.'s research was later enhanced by Grover [31] to no longer require elevated privileges. Using a userland application, they provide an open-source Android monitoring tool for enterprise purposes. All these approaches require software within the REE, which is the main difference to our approach.

8 Conclusions

In this paper, we propose a novel approach for remote forensic telecommunication surveillance which addresses two major downsides of the current practices: Our design increases the evidential value of remote forensic investigations and provides a technique for lawful surveillance of encrypted communication. To achieve these goals, our approach embeds the remote forensic software into the trusted computing base and utilizes characteristics of the ARM TZ, such as the root of trust in secure hardware. Moreover, in our approach, we exfiltrate only a minimal amount of information from the consumer device that is necessary for the surveillance of encrypted communication: the cryptographic key. We argue that this approach is least intrusive to the target device and therefore is the only method, which satisfies legal principles in Europe (Proportionality) and the USA (Balancing Test).

Furthermore, we implement and evaluate TEE-BI, a prototype for our proposed approach. TEE-BI is based on ARMv8-A with ARM TZ technology and, therefore, uses the same foundation as millions of mobile devices around the globe. To demonstrate its practicability, we implemented TEE-BI on real hardware and used an up-to-date Android-based setup for our evaluation. We study TEE-BI's effectiveness, performance, and compatibility as well as evaluate it regarding legal requirements. For the latter, we argue that TEE-BI by design complies with authenticity and integrity, reliability, and verifiability.

Acknowledgements. We would like to thank Maria Maras for her constructive feedback. This research was supported by Deutsche Forschungsgemeinschaft (DFG, German Research Foundation) as part of the Research and Training Group 2475 "Cybercrime and Forensic Computing" (grant number 393541319/GRK2475/1-2019) and the German Federal Ministry of Education and Research (BMBF) as part of the Software Campus project (Förderkennzeichen: 01/S17045).

References

1. Android Open Source Project: Using reference boards. https://source.android.com/setup/build/devices. Accessed 15 Sept 2020
2. BoringSSL. https://boringssl.googlesource.com/boringssl/. Accessed 15 Sept 2020
3. Genode Operating System Framework. https://genode.org/. Accessed 15 Sept 2020
4. German Federal Constitutional Court BVerfGE 120, pp. 274, p. 318–319; Handyside v. The United Kingdom, 24 ECHR (Ser. A) 23 at para. 49 (1976)
5. Lorraine v. Markel American Insurance Company, 2007, United States District Court for the District of Maryland, 241 F.R.D. 534 (D. Md. 2007)
6. Open Portable Trusted Execution Environment. https://www.op-tee.org. Accessed 15 Sept 2020
7. RFC5246 - The Transport Layer Security (TLS) Protocol Version 1.2. https://tools.ietf.org/html/rfc5246. Accessed 15 Sept 2020
8. Skinner v. Ry. Labor Executives' Ass'n, 489 U.S. 602, 629 n. 9 (1989)
9. R. v. Oakes. 1 SCR 103 (1986)
10. Security enclave processor for a system on a chip (2012). https://patents.google.com/patent/US8832465B2/en. Accessed 15 Sept 2020
11. Abeyratne, R.: More structure, more deference: proportionality in Hong Kong. In: Yap, P.J. (ed.) Proportionality in Asia (2019)
12. ARM: Arm®R architecture reference manual Armv8, for Armv8-A architecture profile documentation. https://developer.arm.com/docs/ddi0487/latest. Accessed 15 Sept 2020
13. ARM: ARM security technology: Building a secure system using trustzone technology (2008). https://static.docs.arm.com/genc009492/c/PRD29-GENC-009492C_trustzone_security_whitepaper.pdf. Accessed 15 Sept 2020
14. Azab, A.M., et al.: Hypervision across worlds: real-time kernel protection from the arm trustzone secure world. In: Proceedings of the 2014 ACM SIGSAC Conference on Computer and Communications Security, pp. 90–102. CCS 2014. Association for Computing Machinery, New York (2014). https://doi.org/10.1145/2660267.2660350
15. Barak, A.: Proportionality - Constitutional Rights and their Limitations, pp. 181–208, Concerning the Legal Sources See pp. 211–241. Cambridge University Press, Cambridge (2012)
16. Casey, E.: Digital Evidence and Computer Crime - Forensic Science, Computers and the Internet, 3rd edn. Academic Press, Cambridge (2011). http://www.elsevierdirect.com/product.jsp?isbn=9780123742681. Accessed 15 Sept 2020
17. Cohen-Eliya, M., Porat, I.: Proportionality and Constitutional Culture. Cambridge University Press, Cambridge (2013)

18. Cupa, B.: Trojan horse resurrected - on the legality of the use of government spyware. In: Webster, C., William, R. (eds.) Living in Surveillance Societies: The state of Surveillance: Proceedings of LiSS Conference, vol. 3. pp. 419–428. CreateSpace Independent Publishing Platform (2013)

19. Dent, A.W.: Secure boot and image authentication (2019). https://www.qualcomm.com/media/documents/files/secure-boot-and-image-authentication-technical-overview-v2-0.pdf. Accessed 15 Sept 2020

20. Dewald, A., et al.: Analyse und vergleich von BckR2D2-I und II. In: Suri, N., Waidner, M. (eds.) Sicherheit 2012: Sicherheit, Schutz und Zuverlässigkeit, Beiträge der 6. Jahrestagung des Fachbereichs Sicherheit der Gesellschaft für Informatik e.V. (GI), 7.-9. März 2012 in Darmstadt. LNI, vol. P-195, pp. 47–58. GI (2012). https://dl.gi.de/20.500.12116/18287. Accessed 15 Sept 2020

21. European Telecommunications Standards Institute: Handover interface for the lawful interception of telecommunications traffic (1999). https://www.etsi.org/deliver/etsi_ts/101600_101699/101671/03.11.01_60/ts_101671v031101p.pdf. Accessed 15 Sept 2020

22. European Union, Directorate-General for Internal Policies: Legal frameworks for hacking by law enforcement: Identification, evaluation and comparison of practices (2017). http://www.europarl.europa.eu/supporting-analyses. Accessed 15 Sept 2020

23. Freiling, F., Safferling, C., Rückert, C.: Quellen-TKÜ und Online-Durchsuchung als neue Maßnahmen für die Strafverfolgung: Rechtliche und technische Herausforderungen. Juristische Rundschau **2018**, 9–22 (2018)

24. Fröwis, M., Gottschalk, T., Haslhofer, B., Rückert, C., Pesch, P.: Safeguarding the evidential value of forensic cryptocurrency investigations. Forensic Sci. Int. Digital Invest. https://doi.org/10.1016/j.fsidi.2019.200902

25. Garfinkel, T., Rosenblum, M., et al.: A virtual machine introspection based architecture for intrusion detection. In: Ndss. vol. 3, pp. 191–206. Citeseer (2003)

26. GlobalPlatform: TEE sockets API specification v1.0.1 (2017). https://globalplatform.org/specs-library/tee-sockets-api-specification-v1-0-1/. Accessed 15 Sept 2020

27. Goodison, S.E., Davis, R.C., Jackson, B.A.: Digital evidence and the US criminal justice system: identifying technology and other needs to more effectively acquire and utilize digital evidence, pp. 9–10. RAND Corporation (2015). www.jstor.org/stable/10.7249/j.ctt15sk8v3. Accessed 15 Sept 2020

28. Google: Protected confirmation (2020). https://source.android.com/security/protected-confirmation. Accessed 15 Sept 2020

29. Google Widevine: Widevine - leading content protection for media (2019). https://www.widevine.com/. Accessed 15 Sept 2020

30. Grabenwarter, C.: ECHR - Commentary, Art. 8 para. 3, 4, 28 (2014)

31. Grover, J.: Android forensics: automated data collection and reporting from a mobile device. Digital Invest. **10**, S12–S20 (2013)

32. Guerra, M., Taubmann, B., Reiser, H.P., Yalew, S., Correia, M.: Introspection for ARM TrustZone with the ITZ library. In: 2018 IEEE International Conference on Software Quality, Reliability and Security (QRS), pp. 123–134. IEEE (2018)

33. Hayton, R.: The benefits of trusted user interface (TUI) (2019). https://www.trustonic.com/news/blog/benefits-trusted-user-interface/. Accessed 15 Sept 2020

34. Hebbal, Y., Laniepce, S., Menaud, J.M.: Virtual machine introspection: techniques and applications. In: 2015 10th International Conference on Availability, Reliability and Security, pp. 676–685. IEEE (2015)

35. Huawei Technologies: Emui 8.0 security technical white paper (2017). https://consumer-img.huawei.com/content/dam/huawei-cbg-site/en/mkt/legal/privacy-policy/EMUI8.0SecurityTechnologyWhitePaper.pdf. Accessed 15 Sept 2020
36. Lengyel, T.K., Kittel, T., Eckert, C.: Virtual machine introspection with Xen on ARM. In: Workshop on Security in highly connected IT systems (SHCIS) (2015)
37. Lumme, M., Eloranta, J., Jokinen, H.: Interception system and method (1999). https://patents.google.com/patent/US20020049913. Accessed 15 Sept 2020
38. Maras, M.H.: Computer Forensics, 2nd edn. Jones & Bartlett Learning, Burlington (2015)
39. Marquis-Boire, M., Marczak, B., Guarnieri, C., Scott-Railton, J.: For their eyes only. The commercialization of digital spying. Citizen Lab report, September 2013. https://citizenlab.org/storage/finfisher/final/fortheireyesonly.pdf. Accessed 15 Sept 2020
40. Neumann, C., Kaye, D., Jackson, G., Reyna, V., Ranadive, A.: Presenting quantitative and qualitative information on forensic science evidence in the courtroom. Chance **29**, 37–43 (2016)
41. Payne, B.D.: Simplifying virtual machine introspection using LibVMI. Sandia report, pp. 43–44 (2012)
42. Qualcomm: Qualcomm mobile security (2018). https://www.qualcomm.com/solutions/mobile-computing/features/security. Accessed 15 Sept 2020
43. Rueckert, C.: Cryptocurrencies and fundamental rights. J. Cybersecur. **5**, 6 (2019)
44. Samsung: Trustonic for KNOX (2015). https://news.samsung.com/global/samsung-and-trustonic-launch-trustonic-for-knox-delivering-a-whole-new-level-of-trust-enhanced-experiences-on-samsung-mobile-devices. Accessed 15 Sept 2020
45. Samsung: Samsung TEEGRIS (2020). https://developer.samsung.com/teegris/overview.html. Accessed 15 Sept 2020
46. Samuel, J., Mathewson, N., Cappos, J., Dingledine, R.: Survivable key compromise in software update systems. In: Proceedings of the 17th ACM Conference on Computer and Communications Security, CCS 2010, Chicago, Illinois, USA, 4–8 October 2010, pp. 61–72 (2010). https://doi.org/10.1145/1866307.1866315
47. Sieber, U., von zur Mühlen, N. (eds.): Access to Telecommunication Data in Criminal Justice. A Comparative Analysis of European Legal Orders. Duncker & Humblot, Berlin (2016)
48. Strossen, N.: The fourth amendment in the balance: accurately setting the scales through the least intrusive alternative analysis. 63 NYUL Rev. 1173 (1988)
49. Stüttgen, J., Cohen, M.: Robust Linux memory acquisition with minimal target impact. Digital Invest. **11**, S112–S119 (2014)
50. Sun, H., Sun, K., Wang, Y., Jing, J.: Reliable and trustworthy memory acquisition on smartphones. IEEE Trans. Inf. Forensics Secur. **10**(12), 2547–2561 (2015)
51. Sylve, J., Case, A., Marziale, L., Richard, G.G.: Acquisition and analysis of volatile memory from android devices. Digital Invest. **8**(3–4), 175–184 (2012)
52. Taubmann, B., Alabduljaleel, O., Reiser, H.P.: DroidKex: fast extraction of ephemeral TLS keys from the memory of Android apps. Digital Invest. **26**, S67–S76 (2018)
53. Thing, V.L., Ng, K.Y., Chang, E.C.: Live memory forensics of mobile phones. Digital Invest. **7**, S74–S82 (2010)
54. WikiLeaks: Spyfiles 4. https://wikileaks.org/spyfiles4/. Accessed 15 Sept 2020
55. Winter, L.B.: Remote computer searches under Spanish law: the proportionality principle and the protection of privacy. Zeitschrift für die gesamte Strafrechtswissenschaft **129**(1), 205–231 (2017)

Evidence Gathering in IoT Criminal Investigation

François Bouchaud[1]([✉]), Thomas Vantroys[2], and Gilles Grimaud[2]

[1] IRCGN - Forensic Science Laboratory Gendarmerie Nationale, Cergy, France
`francois.bouchaud@gendarmerie.interieur.gouv.fr`
[2] Univ. Lille, CNRS, Centrale Lille, UMR 9189 - CRIStAL, 59000 Lille, France
{`thomas.vantroys,gilles.grimaud`}`@univ-lille.fr`

Abstract. The Internet of Things (IoT) is a new paradigm. It enables communication between physical "things" through a common and distributed architecture. It is based on objects deeply rooted in the intimate lives of users. The devices are constantly scanning and interacting with this physical world. They bear witness to past events and are therefore a rich source of information for criminal investigations. The collection of evidence from the connected infrastructure is a decisive phase of the success of the police investigation. It is about removing objects from their initial environment and placing them in a controlled and secured area. This action allows the evidence to be preserved for later examination. It is crucial, but nevertheless difficult. It can alter or destroy valuable data during manipulation. Moreover, the difficulty lies in the heterogeneous nature of the devices and their strong dependence on the environment. This paper focuses on the collection of IoT devices at the local level, linked to an investigative strategy. It presents several tools and methods to retrieve the objects and proposes to evaluate its relevance in a use case.

Keywords: Internet of Things · IoT Investigations · Collection and sealing

1 Introduction

In the Internet of Things (IoT) markets, new devices and services are being created to make our lives easier and more connected. Manufacturers and service providers are offering their customers a wide range of offers and options. This IoT infrastructure organizes communication between physical "things" through a common and distributed network [9]. It opens up to the Internet. Technically, these connected objects are exploited by several operating systems and connect to various network technologies at the same time. To communicate, some solutions require specific gateways. These characteristics of heterogeneity, interactivity and dynamism make the architecture more complex than a conventional sensor network. However, it creates value in the services and exchanged data.

S. Goel et al. (Eds.): ICDF2C 2020, LNICST 351, pp. 44–61, 2021.
https://doi.org/10.1007/978-3-030-68734-2_3

From a forensic point of view, this development affects the investigation procedure and these technical acts. Digital forensics (DF) has become an important science for tracking malicious or undesirable activities and finding perpetrators. It is the discipline of identifying, acquiring, analyzing and searching for evidence from a digital source [18]. It aims to introduce cohesion and consistency into the vast field of extracting and examining traces from a crime scene. The search for truth is conducted in such a way that the original incriminating traces are not compromised. Dedicated tools, hardware or software, are available to assist the investigator. However, due to the many dependencies between objects and data management policies, the collection and the analysis of this ecosystem challenges the investigator. Collecting evidence from a connected infrastructure is a decisive phase in the success of a police investigation. It involves removing objects from their original environment and placing them in a controlled and secured area. This action is crucial and difficult. It can alter or destroy valuable data.

This article proposes a collection framework to take into account a criminal scene with IoT devices. Contrary to the study of computers and telephones, connected objects refer to a notion of iteration of selection. Moreover, heterogeneous devices make up the crime scene, having strong dependencies on the environment.

Section 2 of this article highlights the need to collect a connected object and data from its communication infrastructure; Sect. 3 covers previous work in the field of digital forensic collection; Sect. 4 describes the collection framework for the IoT environment; Sect. 5 tests them in a use case; Sect. 6 presents the operational impact factor; Sect. 7 presents the conclusion of the article and the next step of this research.

2   The Need for a Forensic Data Collection Framework

This section defines the collection requirements of a connected object and associated data in the context of the criminal investigation. In addition, it presents encountered difficulties.

2.1   Connected Objects as Evidence Receptacles

The Internet of Things is a complex whole. Its visible and physical part is a local ecosystem defined by the objects, gateways and mobile terminals of connected users. Thus, the concept of "local" is linked to the location and environment of the people involved in the incident. Connected object are "small" object integrating sensors or actuators, with processing logic by a microcontroller. It is generally self-sufficient in energy, powered by a battery. It can include several physical interfaces such as connectors, sockets and buttons, but also wireless communication modules. It collects local data and transmits it to a cloud computing service over the network. Similarly, it receives commands from a management server and returns operational reports. Gateways and user terminals are more conventional in their operation and architecture, acting as an interface between systems or externally. Their operating systems offer a significant abstraction between the software and the hardware on which it runs.

From a forensic perspective, each module of the infrastructure contains usable data. In Oriwoh et al. [20], the authors list potential sources of evidence on the architecture of the Internet of Things. The search for traces is triggered by criminal activity or by the normal operation of devices. It represents a phenomenon or event in a given context. On the basis of this information, the justice system seeks to determine the causes and circumstances of the incident. Digital forensic procedures recommended by the National Institute of Standards and Technology (NIST) are internationally accepted [15]. It is an "application of science to the identification, collection, examination, and analysis of data while preserving the integrity of the information and maintaining a strict chain of custody for the data". These four successive steps are applicable in the IoT environment. Traces must therefore be collected with care and rigor. This technical operation is carried out by taking into account the needs of the investigation in the search for the truth.

This technical operation is a critical phase, especially in the context of a connected environment. Indeed, the collection is constrained by the technical characteristics of this heterogeneous and distributed environment.

2.2   Problem

Evidence gathering is a challenge for the community of digital forensics. Several scientific works list the difficulties inherent in this subject. In Zareen et al. [27], the authors describe them according to three characteristics: architecture, technology and applications. In particular, this article highlights the difficulty of acquiring data due to the heterogeneity of objects. For example, smart devices have a variety of different operating systems [13]. This element has an impact on collection, particularly in the development of a universal approach. According to Miorandi et al. [17], the evidence extraction process may also be more complicated than traditional computing. This is due to the data formats, protocols and involved physical interfaces. Many dependencies between objects complicate the collection. A change in the environment can lead to the writing of logs or the loss of information [23].

Digital evidence is inherently fragile. It can be altered, damaged or destroyed by improper handling or examination [22]. In addition, it is not easily copied and stored in its original state [4]. There is a risk of a remote shutdown of devices or overwriting of evidence. Care must therefore be taken to document and adapt the collection method to the encountered constraints. These operations must be carried out according to the physical characteristics of the object to be studied and the sought data. Faced with this observation, a question arises. What protection measures must be taken to guarantee the non-alteration and optimal conservation of the stored data ? The challenge is to transfer a connected object from its natural environment to a new controlled containment zone without damaging the container and contents.

The scientific community proposes various solutions to take into account the environment and exploit the data.

3   Previous Work

In this section, we present a state of the art of forensic collection of connected objects. We explore the operational limitations of these approaches.

3.1   Literature Review

The process of collecting objects is irreversible because they are removed from the environment. It requires the establishment of controlled sampling protocols [10,11]. Analytical quality assurance from the crime scene to the laboratory must be implemented [8]. It is no longer based solely on legal considerations. For example, work must be done on sealing, traceability of operations and continuity of evidence.

Several strategies have been developed by the scientific community to collect data in a connected environment. Some work proposes interfacing with existing infrastructure. In Zawoad et al. [28], the authors describe the Forensics Aware IoT (FAIoT) model. It is a kind of central repository of reliable evidence. From a specific Programmable Logic Controller (PLC), investigators access data on IoT platforms. This approach requires collaboration between private companies and the police to implement this access. There is an inherent bias in data processing. Only locally synchronized data is accessible. In Copos et al. [7], the authors collect traffic data from the intelligent home network. This solution requires a good knowledge of the network and its accessibility.

In Oriwoh et al. [19] and Perumal et al. [21], the authors present an approach to take the whole environment into account. It is divided into three study areas: the local environment composed of objects and gateways, the Internet with IoT platforms and the service interface for customers (Fig. 1). This approach is relevant in the forensic context. It structures the analysis process on the basis of existing solutions.

Indeed, data collection in the cloud consists of requisitions from operators. The client interface includes the application environment and web portals. It is processed using digital forensic tools. However, device located in zone 3 (gateway) can also play a role in local environment (zone 1), such as mobile phones. It acts as a gateway across a shared network. It also serves as an interface for service consumers. The local area network is often seen as a black box of heterogeneous devices. It is unique in its configuration, topology and the objects that make it up.

3.2   Specific Constraints

Often, devices cannot be turned off to preserve hours of modified, created and accessible data, as suggested in [19]. There are two working hypotheses. The first is to acquire the data directly. This is called live forensic acquisition [1,14,25,26]. This approach applies only to known devices. It requires privileged access to the target system. In the second case, it is not possible to retrieve the information without tampering with the system. It is necessary to maintain the device in the found state for further processing. This problem is dealt with before the device is sealed. However, the device can be turned off when the lost data is of no interest or affects the rest of the investigation.

Sometimes data is scattered across several devices on the same network. It is also stored on external services [2]. This note refers to dependencies between devices. Thus, it is necessary for the investigator to master the topology of the network and its sub-networks. An analysis phase should include the study of the path taken by the data. This work allows understanding their coherence with the system. The collection phase is developed in one reading per branch to maintain the dependencies.

Another challenge is the legal limits of the investigation. Some of the most legal aspects are listed by Ruan et al. [24] and Oriwoh et al. [19]. Data travels between multiple devices or services in the cloud. It is often difficult to find the data when it is on servers in a third country. This is made impossible in the absence of agreement between countries.

In response to these constraints, we propose a framework to facilitate the retrieval and storage of data from a crime scene.

4   Collection Framework and Tools

In this section, we present the framework for data collection. This phase can be broken down into several actions. First, we take charge of the crime scene by isolating different networks. We study the roles and dependencies between objects. Then we collect and extract them, according to network topologies. Finally, we package them. This approach is defined according to the operational constraints and the implementation strategy.

4.1   Crime Scene Data Collection

In this subsection, we study the process of handling connected objects at a crime scene. It is defined according to the dependencies between objects and their technical characteristics. Beforehand, we assume that the IoT environment is divided into three study areas: local (1), online (2) and service interface (3) (Fig. 1). Thus, in the collection phase, we focus on zones 1 and 3. Only data from these zones are directly accessible to investigators. Access to the data on the online platform (2) therefore requires the intervention of a third party by requisition.

Global Approach. This methodology focuses on the examination of the crime scene as a whole. It consists of three successive steps. The first is the identification of local equipment in order to obtain a mapping of the connected environment.

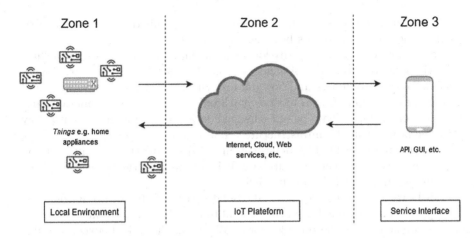

Fig. 1. Zones of Digital Forensics derived from Oriwoh et al. [19]

The second is to determine the technical characteristics of the equipment and its normal operation. The third step is to isolate the networks in order to limit interactions, data leaks and to facilitate data extraction (Fig. 2).

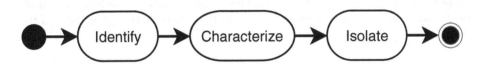

Fig. 2. Crime scene examination methodology

First, we are looking for different equipments. Then we determine their role in the infrastructure: connected objects or gateways. There are two categories of connected objects. The first one includes devices that communicate directly with the outside world. The second contains objects that depend on a third party to communicate. In addition, there are several types of gateways. This distribution is defined according to the provided services. The first group provides access to the Internet or to external networks in zone 2. The second provides the link between IoT-specific protocols and other classical protocols. They constitute network nodes of zone 1. Hybrid solutions are also present. This articulation is deduced from the study of communications, protocols and families of devices. Objects based on short-range networks (Bluetooth, ZigBee, Wi-Fi, etc.) communicate with the external network using a local gateway. Objects based on long-range networks (SigFox, LoRa, etc.) use an external public gateway managed by private operators. On the basis of this information, we draw up a map of the various networks. We obtain the local environment tree with its different branches. The branches symbolize communications. The base of the trunk is the main gateway to the Internet. The specific gateways for the different protocols are the nodes. The leaves are the connected objects. This tree structure is used to determine the dependencies between the devices.

Second, we identify and classify local equipment according to technical characteristics related to the type of memory (volatile or static) and network dependencies. We want to understand how data is synchronized over the network and the normal operation of the objects. Synchronization can be automatic, semi-automatic or manual. The type of exchanged data, the data management policy and their position in the infrastructure are also important elements in understanding the environment. The identification of objects and their synchronization modes are based on a reference database. It is informed on the basis of feedback from surveys and knowledge of the devices.

Third, we seek to disaggregate and isolate parts of the local environment. This approach is developed from the general to the specific. Local infrastructure must be isolated from the outside world. We break the links between the different areas (1, 2 and 3). The mapping of the infrastructure gives the points of interaction with zone 2. Concretely, the investigator physically disconnects the wired Ethernet communication. He removes the SIM cards or scrambles communications. Interference is a time-limited measure. It is only applied when there is no other way to interrupt the communication. Then we take care of the different networks of the local environment identified during the mapping. The network standards used in IoT today can be classified into three basic network topologies: point-to-point, mesh and star (Fig. 3). The Mesh network can be hierarchical or not. These characteristics have an impact on the collection of equipment and its data.

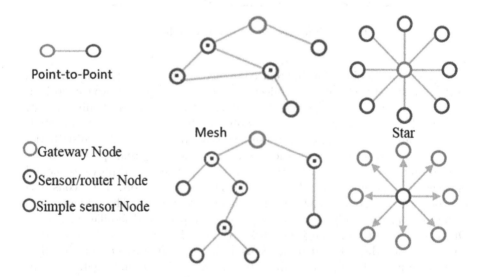

Fig. 3. Network technologies appropriate for the Internet of Things

The point-to-point network establishes a direct connection between the connected object and its gateway. The object accesses the Internet or another network via the gateway. An example of this type of network is a Bluetooth connection between a mobile phone and a connected watch. By breaking the radio link, the gateway and the object are isolated from the network.

The star network consists of a central node to which all other nodes in the network are connected. This hub serves as a common connection point for all other nodes. All the peripheral nodes can therefore communicate with each other via the hub only. An example of this topology is a Wi-Fi network in a house. The hub is the link to the outside world. This architecture makes it easy to add or remove nodes without impacting the network. All the intelligence of the network is concentrated on a single node. This concentric approach facilitates network management. Thus, peripheral nodes can be removed and isolated of the networks one by one. By directly removing the central node, the objects lose connectivity. The network is cut off from the world. However, it can still exchange and store data internally. This network topology is notably developed with the SigFox and LoRa protocols. The object interacts with several gateways. In this case, the recommended solution is to isolate the object from the network.

A mesh network consists of a gateway and connected objects, some of which have routing capabilities. Thus, one object is connected to one or more other objects, acting as nodes in the same network. The gateway allows data to reach the outside world. Thanks to this mesh, the data is potentially relayed by several nodes before reaching its destination. This concept is called a route. Over time, the nodes establish new routes based on their operating states and the physical characteristics of the medium. In some cases, this architecture is hierarchical. The parent node is the master of the network, called the "cluster tree". This structuring is used in home automation according to a relay construction. It compensates for distance issues or noise and obstacles. For example, the Enedis intelligent link network is built on this model [6]. For a hierarchical mesh network, by disconnecting the routers, the connected objects are isolated from the network. However, this operation must start from the ends of the branches to the core of the network. For a classic mesh network, we look for different closed and open loops that make up the network. We isolate the two types of loops. This gives us sub-networks. The open loops are treated according to a hierarchical approach. Closed loops are considered as a connected whole.

The study of the network topology gives a first reading of the collection methodology. Depending on the protocols in place, different containment measures are established. They must take into account dependencies.

Special Case of Targeted Research. Targeted research is a special case of the comprehensive crime scene approach. It is carried out during the examination of a specific object. The aim is to promote efficiency. Thus, this approach includes all the steps described above. However, it focuses on the direct environment of the target object and its dependencies.

A mapping of the network is carried out. It gives an overall view of the environment and the connected present objects. Based on this information, the investigator has the dependency tree between the devices. Instead of studying all the branches, he targets the network he is interested in. He studies the characteristics of the target object and the attached devices. He extracts all these devices from the same branch, with regard to interactions and dependencies. It ignores other devices that interact with the target object.

After reviewing the process of supporting the connected objects in the local infrastructure, we are interested in extracting them from the environment and packaging them. We discuss the sealing of IoT devices and the preservation of the stored data.

4.2　The Sealing

In this section, we develop the concept of sealing and the preparatory acts for proper packaging. The seizure and imposition of legal seals are an act of judicial police. It consists of placing an object or a document at the disposal of justice to be used in the manifestation of the truth. Seizures are carried out following the spontaneous surrender of an object or following a judicial search. Like physical objects, digital data stored in memory media are subject to seizure. The investigator seals either the physical medium containing the data or a copy of the data. Prior to collection, steps are taken at the time of collection to preserve biological traces such as DNA or fingerprints.

The seal must guarantee the integrity of the data present in the device. It protects the content from any physical or digital interaction with the outside. For digital evidence, it protects the content from exposure to electromagnetic fields. Thus, it must be made according to the characteristics and the condition of the object. If the medium cannot be deactivated or must remain activated, the object is packaged in a Faraday cage. As soon as possible, it is permanently powered by an external battery. This action increases the life of the object. The operating time must be estimated according to the capacity of the power supply. This information must be prominently displayed on the seal. If the holder can be deactivated, the object is conditioned in such a way that it cannot be reactivated. The seal must comply with the provisions set out in the Treatises on Digital Forensics [5, 12, 16].

4.3　Process to Follow

The crime scene consists of connected objects and gateways with more or less dependencies. Figure 4 resumes the different operations. After checking their operating status (on or off), the switched-off device is placed directly under seal. In addition, the device switched on without dependencies is disconnected and isolated from the network.

If it has no internal memory, it is placed in a seal in the switched-off state. Indeed, in a second step, the object identifiers can be used in requisitions from operators. If it has a memory, it is processed in the field or in the laboratory. The

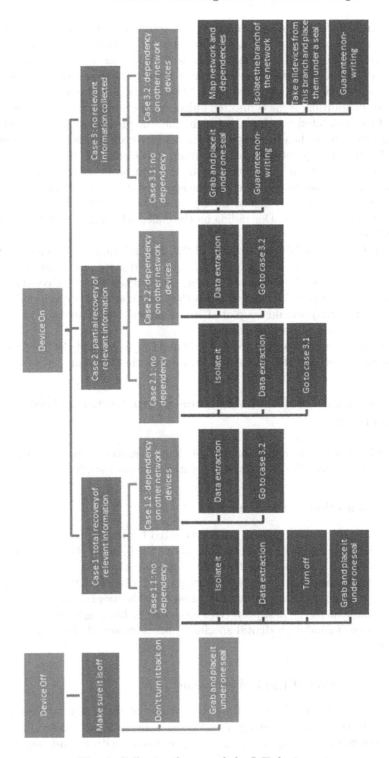

Fig. 4. Collection framework for IoT devices

data retrieval is carried out according to the available tools. For example, many gateways have open communication ports. The extraction is performed according to the availability of services such as with Telnet or a programmable logic controller (PLC). It is therefore performed locally or on the network depending on the scenario or the required data. Nevertheless, local acquisition is always preferred. In addition, some connected objects contain external storage media. A study of the connected watch market highlights the presence of storage and SIM cards in one third of the products. Conventional forensic acquisition methods are applicable to this type of electronic medium. Verification of the extracted data is necessary to establish their integrity for legal purposes. A comparison of the hashes of the original data source and the acquired data is performed. However, this verification is not performed in the case of direct acquisition [3,15]. This action changes the source. Depending on the collected data, the device is turned off or left on.

When it is not possible to extract all the data relevant to the investigation, it is placed in a state as close as possible to its input state. Each device shall be placed in a unique seal. Objects containing dependencies shall be considered as a whole. The treatment is different when the investigator puts them under seal. To limit entry, they should be placed in a common seal. However, an impact study must be carried out beforehand.

Thus, the dependencies between objects and the accessibility of the data with forensic tools motivate the choice of a field acquisition method.

5   Evaluation of Forensic Tools in an Investigative Exercise

This section assesses the collection methodology presented in the previous session on a survey exercise. We conduct an operational impact study.

5.1   Presentation of the Scenario

On April 10, 2018 at 8 a.m., the police is alerted by a neighbor of a burglary in an apartment. The police intervened quickly at the scene of the crime. A patrol arrives at 8:15 am. It discovers that the front door of the apartment is forced. The place also shows many traces of struggle and violence. Objects are broken on the floor. A dead person is found lying on a bed in room 2. The investigators therefore implement the first protective measures by freezing the crime scene. A forensic team, including a digital specialist, takes charge of the crime scene at 9:00 am.

5.2   Presentation of the Environment

The apartment is $45\,\mathrm{m}^2$ $(5\,\mathrm{m} \times 9\,\mathrm{m})$. It consists of three separate rooms: an entrance (room 1), a bedroom (room 2) and a living room (room 3). It contains many connected objects (Fig. 5). It is equipped with a home automation system from an Orvibo kit. It contains two opening sensors (1 and 2) and a motion sensor (3) coupled with a Wi-Fi camera (4). This kit is located in room 1 and controls two external openings. It communicates with the ZigBee protocol via a dedicated hub (5). It is located in room 3. The home automation system also consists of a Philips light bulb (6 and 7) connected to its hub (8). They are located in rooms 2 and 3 of the apartment. Otherwise, four Sen.se Cookies are hidden in different rooms. They turn household objects into connected objects. In our case, the Cookies monitor the water supply level of the coffee machine (9), the room temperature (10), the position of the bicycle (11) and the physical activity of the victim (12). All these objects are connected with a proprietary protocol to the Sen.se Mother (13). It is located in room 3. These different gateways, the Amazon Echo (14), the RaspberryPi0 (15) and the M136W IP camera (16) are connected to the Internet via WinkHub 2 (17).

The victim is on the bed in room 2. She has an Apple Watch 3 (18) on her right arm and an iPhone SE (19) in her pocket. Hidden in the bed is a sleep sensor called the Terraillon Dot (20). Other items in the apartment include a Sens'it (21), a Heroz bracelet (22) and a Nokia scale (23).

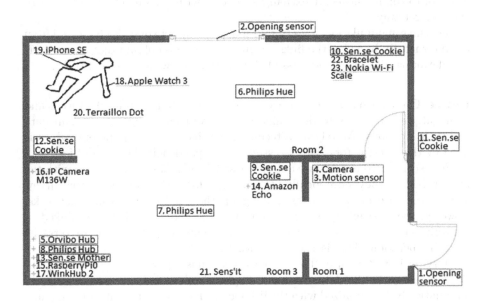

Fig. 5. Home layout with the IoT devices

5.3   Application of the Collection Methodology

Analysis of Local Network. The local infrastructure consists of four networks connected to the Internet (Fig. 6). Each network is treated independently.

The first network contains three connected objects: an Apple Watch 3, a Terraillon Dot and a Nokia scale. The smartwatch and the sleep analyzer are connected to the phone via Bluetooth. The scale uses Wi-Fi or Bluetooth protocol to communicate. The iPhone SE acts as a gateway. It provides Internet access to the connected objects.

By disconnecting the Global System for Mobile (GSM) communications, 4G and Wi-Fi networks from the smartphone, the device group is isolated from the outside environment. Thus, the SIM card is removed as a precautionary measure. The phone is placed in airplane mode.

The second network contains three connected objects: a M136W IP camera, an Amazon Echo and a Rasberry Pi0. It integrates three independent environments: Orvibo, Sen.se and Philips. The WinkHub 2 gateway provides Internet access to different connected objects and environments. It can be seen that a link between the first and second network is broken when the Wi-Fi connection of the iPhone is cut. By disconnecting the Ethernet cable from the WinkHub 2, the second network is isolated from the outside world.

The third and fourth networks are only made up of independent and connected local objects: Heroz and Sens'it. Heroz communicates via Bluetooth. However, in our case it is not connected to any gateway. Sens'it uses the SigFox protocol to communicate. It exchanges directly with the outside world through external gateways.

This first manipulation gives us four independent networks disconnected from the Internet. By breaking the links, we limit a migration of information to external platforms. We also avoid possible interactions between these networks.

Device Characterization. Studying the normal functioning of objects and their gateways helps us to determine the environments containing useful data and their locations. We rely on a technical database of the equipment, which is filled by the investigators. We also study the dependencies between objects.

Some connected objects use automatic synchronization of their data with the network. Thus, they store locally little useful information related to the survey. This is the case of the objects making up the Philips and Sen.se networks. However, the relevant data are contained in the gateways. They are linked to network activity and system configurations. Some objects are more versatile in their operation. This is the case with the objects of the first network and the Orvibo infrastructure. Thus, each object must be treated individually. In the first network, the data from the Apple Watch 3 and the Nokia scale are automatically synchronized with the iPhone SE. For the Terraillon Dot, a manual synchronization action must be performed by the user application. Note that the local data are also present in their internal memory.

Therefore, these different objects must be processed individually. The smartphone concentrates a lot of relevant information by acting as a gateway (zone 1) and a user interface via applications (zone 3). For the Orvibo network, all objects synchronize automatically. However, they do not have the same data management policy. The motion and opening sensors do not contain any useful data in memory. The Orvibo camera contains external storage in the form of an

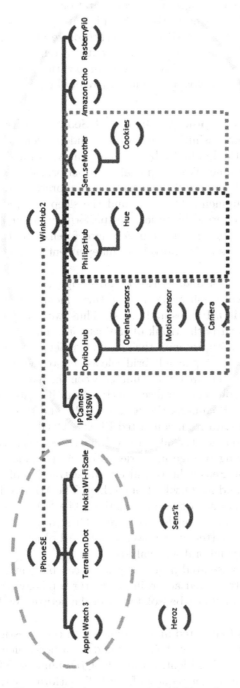

Fig. 6. Global mapping of the IoT environment

SD card. It acts as a buffer in case the network is lost. The gateways contain data about network activity and system configurations.

The other six devices in networks 2, 3 and 4 are processed independently. Heroz, Sens'it and the M136W IP camera synchronize automatically with the network. They do not contain any relevant data in our case. Amazon Echo, RasberryPi0 and WinkHub 2 synchronize some data with the network. They keep the relevant information locally. They must therefore be processed individually.

Analysis of Network Topology, Grab and Seal. Network 1 is structured in a point-to-point relationship. Each object is independent. Thus, connected objects can be isolated individually by disabling the Wi-Fi and Bluetooth connection on the smartphone. We are not able to perform data extraction from the Nokia scale and Terraillon Dot outside the laboratory. In fact, we need specific extraction equipment. The scale and the sleep analyzers are switched off by removing their internal batteries. We perform data extraction from the AppleWatch 3 and iPhone SE with our standard forensic tools. These devices are turned off. All objects in Network 1 are independently sealed for laboratory analysis.

Network 2 consists of a main network and peripheral networks. The main network is a hierarchical mesh network. The three independent edge networks are star networks: Orvibo, Philips and Sen.se. Thus, we start at the end of the branches and move towards the trunk of the network. The Orvibo and Philips objects communicate via ZigBee with their gateways. Sen.se is based on a proprietary protocol. The gateways play a hybrid role as an interface between networks and protocols. In a first step, we cut the link between the main gateway and each environment. Then all objects are disconnected from its gateway. This is also done with the M136W IP camera, the Amazon Echo and the RasberryPi0. We are not able to extract data from connected Philips, Orvibo and Sens'it objects and the Amazon Echo outside the laboratory. In fact, we need specific equipment for a chip off and reading storage memories. We perform data extraction from the Philips, Orvibo and Sens'it hubs. Indeed, the extraction of the Philips hub is done from the PLC and for Orvibo from Telnet. The M136W IP camera does not have any data relevant to the investigation. The SD cards of the Orvibo camera and the RasberryPi0 are also recovered. These devices are turned off by removing their internal batteries or power supply. All objects in network 2 are independently sealed for laboratory analysis.

Network 3 is already isolated from any grid. It can be managed as an offline object. Network 4 is structured according to a star topology. It communicates with external gateways. It must be isolated from the network by being placed in a Faraday cage.

Some devices are not collected in accordance with the investigation strategy. However, it is necessary to know their roles and identifiers, such as the Federal Communications Commission Identification (FCCID) number. This information may be used for analysis or for requests from IoT platform operators.

6   Operational Impact Factor

Several operations are carried out successively to collect devices and data: breaking network links to isolate the local infrastructure from the Internet, removing external cards, extracting data, changing the status of the devices and sealing them. Each action generates or deletes data. This section looks at the impact of these different operations.

Connected objects depend on a local infrastructure. They form a connected whole. Thus, a change in the infrastructure can cause logs to be written to the systems. By breaking the physical or radio links, the impact on writing is limited. It results from a loss of the network. However, we limit the leakage of stored information from the secondary network to the primary network. The study of the Sen'se gateways, Philips and Orvibo, did not reveal any writing in the logs once disconnected. However, an event is created when we disconnect the Amazon Echo in the directory: */system/dropbox/*. These manipulations must therefore be traced in the legal proceedings.

Data extraction can generate traces and loss of information. Direct acquisition leaves a write in the RAM. It modifies a potential source of information. Moreover, the result of a live forensic acquisition is neither repeatable nor reproducible. The only method of acquiring memory without alternation is Crash Dump. Unfortunately, it cannot be activated manually. The acquisition of internal memory during runtime also leads to a more or less significant alteration of the medium. Some methods cause the system to boot or to change to raise privileges or to exploit a security flaw. In order to control the impact of these solutions, operations can be performed in controlled laboratory environments.

A clean shutdown of the operating system necessarily generates a rewriting in the system. It is linked to the recording of application data in the RAM. Conversely, a hard shutdown consists of cutting off the power supply. It protects the memory of new entries. Implementing a system shutdown can result in: writing to event logs, deleting temporary files, purging caches, and system corruption. It may be accompanied by the execution of a script or application leading to the erasure or encryption of data. If the machine has a human-machine interface, we must record the date and time of the machine, the network to which it is connected and the applications running in the background. This operation must be carried out before switching off and sealing the object.

In some cases, the object cannot be deactivated or stopped. Thus, it continues to live and to write data into memory. The risk is that the data may be rewritten on important elements of the investigation after it has been sealed. This is especially the case with an active GPS watch, such as the Apple Watch 3, so it is more interesting to limit its operation. Thus, the investigator may have to stop the applications to freeze the state of the object. This technical act is comparable to putting a mobile phone in airplane mode. These technical operations must be retraced in its procedure. However, keeping objects connected with the seal alive also pose power supply problems. The device must be powered continuously to maintain the volatility of the data in memory.

Thus, any manipulation must be the subject of a note mentioning the act performed and its timestamp.

7   Conclusion

Introducing the Internet of Things (IoT) into the society provides more opportunities for forensic investigations. Connected objects are the actors and direct witnesses of events. However, the objects are heterogeneous and interconnected to the network. Their manipulation generates or alters the contained data. Faced with these results, the investigators must define a methodology to apprehend them. In this article, we present a collection framework. We study the alteration and the impact of the various actions carried out.

The next step in this research is to extract and analyze them. The challenge is to understand the interaction between connected objects and contextualized data in order to respond to a court.

References

1. Adelstein, F.: Live forensics: diagnosing your system without killing it first. Commun. ACM **49**(2), 63–66 (2006)
2. Attwood, A., Merabti, M., Fergus, P., Abuelmaatti, O.: SCCIR: smart cities critical infrastructure response framework. In: 2011 Developments in E-systems Engineering, pp. 460–464. IEEE (2011)
3. Brezinski, D., Killalea, T.: Guidelines for evidence collection and archiving. Network Working Group (1), February 2002. http://www.ietf.org/rfc/rfc3227.txt
4. Carrier, B., Spafford, E.: Getting physical with the digital investigation process. Int. J. Digit. Evid. **2**(2), 1–20 (2003)
5. Casey, E.: Digital Evidence and Computer Crime: Forensic Science, Computers, and the Internet. Academic press, Cambridge (2011)
6. Chauvenet, C., Etheve, G., Sedjai, M., Sharma, M.: G3-PLC based IoT sensor networks for SmartGrid. In: 2017 IEEE International Symposium on Power Line Communications and its Applications (ISPLC), pp. 1–6. IEEE (2017)
7. Copos, B., Levitt, K., Bishop, M., Rowe, J.: Is anybody home? inferring activity from smart home network traffic. In: 2016 IEEE Security and Privacy Workshops (SPW), pp. 245–251, May 2016. https://doi.org/10.1109/SPW.2016.48
8. Crispino, F.: Computerized forensic assistance software (FAS 1.0) for training and standardized investigation in distributed and disconnected services. Forensic Sci. Int. **132**(2), 125–129 (2003)
9. Dorsemaine, B., Gaulier, J., Wary, J., Kheir, N., Urien, P.: Internet of Things: a definition & taxonomy. In: Al-Begain, K., AlBeiruti, N. (eds.) 9th International Conference on Next Generation Mobile Applications, Services and Technologies, NGMAST 2015, Cambridge, United Kingdom, 9–11 September 2015, pp. 72–77. IEEE (2015). https://doi.org/10.1109/NGMAST.2015.71
10. Dovaston, D.: The police perspective. Sci. Justice **40**(2)(1), 150–151 (2000)
11. Gallop, A.: Private practice public duty. Sci. Justice **40**(2)(1), 104–108 (2000)
12. Granja, F.M., Rafael, G.D.R.: The preservation of digital evidence and its admissibility in the court. Int. J. Electron. Secur. Digit. Forensics **9**(1), 1–18 (2017)

13. Hahm, O., Baccelli, E., Petersen, H., Tsiftes, N.: Operating systems for low-end devices in the internet of things: a survey. IEEE Internet Things J. **3**(5), 720–734 (2016)
14. Inoue, H., Adelstein, F., Joyce, R.: Visualization in testing a volatile memory forensic tool. Digital Invest. **8**, S42–S51 (2011)
15. Kent, K., Chevalier, S., Grance, T., Dang, H.: Guide to integrating forensic techniques into incident response. NIST Spec. Publ. **10**(14), 800–86 (2006)
16. Kornblum, J.: Preservation of fragile digital evidence by first responders. In: Digital Forensics Research Workshop (DFRWS), pp. 1–11 (2002)
17. Miorandi, D., Sicari, S., De Pellegrini, F., Chlamtac, I.: Internet of Things: vision, applications and research challenges. Ad Hoc Netw. **10**(7), 1497–1516 (2012)
18. Nelson, B., Phillips, A., Steuart, C.: Guide to Computer Forensics and Investigations. Cengage Learning, Boston (2014)
19. Oriwoh, E., Jazani, D., Epiphaniou, G., Sant, P.: Internet of Things forensics: challenges and approaches. In: 9th IEEE International Conference on Collaborative Computing: Networking, Applications and Worksharing, pp. 608–615, October 2013. https://doi.org/10.4108/icst.collaboratecom.2013.254159
20. Oriwoh, E., Sant, P.: The forensics edge management system: a concept and design. In: 2013 IEEE 10th International Conference on Ubiquitous Intelligence and Computing and 2013 IEEE 10th International Conference on Autonomic and Trusted Computing, pp. 544–550. IEEE (2013)
21. Perumal, S., Norwawi, N., Raman, V.: Internet of Things (IoT) digital forensic investigation model: top-down forensic approach methodology. In: 2015 Fifth International Conference on Digital Information Processing and Communications (ICDIPC), pp. 19–23, October 2015. https://doi.org/10.1109/ICDIPC.2015.7323000
22. Pichan, A., Lazarescu, M., Soh, S.: Cloud forensics: technical challenges, solutions and comparative analysis. Digital Invest. **13**, 38–57 (2015)
23. Qin, Y., Sheng, Q., Falkner, N., Dustdar, S., Wang, H., Vasilakos, A.: When things matter: a survey on data-centric internet of things. J. Netw. Comput. Appl. **64**, 137–153 (2016). https://doi.org/10.1016/j.jnca.2015.12.016, http://www.sciencedirect.com/science/article/pii/S1084804516000606
24. Ruan, K., Carthy, J., Kechadi, T., Crosbie, M.: Cloud forensics. In: Peterson, G., Shenoi, S. (eds.) DigitalForensics 2011. IAICT, vol. 361, pp. 35–46. Springer, Heidelberg (2011). https://doi.org/10.1007/978-3-642-24212-0_3
25. Thing, V.L., Ng, K.Y., Chang, E.C.: Live memory forensics of mobile phones. Digital Invest. **7**, S74–S82 (2010)
26. Vömel, S., Freiling, F.: A survey of main memory acquisition and analysis techniques for the windows operating system. Digital Invest. **8**(1), 3–22 (2011)
27. Zareen, M., Waqar, A., Aslam, B.: Digital forensics: latest challenges and response. In: 2013 2nd National Conference on Information Assurance (NCIA), pp. 21–29. IEEE (2013)
28. Zawoad, S., Hasan, R.: FAIot: towards building a forensics aware eco system for the Internet of Things. In: 2015 IEEE International Conference on Services Computing, pp. 279–284, June 2015. https://doi.org/10.1109/SCC.2015.46

Effective Medical Image Copy-Move Forgery Localization Based on Texture Descriptor

Jiaqi Shi, Gang Wang$^{(\boxtimes)}$, Ming Su, and Xiaoguang Liu

College of CS, TJ Key Lab of NDST, Nankai University, Tianjin, China
{shijq,wgzwp,suming,liuxg}@nbjl.nankai.edu.cn

Abstract. Medical images are vulnerable to be maliciously tampered during network transmission, affecting diagnosis of doctors. Moreover, some images in medical research papers are intentionally manipulated, which reduce the credibility of the conclusions. Therefore, it is essential to research an effective and robust algorithm for medical image tamper detection ans localization. In this paper, we propose a copy-move forgery localization algorithm for medical images called MITD-CMFL. Due to texture structure information is complex and important for medical images, we obtain textural images from noise-reduced images by utilizing texture descriptor to gain more accurate features. It is difficult to extract a sufficient number of feature points with strong representation ability in smooth regions to characterize textures, we extract SIFT keypoints in texture images and decrease the contrast threshold. The experiments conducted on 2,898 tampered breast cancer images randomly selected from DDSM dataset show the pixel-level F_1 of MITD-CMFL reaches up to 95.07% under plain copy-move attack, and the method has superior performance even under typical image transformations compared to the state-of-the-art algorithms.

Keywords: Medical images · Copy-move · Forgery localization · Texture · DDSM dataset

1 Introduction

The telemedicine system is rapidly emerging with the vigorous development of computer networks. Through this system, doctors can judge health status of their patients according to the digital medical images. Especially modern image editing software have been able to achieve the degree of realism, sensitive information of patients in the telemedicine system may be maliciously tampered during network transmission. The lesion regions may be spread or covered up,

This work is partially supported by National Science Foundation of China (61872201, 61702521, U1833114); Science and Technology Development Plan of Tianjin (18ZXZNGX00140, 18ZXZNGX00200).

causing doctors to misdiagnose. Furthermore, from 1995 to 2004, 20,621 medical research papers published in 40 different journals in the fields of microbiology, immunology, cancer biology, and general biology, 3.8% of the papers contained problematic figures, with at least half exhibiting features suggestive of deliberate manipulations [3]. If the medical images in scientific papers are honest wrong or intentional falsification, it will make unscientific conclusions, reduce the credibility of the articles, and seriously affect the integrity of the authors. Based on the above two points, it is significant to identify the authenticity and locate tampering regions of medical images. Since medical images involve smoother regions and more complex texture structure information compared with nature images, the accuracy and practicality of medical image tamper detection and localization technologies still face significant challenges.

Digital image forensics methods are divided into *active tampering* and *passive tampering*. In the literature, most of the medical image tampering localization algorithms utilize the watermarking technique in active tampering [7,16,27,29]. Although the watermarking forensics methods achieve the goal of pixel-level forgery localization, the watermarking is embedded in the medical image in the form of additional information, which impairs the visual quality of the image. More importantly, doctors may misdiagnose and endanger the health status of patients. Even in reversible watermarking, additional preprocessing steps are required.

There are many existing passive tampering methods, where *copy-move* is one common manipulation which refers to duplicate one or more areas to other locations in the same image in order to conceal or duplicate some information. The copied areas may be rotated or scaled before pasting. The forgery detection methods for copy-move are divided into three groups: *blocked-based* [2,5,6,8,14,17,19,21,24,26,32], *keypoint-based* [1,4,11,13,15,18,22,28], and *keypoint-segmentation-based* [12,20,30,31]. For the block-based copy-move forgery detection algorithms, the original images are first divided into overlapping regular image blocks, then features are extracted separately for each block. At present, common block features include Discrete Cosine Transform (DCT) [8,26], Discrete Wavelet Transform (DWT) [17], Principal Component Analysis (PCA) [19], Singular Value Decomposition (SVD) [32], and other approaches. However, the robustness of these features are unsatisfactory to image scaling and rotation. Techniques based on circular harmonic transformation, like Zernike moment [21], Polar Cosine Transform (PCT) [14], Log Polar Transformation [24], Fourier-Merlin Transform [2], are performed well in rotation and scale invariant, which further improve the robustness of the block-based forgery detection approaches. In order to achieve higher robustness, Davide et al. proposed a fast approximation nearest neighbour search algorithm [6] suitable for computing image dense fields, but taking longer processing times. The keypoint-based methods are more robust to geometric attacks. The Scale-Invariant Feature Transform (SIFT) is the classic and popular keypoint extraction method [1,4,11], but has a higher computational cost. Many approaches improved the detection speed by improving SIFT algorithm [22,28]. Both SIFT algorithm and improved SIFT algorithm generally have a disadvantage that they cannot extract large and accurate keypoints when the regions are small or smooth. Li et al. [13] solved this problem well by lowering SIFT contrast threshold and rescaling the input image size. In recent years, the algorithms combining block-based and keypoint-based technologies have emerged, which avoid the high computational complexity of block-based technologies and the low recall rate of keypoint-based technologies. [20] integrated image segmentation and SIFT algorithm for the first time. Mohsen et al. [30] combined with PCT features and Simple Linear Iterative Clustering (SLIC) image segmentation, which located tampering regions more accurately. Li et al. [12] segmented the image into non-overlapping blocks and performed copy-move forgery detection algorithm in two stages.

The forgery detection methods mentioned above are all directed at natural images, which are not good at medical images. Medical images are smoother than natural images, whose texture and structure information is significant. The general forensic approaches perform normally when detecting smooth regions, and they can not extract high discriminating features in complex texture structures. There are currently few articles devoted to detecting medical images [9, 23, 25]. Surbhi et al. [23] located image copy-move forged regions by dividing medical images into overlapping blocks and calculating the Central Symmetric Local Binary Pattern of each block as the features, but the method could not resist geometric attacks. Guzin et al. [25] extracted the medical image texture information by using the Local Binary Pattern Rotational Invariant (LBPROT), and extracted SIFT feature points in the texture image for matching the copy-move regions. Ahmed et al. [9] proposed a medical image forgery detection system which used Wiener-filter to extract noise maps from images and utilized multiresolution regression filters on noise maps. Unfortunately, the system only detects whether the medical image has been tampered with and cannot locate the tamper regions. Due to the particularity of medical images and the low applicability of existing tamper detection approaches, developing a forgery detection scheme suitable for medical images is imperative.

In this paper, we propose an efficient and robust copy-move forgery localization scheme for medical images combining image blocks and keypoints. The main contributions are as follows:

- We obtain texture images by applying LBPROT texture descriptor to highlight texture structural information of medical images.
- We decrease the contrast threshold of SIFT and extract SIFT keypoints in LBPROT images to ensure that plenty of feature points which have high discrimination in smooth regions can be extracted.
- Experimental results on the forged DDSM dataset demonstrate that the proposed MITD-CMFL achieves higher F_1 compared with the existing schemes, even under rotation, scaling, adding Gaussian noise, and JPEG compression.

The remainder of this paper is organized as follows. A novel forgery detection and localization method called MITD-CMFL is detailed in Sect. 2. Section 3 analyzes experimental results and performance comparisons. Finally, the conclusion is in Sect. 4.

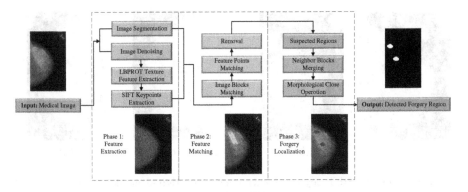

Fig. 1. Framework of the proposed MITD-CMFL.

2   Proposed Method

The algorithm MITD-CMFL follows the classic image forgery detection workflow. The process framework is shown in Fig. 1. It is roughly divided into three parts: feature extraction, feature matching, and forgery localization.

2.1   Feature Extraction

Feature extraction is a key step in our method. The quality of feature discrimination directly affects the accuracy of forgery detection and localization, especially for medical images with rich texture information. The proposed MITD-CMFL extracts texture feature points on the original image while segmenting this image into small patches.

Image Segmentation. We utilize SLIC method to segment the medical image into non-overlapping and irregular superpixel patches according to the texture structure and content characteristics, the obtained patches are meaningful and follow the boundary well. The SLIC initial sizes of different images are different. In general, the proper initial size of the patches is important to gain convincing forgery detection results for different shapes of forgery regions. When the initial size is too small, it will have a large computational expense; otherwise, the forgery detection results will not be sufficiently accurate. We adjust the initial size of superpixel according to the image size, which can achieve balances between localization accuracy and computational cost.

Image Denoising. In reality, medical images are often affected by imaging equipment and external environmental noise during acquisition, conversion, and transmission, resulting in degradation. Most real medical images are noisy images. The medical image to be tested is subjected to mean filtering, which eliminates irrelevant information and extracts useful image features.

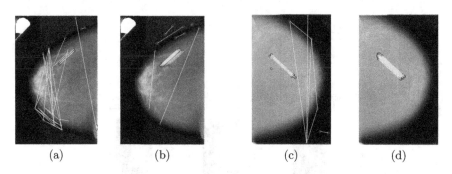

(a)	(b)	(c)	(d)

Fig. 2. (a) and (c): SIFT keypoints extracted from original medical images; (b) and (d): SIFT keypoints extracted from LBPROT texture images.

LBPROT Texture Feature Extraction. Noise reduction results in loss of information such as texture and edges, but LBPROT can enhance images and increase the contrast between foreground and background so that creating a relatively clean input for the subsequent extraction of SIFT features and achieving better detection results.

Doctors diagnose the disease through image texture analysis. The texture information of the image cannot be ignored in medical image forgery detection. On the contrary, the complex texture structure information helps the forgery localization to be more precise. It is a serious challenge that how to extract high discriminating features in smooth and texture-rich medical images. LBPROT can extract the texture information of smooth regions from medical images effectively. As shown in Fig. 2(a) and Fig. 2(c), these pictures are obtained by directly extracting SIFT keypoints in the original medical images and then applying simple threshold matching. It can be seen that there are some mismatched feature points and the number of feature points that are correctly matched is not much. Figure 2(b) and Fig. 2(d) show SIFT keypoints extracted and matched in the LBPROT texture map. Since LBPROT can enhance the texture structure information, the feature points can be matched more accurately and in larger quantities in contrast.

SIFT Keypoints Extraction. LBP operator eliminates the problem of lighting changes to a certain extent, and the low dimension of texture features makes the calculation fast. The LBPROT makes the LBP operator more robust by introducing a rotation invariant definition. But it also makes the LBP lose the direction information. We need to address this shortcoming to ensure the accuracy and robustness of the proposed algorithm. Due to the SIFT algorithm has direction information and has excellent robustness against various attacks, we combine SIFT keypoints to characterize image blocks which overcome the shortcomings of LBPROT. SIFT and LBPROT can complement each other which both are indispensable to ensure the accuracy and robustness of the algorithm.

In the proposed MITD-CMFL, each image block consists of a set of SIFT feature points. Because of the rich texture information of medical images, the SIFT algorithm is applied to the LBPROT texture image to extract feature points, so that the obtained keypoints have higher ability to represent image texture information and stronger discrimination. Medical images are smoother compared with nature images, in smooth areas, the extreme contrast values are often very low. Any extreme value with a contrast value less than the threshold is rejected as the final SIFT keypoint. As a result, the number of SIFT keypoints detected in smooth areas will be reduced. A small number of feature points obviously cannot be accurately located in forged regions. To guarantee that a sufficient number of feature points can be generated in smooth regions, we decrease the SIFT contrast threshold (set to 0.6 in our experiments), allowing for a large number of extreme values with low contrast values.

2.2   Feature Matching

In this subsection, we propose a simple feature matching scheme. Typically, our method comprises three steps.

Step 1): we match the SIFT keypoints extracted from the LBPROT texture image with the superpixel blocks obtained by SLIC segmentation according to the position information, and obtain a many-to-one relationship diagram between the feature points P and the image blocks B as shown in (1):

$$\{P_m, P_n, \cdots \in B_i \;\; m, n, i = 1, 2, \cdots\}, \tag{1}$$

where P_m represents the m-th SIFT keypoint; B_i is the i-th image block.

Step 2): we calculate the distance d between the feature points in different image blocks as shown in (2):

$$d(P_a, P_b) = \sqrt{\sum_{s=1}^{128}(f_a^s - f_b^s)^2},$$

$$a, b = 1, 2, \cdots, N, \; and \; a \neq b, \tag{2}$$

$$P_a \in B_i, \; P_b \in B_j, \; i \neq j,$$

where f_a^s represents the s-th dimension SIFT descriptor of the a-th feature point, and each SIFT keypoint has a 128-dimensional feature descriptor; N denotes the total number of SIFT keypoints; where P_a and P_b belong to different image blocks, respectively.

The matching between the feature points is successful if the distance is not greater than the threshold T_P (the threshold is set to 0.5), that is, $d(P_a, P_b) \leq T_P$. Then we mark the feature points whose matching is successful.

Step 3): we record the number of feature points successfully matched between each pair of image patches as the matching coefficient. It is necessary to remove the image block pair if the matching coefficient is smaller than the threshold T_B (the threshold is set to 2), which means deleting the feature points in the two image blocks that were successfully matched in step 2).

2.3   Forgery Localization

After the feature matching, the marked feature point pairs are obtained, but this is only the approximate location of the forged regions, and we need to locate precise forged regions. Forgery localization of our method involves three steps.

Step 1): we perform SLIC superpixel segmentation again, but this time the SLIC initial size is small (set to 20 in the experiments), which can result in small superpixel blocks. We replace the matching feature point pairs with small super-pixel blocks, so that the separated pixels are converted into suspected regions with strong connectivity.

Step 2): for each suspected region, we compare it with the superpixel blocks adjacent to it. We check whether their color features are similar. Specifically, we calculate the mean value R of the pixels in the suspected region and the mean value S_i of the pixels in the i-th adjacent superpixel block. If $|R - S_i| \leq T_s$ (the threshold T_s is set to 5), the superpixel block is included in the suspected regions.

Step 3): we apply the morphological close operation into the suspected regions. A circular structural element is used in the closing operation whose radius is related to the size of the suspected regions. The close operation can fill the gaps in the merged regions in step 2) while maintaining the shape of the region unchanged.

3   Experiment Results

In this section, we conduct a series of experiments to evaluate the detection and localization performance of the proposed method for medical image copy-move forgery. The medical image dataset we used is the DDSM database [10] established by medical institutions to store breast cancer images and the lesion regions are marked by expert radiologists. The database includes more than 10,000 medical images in 2,620 cases. We randomly copy an area that has arbitrary shape in the cancer regions of the medical image and paste it to any random position of the same image, which do not leave a mark and the naked eyes cannot distinguish whether it is tampering or not and tampering with the localization.

Our experimental evaluation indicators are divided into image-level and pixel-level. Image-level indicators focus on assessing the ability of medical images to be correctly identified as forged or genuine. Pixel-level indicators analyze the performance for the accuracy of medical image forgery localization. In the following experiments, the three characteristics F_1 scores, True Positive Rate (TPR), and False Positive Rate (FPR) are used to evaluate the performance of the proposed MITD-CMFL, which are respectively defined as:

$$F_1 = \frac{2TP}{2TP + FP + FN},$$

$$TPR = \frac{TP}{TP + FN}, FPR = \frac{FP}{TN + FP}. \tag{3}$$

Table 1. Forgery localization performance of different methods.

Methods	Image level			Pixel level		
	F_1(%)	TPR(%)	FPR(%)	F_1(%)	TPR(%)	FPR(%)
FE-CMFD-HFPM [13]	99.92	99.85	0.00	90.01	98.10	0.19
Segment-CMFD [20]	99.63	99.27	0.00	58.68	79.61	1.27
Iterative-CMFD [30]	99.78	99.56	0.00	42.96	98.94	4.81
CMFD-PM [6]	99.85	99.71	0.00	86.23	87.35	0.07
RITD-MITD [23]	99.84	99.68	0.00	77.61	97.91	0.43
MITD-PIA [25]	99.81	99.63	0.00	81.93	95.65	0.29
MITD-CMFL	**100.00**	**100.00**	**0.00**	**95.07**	**98.81**	**0.08**

The F_1 score is a performance indicator of the integrated TPR and FPR. The higher the F_1, the better the performance of the algorithm. In this work, we use F-image and F-pixel to represent the F_1 scores at the image level and the pixel level, respectively. At the image level, TPR is the probability of detecting a forged image, which is defined as the ratio of the number of correctly detected fake images to the actual number of forged images; FPR is defined as the ratio of the number of correctly detected pristine images to the actual number of genuine images. Where TP (true positive) indicates the number of correctly detected fake images; TN (true negative) is the number of correctly detected genuine images; FN (false negative) calculates the number of undetected forged images; and FP (false positive) is the number of wrongly detected pristine images. In the pixel level, TPR is the probability that the relevant regions are detected, which is defined as the ratio of the number of correctly detected forged pixels to the number of forged pixels in the ground-truth fake image; FPR is expressed as the ratio of the number of genuine pixels detected correctly to the actual number of pristine pixels. Where TP, TN, FN, and FP represent the number of correctly detected fake pixels, correctly detected pristine pixels, wrongly undetected forged pixels, and missing detected genuine pixels. In general, a higher TPR and a lower FPR simultaneously indicate superior performance.

All experiments in this paper are conducted on the PC with Core-i7 and 12-GB RAM, operating in the MATLAB R2016a.

3.1 Evaluation Under Plain Copy-Move Attack

In this subsection, we evaluate the proposed MITD-CMFL under plain copy-move attack, namely no further attack is performed on the copy-move regions. The experiments of the subsection are performed on 1362 medical images randomly selected from DDSM. We selected six different copy-move forgery detection schemes as the baselines, including block-based [6,23], keypoint-based [13,25], and keypoint-segmentation-based [20,30]. Among them, [23] and [25] are algorithms for tampering localization of medical images. Table 1 lists the results on medical images of the DDSM dataset obtained by different copy-move

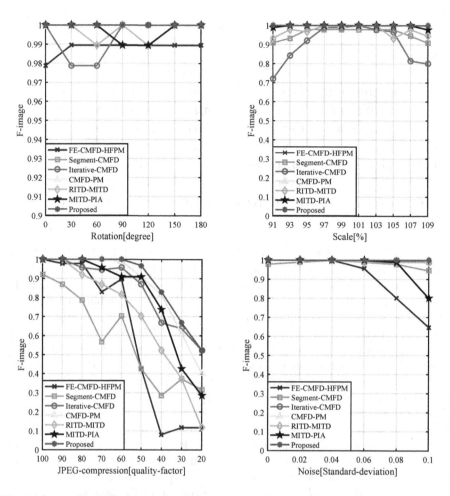

Fig. 3. Image level F_1 curves for different methods against rotation, scaling, JPEG compression, and Gaussian noise addition.

forgery detection methods. The algorithm FE-CMFD-HFPM improves the number of keypoints extracted in smooth regions, but cannot provide good support for texture information. The methods RITD-MITD and MITD-PIA are aimed at medical image tampering detection which extract the texture features of images. But other parts of RITD-MITD do not combine well with the texture information, and do not give full play to the advantages of texture features. Since medical images are relatively smooth, MITD-PIA cannot guarantee that enough keypoints with high discriminative ability in smooth regions are extracted to characterize texture features. The other three algorithms have poor detection capabilities which are unable to adapt to rich texture features and smooth regions of medical images. The proposed algorithm MITD-CMFL greatly overcomes such limitation which not only realizes the importance of texture information of med-

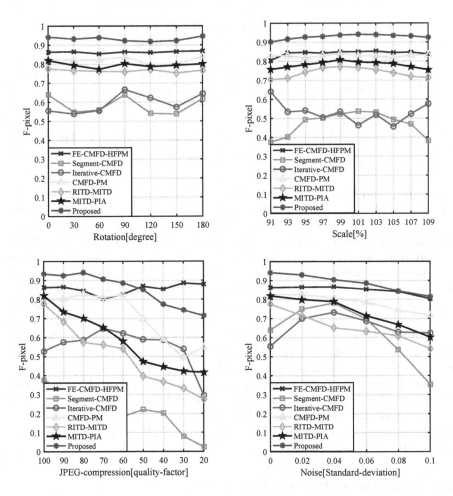

Fig. 4. Pixel level F_1 curves for different methods against rotation, scaling, JPEG compression, and Gaussian noise addition.

ical images, but also can well handle the problem of small number of SIFT feature points in smooth regions and weak representation ability. MITD-CMFL has considerable performance compare to other algorithms and achieves 95.07% high-precision tampering localization results.

3.2 Evaluation Against Different Attacks

In this subsection, we test the performance of MITD-CMFL against various attacks. The dataset used is 48 medical images randomly selected from the DDSM. We use image editing software to generate an image set containing 1536 images in total under different attacks comprising rotation, scaling, JPEG compression, and Gaussian noise addition. The details are as follows:

- Rotation: The rotation angle of each copied region ranges from 0° to 180° by a step size 30°. There are $7 \times 48 = 336$ medical images in total;
- Scaling: Each copied region is scaled from 91% to 109% of the scale factor with a step size of 2%, which can generate $10 \times 48 = 480$ medical images;
- JPEG compression: JPEG compression for each medical image using quality factor (QF) between 20 and 100 by a step size 10, in this case, we test $9 \times 48 = 432$ medical images;
- Gaussian noise addition: Gaussian noise is added to each medical image with standard value from 0 to 0.1 and the step size is 0.02. This produces a total of $6 \times 48 = 288$ medical images.

Figure 3 and Fig. 4 respectively show the F_1 curves for the image level and the pixel level against different attacks. At the image level, our proposed algorithm is completely superior to other algorithms. At the pixel level, our scheme is more sensitive to JPEG compression with the QF less than 60. After JPEG compression, especially when the QF is low, medical images lose their texture structures in a distorted manner, but texture information is the guarantee of detection accuracy. In addition, it exhibits better stability under other attacks. Although the stability of JPEG compression is slightly inferior to the method FE-CMFD-HFPM at the pixel level, the F1-measure curve at the image level of the FE-CMFD-HFPM indicates that its performance of correctly detecting whether the forged medical image is poor. Especially when the QF is less than 60, the detection performance is rapidly degraded, and it is basically impossible to resist this attack. Taken together, the proposed MITD-CMFL achieves better robustness gains over all the cases against the competing algorithms. The tampering localization algorithm RITD-MITD and MITD-PIA specifically for medical images cannot well resist these common attacks, which is a fatal disadvantage for medical images.

3.3 Evaluation of Different Phases

In this subsection, we test how the feature extraction scheme affects the performance of MITD-CMFL. The dataset for this part of the experiments is the same as Subsect. 3.1. Since the experiments involved in this subsection have little effect on the image-level evaluation indicators, we only show the experimental results at the pixel level.

The Initial Block Size of Superpixels in SLIC. The choice of initial block size of superpixels in SLIC affects the tampering localization accuracy and detection speed of the proposed algorithm. A larger initial block reduces the localization accuracy, while a smaller initial block brings a greater computational cost. In order to choose a suitable initial block size, we weigh the localization accuracy and detection speed. As shown in Fig. 5, during the process of changing the initial block from large to small, the accuracy of tampering localization is continuously improved, and the calculation cost is continuously increased. When the segmented image blocks are large, the probability of un-tampered regions being

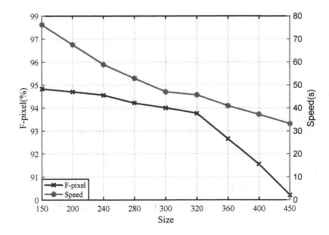

Fig. 5. F-pixel and speed of MITD-CMFL for different initial block sizes of superpixels in SLIC.

judged as tampered regions increases, which will cause the *FPR* to increase, and eventually reduce the *F-pixel*. When the initial blocks are small, the number of segmented image blocks increases, and the amount of SLIC calculations increases. Most importantly, the computational cost of the feature block matching process after segmentation will increase sharply. Considering that when the initial blocks are less than 300, the calculation cost rises sharply, but the improvement in positioning accuracy brought by it is not so obvious. After weighing, we chose 300 as the initial block size of SLIC in the proposed algorithm. Because the medical images in the DDSM dataset used for experiments are relatively large, more than 80% of the images are larger than 3000×3000, the overall calculation speed of the algorithm is relatively slow.

Table 2. The performance of different noise reduction methods.

Methods	$F_1(\%)$	$TPR(\%)$	$FPR(\%)$
MITD-CMFL+Mean filtering	**95.07**	**98.81**	**0.08**
MITD-CMFL+Wiener filtering	85.12	75.80	0.008
MITD-CMFL+Median filtering	79.56	66.89	0.01

The Noise Reduction Methods Table 2 shows the performance of different noise reduction methods on our algorithm. We compare three different noise reduction methods including mean filtering, Wiener filtering, and median filtering. We use *MITD-CMFL+Mean filtering*, *MITD-CMFL+Wiener filtering*, and *MITD-CMFL+Median filtering* represent these noise reduction methods respectively. According to the results in Table 2, we can see that the forgery detection

Table 3. Forgery localization performance of different methods with or without mean filtering.

Methods	With mean filtering			Without mean filtering		
	$F_1(\%)$	$TPR(\%)$	$FPR(\%)$	$F_1(\%)$	$TPR(\%)$	$FPR(\%)$
FE-CMFD-HFPM [13]	89.99	98.07	0.19	90.01	98.10	0.19
Segment-CMFD [20]	57.93	86.35	1.34	58.68	79.61	1.27
Iterative-CMFD [30]	41.91	98.64	3.96	42.96	98.94	4.81
CMFD-PM [6]	85.71	87.01	0.06	86.23	87.35	0.07
RITD-MITD [23]	77.83	97.52	0.41	77.61	97.91	0.43
MITD-PIA [25]	84.14	96.87	0.18	81.93	95.65	0.29
MITD-CMFL	**95.07**	**98.81**	**0.08**	**91.17**	**85.79**	**0.02**

method with mean filtering can extract more useful image features for MR medical image. Median filtering is easy to cause medical images discontinuity, and Wiener filtering is a non-stationary random process that is less friendly to noise reduction.

Noise reduction is a pre-treatment process for medical images, and noise reduction is an optional option, but it results in loss of information such as texture and edges. LBPROT texture descriptor can enhance images and increase the contrast between the foreground and the background so that creating a relatively clean input for the subsequent extraction of the SIFT features and achieving better localization results. Since both MITD-PIA and the proposed MITD-CMFL extract the texture features of medical images through LBPROT, we can observe from the Table 3 that the tampering localization accuracy of these two algorithms is improved after the mean filtering, while noise reduction has no effect on the other algorithms or reduces their performance.

Table 4. Forgery localization performance of different texture descriptors.

Methods	$F_1(\%)$	$TPR(\%)$	$FPR(\%)$
MITD-CMFL+NO_LBP	86.91	79.21	0.02
MITD-CMFL+LBP	90.20	85.51	0.01
MITD-CMFL+LBPEQU	47.42	41.07	0.002
MITD-CMFL+LBPROT	**95.07**	**98.81**	**0.08**

The LBP Operators. In the field of medical information, research on the physical characteristics of medical images is helpful to improve the positioning accuracy of image tampering detection. LBP is an indispensable step for MITD-CMFL owing to medical images have rich texture information, which can emphasize texture structures of medical images. Different LBP texture descriptors have different effects on MITD-CMFL. As shown in Table 4, we have no LBP (*MITD-CMFL+NO_LBP*), LBP basic descriptor (*MITD-CMFL+LBP*), LBP equivalent descriptor (*MITD-CMFL+LBPEQU*), and rotation-invariant LBP descriptor (*MITD-CMFL+LBPROT*) are tested. The texture structure information of medical images is more complicated and more important than natural images, so it is necessary to specifically extract texture information. LBPROT is the best choice among different LBP descriptors which extends the 3×3 neighbourhood to any neighbourhood and replaces the square neighbourhood with a circular neighbourhood, it can adapt to texture features of different scales and achieve the grayscale and rotation invariant. Therefore, the extracted SIFT feature points representation ability under LBPROT descriptor is stronger, and the forgery localization performance is better.

4 Conclusion

Medical images are smooth and have complex texture structures. Accordingly, we propose an effective and robust method MITD-CMFL for medical image copy-move forgery detection and localization. MITD-CMFL combines block-based and keypoint-based technologies, which segments the medical image into semantically independent patches by using SLIC and matches the block features consisting of SIFT keypoints. LBPROT can reflect texture information of medical images, so that the obtained SIFT keypoints from texture images have high discriminating ability. To extract a larger number of feature points even in smooth regions of medical images, we decrease the SIFT contrast threshold. Experimental results demonstrate the proposed MITD-CMFL achieves higher success rate of detection and higher accuracy of localization. Despite these, there is much room for improving the robustness against JPEG compression and increasing the practicality of our method.

References

1. Amerini, I., Ballan, L., Caldelli, R., Del Bimbo, A., Serra, G.: A sift-based forensic method for copy-move attack detection and transformation recovery. IEEE Trans. Inf. Forensics Secur. **6**(3), 1099–1110 (2011)
2. Bayram, S., Sencar, H.T., Memon, N.: An efficient and robust method for detecting copy-move forgery. In: 2009 IEEE International Conference on Acoustics, Speech and Signal Processing, pp. 1053–1056 (2009)
3. Bik, E.M., Casadevall, A., Fang, F.C.: The prevalence of inappropriate image duplication in biomedical research publications. MBio **7**(3), e00809–16 (2016)
4. Chen, C.-C., Lu, W.-Y., Chou, C.-H.: Rotational copy-move forgery detection using SIFT and region growing strategies. Multimedia Tools Appl. **78**(13), 18293–18308 (2019). https://doi.org/10.1007/s11042-019-7165-8
5. Cozzolino, D., Poggi, G., Verdoliva, L.: Copy-move forgery detection based on patchmatch. In: 2014 IEEE International Conference on Image Processing (ICIP), pp. 5312–5316 (2014)

6. Cozzolino, D., Poggi, G., Verdoliva, L.: Efficient dense-field copy-move forgery detection. IEEE Trans. Inf. Forensics Secur. **10**(11), 2284–2297 (2015)

7. Eswaraiah, R., Reddy, E.S.: Robust medical image watermarking technique for accurate detection of tampers inside region of interest and recovering original region of interest. IET Image Process. **9**(8), 615–625 (2015)

8. Fridrich, A.J., Soukal, B.D., Lukáš, A.J.: Detection of copy-move forgery in digital images. In: Proceedings of Digital Forensic Research Workshop (2003)

9. Ghoneim, A., Muhammad, G., Amin, S.U., Gupta, B.: Medical image forgery detection for smart healthcare. IEEE Commun. Mag. **56**(4), 33–37 (2018)

10. Heath, M., Bowyer, K., Kopans, D., Moore, R., Kegelmeyer, P.: The digital database for screening mammography. In: Proceedings of the Fourth International Workshop on Digital Mammography (2000)

11. Jin, G., Wan, X.: An improved method for sift-based copy-move forgery detection using non-maximum value suppression and optimized j-linkage. Signal Process. Image Commun. **57**, 113–125 (2017)

12. Li, J., Li, X., Yang, B., Sun, X.: Segmentation-based image copy-move forgery detection scheme. IEEE Trans. Inf. Forensics Secur. **10**(3), 507–518 (2014)

13. Li, Y., Zhou, J.: Fast and effective image copy-move forgery detection via hierarchical feature point matching. IEEE Trans. Inf. Forensics Secur. **14**(5), 1307–1322 (2018)

14. Li, Y.: Image copy-move forgery detection based on polar cosine transform and approximate nearest neighbor searching. Forensic Sci. Int. **224**(1–3), 59–67 (2013)

15. Manu, V., Mehtre, B.M.: Copy-move tampering detection using affine transformation property preservation on clustered keypoints. Signal Image Video Process. **12**(3), 549–556 (2018)

16. Memon, N.A., Chaudhry, A., Ahmad, M., Keerio, Z.A.: Hybrid watermarking of medical images for ROI authentication and recovery. Int. J. Comput. Math. **88**(10), 2057–2071 (2011)

17. Muhammad, G., Hussain, M., Bebis, G.: Passive copy move image forgery detection using undecimated dyadic wavelet transform. Digital Invest. **9**(1), 49–57 (2012)

18. Muzaffer, G., Ulutas, G.: A fast and effective digital image copy move forgery detection with binarized sift. In: 2017 40th International Conference on Telecommunications and Signal Processing (TSP), pp. 595–598 (2017)

19. Popescu, A.C., Farid, H.: Exposing digital forgeries by detecting duplicated image regions. Technical Report TR2004-515, Department of Computer Science, Dartmouth College, pp. 1–11 (2004)

20. Pun, C.M., Yuan, X.C., Bi, X.L.: Image forgery detection using adaptive oversegmentation and feature point matching. IEEE Trans. Inf. Forensics Secur. **10**(8), 1705–1716 (2015)

21. Ryu, S.J., Kirchner, M., Lee, M.J., Lee, H.K.: Rotation invariant localization of duplicated image regions based on Zernike moments. IEEE Trans. Inf. Forensics Secur. **8**(8), 1355–1370 (2013)

22. Shahroudnejad, A., Rahmati, M.: Copy-move forgery detection in digital images using affine-sift. In: 2016 2nd International Conference of Signal Processing and Intelligent Systems (ICSPIS), pp. 1–5 (2016)

23. Sharma, S., Ghanekar, U.: A rotationally invariant texture descriptor to detect copy move forgery in medical images. In: 2015 IEEE International Conference on Computational Intelligence & Communication Technology, pp. 795–798 (2015)

24. Tejas, K., Swathi, C., Rajesh, K.M.: Copy move forgery using Hus invariant moments and log polar transformations (2018)

25. Ulutas, G., Ustubioglu, A., Ustubioglu, B., Nabiyev, V.V., Ulutas, M.: Medical image tamper detection based on passive image authentication. J. Digital Imaging **30**(6), 695–709 (2017)
26. Wang, H., Wang, H.: Perceptual hashing-based image copy-move forgery detection. Secur. Commun. Netw. (2018)
27. Wu, J.H., et al.: Tamper detection and recovery for medical images using near-lossless information hiding technique. J. Digital Imaging **21**(1), 59–76 (2008)
28. Yang, B., Sun, X., Guo, H., Xia, Z., Chen, X.: A copy-move forgery detection method based on CMFD-SIFT. Multimedia Tools Appl. **77**(1), 837–855 (2017). https://doi.org/10.1007/s11042-016-4289-y
29. Zain, J.M., Fauzi, A.R.: Medical image watermarking with tamper detection and recovery. In: 2006 International Conference of the IEEE Engineering in Medicine and Biology Society, pp. 3270–3273 (2006)
30. Zandi, M., Mahmoudi-Aznaveh, A., Talebpour, A.: Iterative copy-move forgery detection based on a new interest point detector. IEEE Trans. Inf. Forensics Secur. **11**(11), 2499–2512 (2016)
31. Zhao, F., Shi, W., Qin, B., Liang, B.: Image forgery detection using segmentation and swarm intelligent algorithm. Wuhan Univ. J. Nat. Sci. **22**(2), 141–148 (2017)
32. Zhao, J., Guo, J.: Passive forensics for copy-move image forgery using a method based on DCT and SVD. Forensic Sci. Int. **233**(1–3), 158–166 (2013)

A Partial Approach
to Intrusion Detection

John Sheppard[(⊠)] [iD]

Waterford Institute of Technology, Waterford, Ireland
jsheppard@wit.ie

Abstract. The need for intrusion detection continues to grow with the advancement of new and emerging devices, the increase in the vectors of attack these bring, and their computational limitations. This work examines the suitability of a traditional data mining approach often overlooked in intrusion detection, partial decision trees, on the recent CICIDS 2017 dataset. The approach was evaluated against recent deep learning results and shows that the partial decision tree outperformed these deep learning techniques for the detection of DDoS and Portscan attacks. Further analysis of the complete dataset has been performed using this partial technique. The creation of a reduced feature version of the dataset is proposed using PCA and is evaluated using a partial decision tree. It shows that a ten feature version of the dataset can produce a detection rate of 99.4% across the twelve classes, with a 77% reduction in training time.

Keywords: IDS · Data mining · Partial decision trees · CICIDS · PCA

1 Introduction

The critical importance of Intrusion Detection Systems (IDS) and the suitability of anomaly detection classification models are highlighted in [1] and [2] and reinforced in recent surveys conducted by [3–6], and [7]. Recurring issues associated with intrusion detection include the problem of high dimensionality associated with intrusion detection datasets [8–10], along with the application and evaluation of data mining algorithms for intrusion detection [8,11].

Intrusion Detection is founded upon the belief that the actions of an intruder deviate from those of a normal user in a measurable manner. The measure of the deviation, however, may not be clear and there may exist some overlap between the two behavioural styles. An IDS is a system used for detecting such intrusions. An IDS attempts to detect illegitimate users gaining access to a network or system, and legitimate users misusing resources. In [12] Denning proposed four reasons for the development of such systems. Even with the advancement of technology these motivating factors are still valid. They are:

© ICST Institute for Computer Sciences, Social Informatics and Telecommunications Engineering 2021
Published by Springer Nature Switzerland AG 2021. All Rights Reserved
S. Goel et al. (Eds.): ICDF2C 2020, LNICST 351, pp. 78–97, 2021.
https://doi.org/10.1007/978-3-030-68734-2_5

1. the majority of Information Technology (IT) systems suffer from security vulnerabilities; it is not always feasible to identify and fix theses issues due to technological or financial constraints;
2. where vulnerabilities have been identified in these systems it is not easy to replace these systems due to either financial constraints or due to a trade-off in usability;
3. it is not possible to build a completely secure system especially considering the two very independent and non-integrated worlds of software development and security where it has been tradition to develop and release software as quickly as possible and patch problems later;
4. even if systems are secured externally, attacks can occur internally through avenues such as privilege escalation or misuse.

To tackle these problems there has been a wealth of work based on the application of Artificial Intelligence (AI) techniques to fabricated datasets. Models produced by researchers in the past have been weakened through the analysis of the datasets on which these models were based. In 2018 the CICIDS 2017 dataset was released, and an attempt was made to address the issues that had been discovered in earlier datasets. This work focuses on the performance of traditional data mining, and deep learning techniques on this dataset in terms of accuracy, false alarm rates and speed.

In this work a Partial Decision Tree approach has been used on the CICIDS 2017 dataset for the first time. It has been chosen for its speed and accuracy. Decision tree techniques have been commonly used on various different IDS datasets. Partial Decision Trees have been are applied here as they tend to produce higher accuracy rates than separate and conquer techniques, while being faster than divide and conquer approaches.

1.1 Contribution of This Work

The contribution of this work can be summarized as follows:

- An evaluation of a partial decision tree approach to the complete CICIDS 2017 dataset, and to a Principal Component Analysis (PCA) reduced feature version of this dataset.
- An evaluation of a partial decision tree versus a deep learning approach for the detection of Denial of Service (DoS), Distribute Denial of Service (DDoS) and Probing attacks using the CICIDS 2017 dataset.

1.2 Structure of This Work

Section 2 presents the related research in the area of IDS. Section 3 details the dataset used. Section 4 presents the methodology used. Section 5 presents the results of the approach taken. Section 6 discusses the findings. Section 7 summarises the conclusions of the paper, and identifies future work that needs to be addressed in the area.

2   Related Work

Intrusion detection systems can take several forms. In accordance with the National Institute for Standards and Technology (NIST) [13] these are Network Intrusion Detection Systems (NIDS), Host Intrusion Detection Systems (HIDS), Network Baseline Analysers (NBA) and Wireless Intrusion Detection Systems (WIDS). These systems are characterised by different monitoring and analysing approaches. These approaches can be described in terms of a generic process model. This model has three fundamental components, (i) information sources, (ii) analysis engine (iii) response [14].

For research purposes, the community has worked on the development of different datasets to replicate the information source phase, and to give researchers a benchmark for the analysis phase. A review of eleven of the most popular datasets used in intrusion detection highlighted eleven shortcomings with these datasets [15]. The datasets reviewed were:

- Darpa (Lincoln Laboratory 1998, 1999)
- KDD 99 (University of California, Irvine 1998, 99)
- Defcon Dataset 2000
- CAIDA 2002/2016
- LBNL (Lawrence Berkeley National Laboratory and ICSI - 2004/2005)
- CDX (United States Military Academy 2009)
- Kyoto (Kyoto University - 2009)
- Twente (University of Twente - 2009)
- UMASS (University of Massachusetts - 2011)
- ISCX2012 (University of New Brunswick - 2012)
- ADFA (University of New South Wales - 2013)

Following the review of these datasets, a new dataset was designed taking account of these shortcomings. The release of the CICIDS-17 dataset by the Canadian Institute for Cybersecurity [16] gave the research community a new dataset to work with. The dataset was produced over five days during July 2017. This dataset contained B profile data used to produce benign activity of 25 users across HTTP, HTTPS, FTP, SSH, and email protocols. The first day of data did not contain any attack data. The dataset also contained attacks conducted over the other four days. The implemented attacks include Brute Force FTP, Brute Force SSH, DoS, Heartbleed, Web Attack, Infiltration, Botnet and DDoS. The dataset was made available as .pcap files and as .CSV files for research. Eighty features were constructed from the data. In 2018 the CSE-CICIDS 2018 dataset was released. It has been reviewed and compared with the 2017 version [17]. They found improvements in the sample sizes for some attacks, in particular for Botnet and Infiltration attacks, but that the number of Web attack samples were small at 928 instances. This paper focuses primarily on the detection of Portscan, DoS and DDoS attacks and so the CICIDS 2017 dataset has been used.

This dataset has been analysed using Support Vector Machines (SVM) and deep learning techniques for the detection of port scans by [18]. On a subset of the data consisting of 286467 records, where 127537 were benign and 158930 were port scan attempts. The dataset was split with 67% used for training and 33% used for testing. This gave 191684 samples for training and 94412 for testing. The deep learning model was trained based on 30 passes. It was found that Port Scans could be detected with a deep learning machine with an accuracy of 97.8% while SVMs could only achieve 69.8% accuracy. On a separate version of the dataset containing 80 features, and 26,167 DDoS and 26,805 benign examples, [19] achieved accuracy rates of 60.69% for SVMs and 99.0% for a decision tree approach. However, the decision tree algorithm used is not specified.

Shallow and deep learning methods are an advancement on Artificial Neural Network (ANN) architectures. An ANN which consists of one or two layers is considered to be shallow learning. Deep learning consists of several hidden layers [20]. Deep learning techniques can be categorised into generative and discriminative architectures [21]. Deep learning techniques require larger amounts of data than traditional machine learning algorithms. They also require longer training times and higher performance machines. However deep learning does tend to have the advantage of higher accuracy rates and eliminate the need for the feature extraction phase by identifying high-level features in an incremental manner. Deep learning also tends to solve problems end-to-end.

Generative models depict independence/dependence for distribution graphically. Generative models can be classed as Recurrent Neural Network (RNN), Deep Auto-Encoders, Deep Boltzmann Machines (DBM) and Deep Believe Networks (DBN). Discriminative architectures, such as those used in Convolutional Neural Networks (CNNs) and some RNNs, use discriminative power for classification [31].

To date, much of the literature associated with deep learning in intrusion detection has focused on deep learning techniques evaluated against the KDDCup'99 and the NSL-KDD Dataset. Example of such work include [22–24] and [25]. However these datasets have been critiqued for issues such as a lack of real world data and for suffering from bias as was reported by [26].

A comparative study of traditional machine learning algorithms and deep learning algorithms, was conducted across several IDS datasets including KDD-Cup'99, NSL-KDD, UNSW-NB15 and CICIDS 2017 [27]. The CICIDS 2017 training dataset consisted of 93,500 instances, while the testing dataset contained 28,481. The approaches of Decision Tree, Ada Boost (AB) and Random Forest (RF) classifiers performed better than the other classifiers namely linear regression, Naive Bayes, K-Nearest Neighbour and SVMs. The performance of Decision Trees (DT), AB and RF classifiers remained in the same range across different datasets. The performance of Logistic Regresion (LR), NB, KNN, and SVM-rbf are varied across different datasets. They state that the DT, AB and RF classifiers can detect new attacks. In the binary classification experiment labelled as attack versus normal, the decision tree produced an accuracy rate of 92.9% on the KDDCup 99 dataset, 93% on the NSL-KDD dataset and 93.5% on the CICIDS 2017 dataset. The SVM technique produced accuracy rates 87.7%, 83.7% and 79.9% for the three datasets respectively. Depending on the number of layers used, Deep Neural Networks produced accuracy rates between 92.7% and 93% for the KDDCup data, between 78.9% and 80.1% for the NSLKDD data and between 93.1% and 96.3% for the CICIDS data.

CICIDS 2017 DDoS attacks were examined using Random Forests for feature reduction followed by the use of a deep learning MLP [28]. The dataset consisted of 225,746 instances and an accuracy rate of 91% was achieved using all 80 features and the MLP approach. Using the Random Forest feature reduction technique, the dataset was reduced to the 10 most important features. The retrained MLP model could then achieve 89% accuracy. Training and testing times for the two models were not presented.

The CICDS 2018 dataset was examined using decision trees, Gaussian Naive Bayes, random forest, KNN, SVM and LTSM+AM. These produced accuracy rates of 92.8%, 55.4%, 94.2%, 94.2%, 74.7%, 96.2% respectively. LTSM+AM was also compared with MLP, producing 90.5%, and with LTSM without AM, producing 93.3% [17].

An ANN approach was compared with a Random Forest classifier in [45]. The ANN had an average accuracy score of 96.53% while the random Forest had a score of 96.24.

In [43] a deep fully connected feed forward neural network was employed on the full CICIDS 2017 dataset. This deep learning approach achieved an accuracy rate of 96.77%. When IP addresses were included as a feature in the dataset an accuracy of 99.93% was achieved. Manimurugan et al. applied a range of deep learning techniques to the CICDIS 2017 dataset. Using a Deep Belief Neural network they achieved an accuracy of 96.67% on the DoS and DDoS data and an accuracy rate of 97.71% for Portscan attacks. SVM, RNN, Spiking Neural Network (SNN) and FNN were also employed but found to perform poorer than the DBN [44].

Recently there has been a focus in terms of the application and deployment of IDS to alternate environment with different computational powers. Environments investigated include Internet of Things (IoT), Cloud-based and Fog-based [3]. The need for improved AI techniques in these areas in expected to grow in the future.

IoT IDS suffer from high false alarm rates due to overlapping and suspicious instances [34,35]. Sources of data with IoT IDS can include telemetry data of sensors and actuators connected to the internet. There is a need for further research into the development of new post-processing techniques for IoT networks for correlating NIDS alerts, reducing false alarm rates and for visualisation of network data [36]. [37] surveyed the challenges of security in IoT and presented a comprehensive review of current anomaly-based IoT IDSs. [38] proposed a lightweight machine learning NIDS for IoT environments using a combination of Fuzzy C-means Clustering (FCM) and PCA, while [39] presents a NIDS with low computational and resource requirements using decision trees. A data mining approach for an IoT NIDS using PCA and Suppressed Fuzzy Clustering (SFC) techniques proved to be well suited to high dimensional spaces producing high levels of accuracy [40].

Cloud IDS are used by organisations that send data and processing tasks to public cloud services. Existing NIDS are not capable of detecting internal malicious activities. The detection of internal malicious activities is a challenging task due to their complexity and the remotely located modules [41]. Mobile edge IDS, or Fog-based IDS, suffer from decentralised and distributed issues such as synchronisation, provider integration and VM access to host and context information [42].

3   Dataset

The Canadian Institute for Cybersecurity (CIC) has been developing more recent datasets with up to date attacks. For this work the CICIDS 2017 dataset was chosen for use based on the shortcomings of other datasets in the area. In [15] eleven of the most cited and studied datasets were evaluated, and eleven shortcomings of these datasets were identified. The CICIDS 2017 and CICIDS 2018 datasets were developed taking these considerations into account to improve the quality of the dataset. These shortcomings found that:

1. To represent the real world a completely configured network is needed.
2. A realistic looking mix of pseudo-realistic, or synthetic traffic in a dataset.
3. Attention should be given to whether the dataset is labelled, partial labelled or unlabelled.
4. All network interactions are needed, such as interactions between internal networks.
5. All traffic should be captured and should remain in the dataset. They found issues with other datasets where non-functional or unlabelled data was removed.
6. Normal and anomalous data needs to be present.
7. There is a need to be able to analyse and test IDSs against up to date attacks in an off-line environment.
8. Payloads are often removed due to privacy concerns. However this prevents research in to techniques such as deep packet inspection.
9. There is a need for datasets that use a single source, and datasets that use multiple combined sources of data such as network traffic and operating system logs.
10. One of the biggest issues in the creation of an IDS dataset is feature extraction and construction.
11. Most IDS datasets suffer from incomplete documentation.

Taking these considerations into account, in January 2018 CIC released CIC-IDS 2017 [16]. The dataset was developed over five days during July 2017. This dataset contained B profile data used to produce benign activity of 25 users across HTTP, HTTPS, FTP, SSH, and email protocols. The first day of data did not contain any attack data. The dataset also contained attacks conducted over the other four days. The attacks were categorised seven major groups based on the 2016 McAfee report, Browser-based, Brute force, DoS, Scan or enumeration, Backdoors, DNS, and other attacks (e.g., Heartbleed, Shellshock, and Apple SSL library bug). The dataset was made available as .pcap files and as .CSV files for research. Eighty features were constructed from the data using the CICFlowMeter-V3.

CICIDS 2017 was followed by CSE-CICIDS 2018, an updated version with more instances. [17] presented the increase in traffic flows as seen in Table 1. As the download size of the CSE-CICIDS 2018 dataset is over 220 Gb in size it was decided to focus on the CICIDS 2017 dataset for this research.

Table 1. Statistics of redundant records in the testing data

	Normal	DDOS	PortScan	BOT	Inf	Web Attack	BF	DOS
CIC-IDS-2017	1743179	128027	158930	1966	36	2180	13835	252661
CSE-CIC-IDS-2018	6112151	687742	–	286191	161934	928	380949	654301

4   Methodology

The release of the CICIDS-17 dataset by the Canadian Institute for Cybersecurity [16] gave the research community a new dataset to work with. The experiments that were conducted were,

1. An evaluation of a partial decision tree approach for probing attack detection, using the data employed by [18] to test SVM and Deep Learning techniques. This dataset consisted of benign and probing activity.
2. An evaluation of a partial decision tree approach, using data as used for SVM and Deep Learning techniques in [28]. This dataset consisted of benign and DDoS activity.
3. An evaluation of a partial decision tree approach for the detection of DoS and DDoS attacks.
4. An evaluation of a partial decision tree approach, using the full dataset gathered over the 5 days, and the 12 classes, benign, PortScan, FTP-Patator, SSH-Patator, DoS, DDoS, Heartbleed, Web-Attack-Brute-Force, Web-Attack-XSS, Infiltration, Bot, Web-Attack-Sql-Injection.
5. An evaluation of a partial decision tree approach to 10 feature dataset created by applying Principal Component Analysis (PCA) to the dataset.

Each of these experiments was conducted in the Weka 3-9-1 environment using the default PART parameters. For the Portscan data, the training and testing data were split 67% to 33% to consistent with [18]. For the DDoS and full dataset 10 fold cross validation was used. The results of experiments on the CICIDS 2017 dataset are presented and discussed in Sect. 5.

Classification. One of the most common forms of data mining is classification. Classification differs from prediction in that classification is the forecasting of a discrete or categorical value whereas prediction forecasts a continuous value [29].

Given a database $D = \{t1, t2, ..., tn\}$ of tuples and a set of classes $C = \{C1, C2, ..., Cn\}$, the classification problem is to define a mapping $f : D \rightarrow C$ where each ti is assigned to one class. A class, Cj, contains precisely those tuples mapped to it; that is $Cj = ti | f(ti) = Cj, 1 \leq i \leq n$ and $ti \epsilon D$ [30].

Classification occurs in two phases

1. A model is created on a specific dataset by evaluating a training set in a supervised learning mode. This phase takes as input a training dataset and produces as output a definition of a model which classifies the training set as accurately as possible.
2. Apply the model created in stage one to a test dataset.

Classification algorithms are categorised as Statistical, Distance, Decision Tree, Neural Network and Rule-based.

Decision Tree Techniques. A Decision Tree is constructed from nodes, representing questions, and arcs that represent the possible answers to those questions. The first node is known as the root, and the set of internal nodes, based on the answers, leads to the solution at the end leaf node [32].

A Decision Tree Model consists of three parts;

- A decision tree consisting of edges or branches, and nodes or leaves
- An algorithm for creating the tree
- An algorithm that applies the tree to data to solve the problem being considered

[30] defines a decision tree as:

Given a database $D = \{t_1, ..., t_n\}$ where $t_i = <t_{i1}, ..., t_{ih}>$ and the database schema contains the following attributes $A_1, A_2, ..., A_h$. Also given is a set of classes $C_1, ..., C_m$. A decision tree (DT) or classification tree is a tree associated with D that has the following properties:

- Each internal node is labelled with attribute, A_i
- Each arc is labelled with a predicate that can be applied to the attribute associated with the parent
- Each leaf node is labelled with a class, C_j

Decision trees are easy to use and produce output that can easily be understood and hence easily translated into rulesets. DTs scale well with large datasets and can handle large numbers of attributes [30]. Continuous data needs to be divided into categories though in order to be used. Missing data can prove troublesome as a decision cannot be made as to which branch in the tree should be followed. DTs can also suffer from overfitting though this can be addressed by pruning. Correlations amongst attributes are ignored by DTs.

Attributes are represented as nodes in a DT structure and are referred to as splitting attributes. The arcs which come from these nodes are known as splitting predicates [30]. Algorithms may be differentiated in the way they choose splitting attributes and select their splitting predicates.

The performance of a DT [30] is affected by

- The choice of splitting attribute
- The order of splitting attribute
- The number of splits required over the whole tree
- The structure of the tree in terms of number levels and the degree of branching
- The stopping criteria
- The amount of training data involved
- Any pruning of the tree which may be required

The complexity of the algorithm depends on the product of the number of levels in the tree, and the maximum branching factor at each level. The time complexity to build a tree is $O(hq \ log \ q)$, where h is the number of attributes and q is the size of the training data. The time needed to classify a database of size n is based on the height of the tree. Assuming a height of $O(log \ q)$ this can be calculated as $O(n \ log \ q)$ [30].

The most common decision tree algorithms include C4.5, C5.0 and CART. C4.5 extended ID3. ID3 splits attributes by selecting the attribute with the highest information gain. Entropy is a measure of the amount of uncertainty, surprise or randomness in a dataset. Entropy [30] is defined as

Given probabilities $p_1, p_2, \ldots, p_s$ where $\sum_{i=1}^{s} p_i = 1$, entropy is defined as

$$H(p_1, p_2, \ldots, p_s) = \sum_{i=1}^{s} (p_i log(1/p_i)) \tag{1}$$

A split is calculated from the difference in entropies of the original dataset and the weighted sum of the entropies form each of the subdivided datasets. ID3 determines the gain as

$$Gain(D, S) = H(D) - \sum_{i=1}^{s} P(D_i)H(D_i) \tag{2}$$

Where $H(D)$ finds the amount of order in database state D. When state D is split it produces s new states $S = \{D_1, D_2, \ldots, D_s\}$.

A hybrid algorithm of J48, Meta Paging, RandomTree, REPTree, AdaBoostM1, DecisionStump and NaiveBayes was applied to a dataset which had been filtered using information gain and the vote algorithm can be seen in [8].

Frank & Witten developed an approach for rule induction that combines both the divide and conquer technique for decision trees with the separate and conquer technique for rule learning in an attempt to overcome their limitations. This method of obtaining rules from partial decision trees avoids global optimisation and produces accurate, compact rule sets. It follows the separate and conquer technique in that it, [32].

1. Builds a rule X
2. Removes the instances covered by rule X
3. Continue to create rules recursively for the remaining instances until none are left

PART can be differentiated from the usual separate and conquer technique in its rule production. It creates a pruned decision tree from the current set of instances, and extract the leaf with the largest coverage as rule. The rest of the tree is then discarded. This approach removes the tendency to overprune associated with the separate and conquer approach [32].

Partial decision tree approaches tend to outperform separate and conquer approaches in terms of accuracy. They are comparable to divide and conquer approaches in terms of accuracy, but are faster than divide and conquer techniques such as C4.5. Partial decision tree approaches combine the simplistic approach of separate and conquer with the accuracy of divide and conquer techniques. The complexity of the partial decision tree approach is $O(a \text{ x } n \ log \ n)$. On a noise free dataset, partial decision trees are very fast, as there is no need to prune the tree. This means that as the level of noise in the data increase, there is a decrease in the performance speed [33].

5   Results

Metrics. For domains such as intrusion detection a misclassification can be crucial to the security of the network. In a binary case of normal or intrusion, each prediction has four possible outcomes represented by a confusion matrix.

- True Positive TP, class correctly determined as class 1
- True Negative TN, class correctly determined as class 2
- False Positive FP, class incorrectly classified as class 1
- False Negative FN, class incorrectly classified as class 2

The true positive rate is TP divided by the total number of positives which is $TP + FN$; the false positive rate FP divided by the total number of negatives, $FP + TN$. The overall success rate is the number of successful classifications divided by the total number of classifications as shown below. The error rate is one minus the overall success rate [32].

$$Accuracy = \frac{TP + TN}{TP + TN + FP + FN} \tag{3}$$

Where there are more than two classes to be present, a two dimensional confusion matrix will be created with a row and a column for each class. Correct classifications are indicated by high numbers running down the diagonal diagonal. Any values not present on the diagonal are counts of instances that have been miscalssified. A confusion matrix is often represented using an Operating Characteristic (OC) curve that plots the percentage of false positive on the x axis against the percentage of true positives on the y axis [32].

Two other metrics commonly used in information retrieval, are precision and recall [32]. These are plotted against each other to produce recall-precision curves.

$$recall = \frac{number of relevant documents retrieved}{total number of relevant documents} \tag{4}$$

$$precision = \frac{number of relevant documents retrieved}{total number of documents retrieved} \tag{5}$$

In general a high precision and a high recall are desirable. However a high precision leads to a low recall and vise versa. A trade-off between these is the harmonic mean, or F-measure. This can be defined as

$$F = \frac{2 X recall X precision}{recall + precision} = \frac{2x TP}{2x(TP + FP + FN)} \tag{6}$$

A Partial Approach to the Portscan Data. Table 2 presents the confusion matrix of a partial decision tree approach to the PortScan data from the CICIDS dataset. As with [18], the data was split as 67% training data and 33% testing data. It took 71.93 s to build the model and 0.17 s to test the model on the split data. This produced an accuracy rate of 99.98% and a ruleset of fifteen rules. This model outperformed the SVM and deep learning methods proposed in [18] as can be seen in Table 3.

Table 2. Confusion matrix: PART CICIDS PortScan data

Classified as ->	Normal	Attack
Normal	43387	8
Attack	11	53993

Table 3. Confusion matrix: Part comparison with [18] CICIDS PortScan data

Method	Accuracy	Precision	Recall	F1 Score
PART	99.98	1.0	1.0	1.0
Deep learning	97.80	0.99	0.99	0.99
SVM	69.79	0.80	0.70	0.65

A Partial Approach to the DDoS Data. The second version of the dataset used was the DDoS dataset. It consisted of 225,746 instances and took 63.72 s to build the model. It produced an accuracy rate of 99.99% over 14 rules. Ten of the normal instances were misclassified as being attacks and seven attacks were missed and classified as being normal. [28] analysed the same version of the dataset using an MLP approach and achieved an accuracy rate of 91% as can be seen in Table 7 (Tables 4 and 5).

Table 4. Confusion matrix: PART CICIDS DDoS data

Classified as ->	Normal	Attack
Normal	97708	10
Attack	7	128020

Table 5. Part comparison with [28] CICIDS DDoS data

Method	Accuracy
PART	99.98
MLP	91

A Partial Approach to the DoS/DDoS Data. The third version of the data used consisted of all DoS and DDoS data. This totaled 918,448 instances and produced an accuracy rate of 99.97%. The number of false alarms outweighed the number of missed attacks as can be seen in the confusion matrix in Table 6. The model took 890 s to build and produced 77 rules.

Table 6. Confusion matrix: PART CICIDS DDoS data

Classified as ->	Normal	Attack
Normal	537584	165
Attack	71	380628

A comparison with the results of [44] can be seen in Table 7. The Partial decision tree technique outperformed the Deep Learning techniques that had been employed.

Table 7. Part compared with deep learning techniques [44] for CICIDS DoS/DDoS data

Method	Accuracy	Precision	Recall	F1 score
PART	99.97%	1.000	1.000	1.00
DBN [44]	96.67%	0.952	0.973	0.97
SVM [44]	95.55%	0.943	0.962	0.95
RNN [44]	94.40%	0.939	0.956	0.94
SNN [44]	93.30%	0.920	0.943	0.93
FNN [44]	92.25%	0.911	0.911	0.92

A Partial Approach to the Full DataSet. The results of the third analysis can be seen in Table 8. This table presents the breakdown of the classification of each attack in the dataset. The model produced an accuracy rate of 99.98% and took 7812.19 s to build. The metrics associated with this experiment can be seen in Table 9.

Table 8. Confusion matrix: PART CICIDS full dataset

Classified as ->	A	B	C	D	E	F	G	H	I	J	K	L
(A) normal	2271622	989	6	4	381	17	1	8	9	2	56	2
(B) PortScan	17	158869	2	0	38	0	0	4	0	0	0	0
(C) FTP-Patator	3	0	7934	0	0	0	0	1	0	0	0	0
(D) SSH-Patator	7	0	1	5889	0	0	0	0	0	0	0	0
(E) DoS	65	12	0	0	252574	3	0	5	0	0	0	2
(F) DDoS	19	0	0	0	3	128005	0	0	0	0	0	0
(G) Heartbleed	1	0	0	0	0	0	10	0	0	0	0	0
(H) Web-Attack-Brute-Force	14	2	0	0	1	0	0	1468	22	0	0	0
(I) Web-Attack-XSS	6	3	1	0	4	0	0	582	56	0	0	0
(J) Infiltration	12	0	0	0	0	0	0	0	0	24	0	0
(K) Bot	544	0	0	0	0	0	0	0	0	0	1422	0
(L) Web-Attack-Sql-Injection	1	0	0	0	4	0	0	2	2	0	0	12

A Partial Approach to the PCA Reduced DataSet. The results of the fourth experiment are presented in Table 10. This table shows the breakdown of the classification of each attack in the dataset. The model produced an accuracy rate of 99.4% and took 1767.95 s to build. This dataset was reduced to 10 features using PCA in Weka. The variance used to produced the dataset was 0.95 and the 10 most important new features produced from this were used to create the new dataset. The detailed metrics associated with this partial decision tree experiment can be seen in Table 11.

Table 9. Detailed accuracy rates for the CICIDS 2017 full dataset

Class	TP Rate	FP Rate	Precision	Recall	F-Measure	MCC	ROC area	PRC area
(A) normal	0.999	0.001	1.000	0.999	1.000	0.998	1.000	1.000
(B) PortScan	1.000	0.000	0.994	1.000	0.997	0.996	1.000	0.997
(C) FTP-Patator	0.999	0.000	0.999	0.999	0.999	0.999	1.000	0.999
(D) SSH-Patator	0.999	0.000	0.999	0.999	0.999	0.999	1.000	0.999
(E) DoS	1.000	0.000	0.998	1.000	0.999	0.999	1.000	0.999
(F) DDoS	1.000	0.000	1.000	1.000	1.000	1.000	1.000	1.000
(G) Heartbleed	0.909	0.000	0.909	0.909	0.909	0.909	0.955	0.826
(H) Web-Attack-Brute-Force	0.974	0.000	0.709	0.974	0.821	0.831	0.991	0.825
(I) Web-Attack-XSS	0.086	0.000	0.629	0.086	0.151	0.232	0.984	0.437
(J) Infiltration	0.667	0.000	0.923	0.667	0.774	0.784	0.912	0.638
(K) Bot	0.723	0.000	0.962	0.723	0.826	0.834	0.997	0.927
(L) Web-Attack-Sql-Injection	0.571	0.000	0.750	0.571	0.649	0.655	0.855	0.545
Weighted Avg	0.999	0.001	0.999	0.999	0.999	0.997	1.000	0.999

Table 12 present a comparison of the Full Dataset evaluation, the PCA dataset evaluation and the results produced by [43]. It can be seen that both Partial decision tree models out perform the Deep Neural Network.

6   Discussion

The partial decision tree approach was compared to deep learning approaches for the DDoS and Probing data of the dataset. It outperformed both of these in accuracy. [27] achieved an accuracy rate of 79.9% using SVM and accuracy rates between 93.1% and 96.3% using Deep Neural Networks compared to accuracy scores of 99.98%. The dataset used consisted of 93,500 instances, while the testing dataset contained 28,481, however the authors do not describe how this data was sampled. The partial decision tree method was also evaluated against the work of [18]. This focused on the evaluation of the portscan campaign that had been conducted. It again outperformed the MLP apporach which had an accuracy of 91% in comparison to our model which again scored 99.98%.

Table 10. Confusion matrix: PART CICIDS reduced feature dataset

Classified as ->	A	B	C	D	E	F	G	H	I	J	K	L
(A) normal	2269846	1145	8	80	1393	362	0	113	15	5	130	0
(B) PortScan	145	158733	0	1	37	12	0	2	0	0	0	0
(C) FTP-Patator	10	0	7920	5	2	0	0	1	0	0	0	0
(D) SSH-Patator	73	3	0	5817	1	0	0	3	0	0	0	0
(E) DoS	11266	10	1	1	240992	386	1	4	0	0	0	0
(F) DDoS	334	2	0	0	587	127103	0	0	0	0	1	0
(G) Heartbleed	2	0	0	0	1	1	7	0	0	0	0	0
(H) Web-Attack-Brute-Force	82	3	1	25	1	0	0	1303	92	0	0	0
(I) Web-Attack-XSS	44	2	0	0	2	0	0	518	86	0	0	0
(J) Infiltration	27	0	0	0	1	0	0	0	0	8	0	0
(K) Bot	1064	0	0	0	1	0	0	0	0	0	901	0
(L) Web-Attack-Sql-Injection	13	0	0	4	1	0	0	3	0	0	0	0

Table 11. Detailed accuracy rates for the CICIDS 2017 reduced feature dataset

Class	TP rate	FP rate	Precision	Recall	F-Measure	MCC	ROC area	PRC area
(A) normal	0.999	0.023	0.994	0.999	0.996	0.982	0.999	0.999
(B) PortScan	0.999	0.000	0.993	0.999	0.996	0.995	1.000	0.997
(C) FTP-Patator	0.998	0.000	0.999	0.998	0.998	0.998	0.999	0.997
(D) SSH-Patator	0.986	0.000	0.980	0.986	0.983	0.983	0.999	0.983
(E) DoS	0.954	0.001	0.992	0.954	0.972	0.970	0.999	0.994
(F) DDoS	0.993	0.000	0.994	0.993	0.993	0.993	0.999	0.995
(G) Heartbleed	0.636	0.000	0.875	0.636	0.737	0.746	0.864	0.564
(H) Web-Attack-Brute-Force	0.865	0.000	0.669	0.865	0.754	0.761	0.969	0.739
(I) Web-Attack-XSS	0.132	0.000	0.446	0.132	0.204	0.242	0.954	0.386
(J) Infiltration	0.222	0.000	0.615	0.222	0.327	0.370	0.806	0.146
(K) Bot	0.458	0.000	0.873	0.458	0.601	0.632	0.987	0.686
(L) Web-Attack-Sql-Injection	0.000	0.000	0.000	0.000	0.000	0.000	0.717	0.020
Weighted Avg	0.994	0.019	0.994	0.994	0.993	0.981	0.999	0.998

Table 12. Full dataset comparison with [43]

Method	Accuracy	Precision	Recall	F1 score
PART	99.98%	0.999	0.999	0.999
PART (PCA)	99.4%	0.994	0.994	0.993
DNN [43]	96.77%	0.978	0.968	0.973

In experiment 3 DoS and DDoS data were examined together, and a model was built for DoS/DDoS attack detection. The inclusion of the DoS attacks led to a very slight decline in accuracy over the model produced in the second experiment, and the model now missed 71 attacks which was a further 64 above the DDoS model. 165 patterns of normal usage were misclassified compared to 10 with the DDoS model. [44] evaluated Deep Belief, Recurrent Neural Network, Spike Neural Network and Fullforward Neural Network for the same purpose and found Deep Belief Neural Networks to achieve the highest accuracy at a rate of 96.67%.

The full dataset was analysed using the partial decision tree and all 12 classes. The class used were Normal, PortScan, FTP-Patator, SSH-Patator, DoS, DDoS, Heartbleed, Web-Attack-Brute-Force, Web-Attack-XSS, Infiltration, Bot, Web-Attack-Sql-Injection. The results of this can be seen in Table 8. The model was built in 7812.19 s and achieved an accuracy rate of 99.899%. It contained 235 rules. Web-Attack-Brute-Force, Web-Attack-XSS, Bot and Web-Attack-Sql-Injection performed worst all achieving detection rates of less than 90%. Web-Attack-XSS had the lowest detection rate at 0.086%, however 87.4% of the instances were detected as a brute force web attack rather than a XSS attack. Only 6 of the 666 XSS instances were missed and classed as normal. The class Bot had a detection rate of 72.3%. 544 of the 1,966 instances were missed and classed as normal behaviour. Of the 1,507 Web-Attack-Brute-Force instances, 22 were classed as Web-Attack-XSS, 2 as portscan and 1 as DoS. 14 were missed and classed as normal behaviour. Web-Attack-Sql-Injection achieved a detection rate of 57.1%. However there were only 21 instances of this attack in the entire dataset, and only 1 of these was missed and classed as normal. The detection rate (TP), false alarm rates (FP), precision, recall, harmonic mean (F-Measure), Matthews Correlation Coefficient (MCC), ROC and PRC results are presented in Table 9. 1,475 instances of normal behaviour were classified as an attack. This model was evaluated against the model produced by [43]. The PART model produced an accuracy score of 99.98% in comparison to the Deep Neural Network model.

When the dataset was reduced to 10 features and 12 classes the accuracy of the model fell to 99.36% but the time to build the model dropped from 8812.19 s to 1767.95 s. This was a drop of 77% in the time taken with a fall in accuracy of just 0.5%. Except for Web-Attack XSS, there was a drop in the detection rate of each attack. There was an increase in all instances of normal behaviour being misclassified for each attack class. There was also an increase in the number of attacks missed for each class. This model was also found to outperform the depp learning model found in [43].

7 Conclusion

Data mining has become an important tool in the intrusion detection community toolbox. Intrusion detection systems have steadily moved to using the approach of a hybrid of data mining techniques to build intrusion detection systems. These components, or modules, can be used to detect different types of attacks and usually form one of several stages. A well designed IDS should be made up of interchangeable rules modules which can be used with varying architectures. These rules modules should have a shorter life span than the architecture itself and will change as the attacks advance.

The partial decision tree approach was evaluated on the CICIDS 2017 dataset. Five versions of this dataset were used in this work, the Portscan data, the DDoS data, the DoS/DDoS data, the twelve class dataset with all features present, and a reduced version of the dataset with 10 features produced from a PCA analysis of the data. The results were compared with deep learning and SVM approaches found in the literature. In each instance the partial decision tree approach out performed the deep learning and SVM approaches in terms of accuracy. The PART algorithm achieved accuracy rates of 99.98% on the Portscan data, 99.99% on the DDoS data and 99.89% on the entire dataset. The accuracy fell slightly when the dataset was reduced however the time taken was significantly reduced as was the size of the data.

7.1 Future Work

Future work in the area of intrusion detection involves the further evaluation of the features currently available in the dataset, and the investigation of new features that could be created from the raw .pcap files that are also available to researchers. The evaluation of hybrid approaches between traditional data mining and deep learning techniques also warrants further investigation. Recent work has seen the expansion of deployment architectures to be more specific to domains such as IoT, vehicle, cloud and mobile computing environments. More work is needed in these areas regarding the creation of datasets, the suitability of current analysis and detection methods in these different environments, and the correlation of results from detection engines speaking to one another. Work is also needed in the area of eXplainable AI for network forensics and IDS.

References

1. Du, X., et al.: SoK: exploring the state of the art and the future potential of artificial intelligence in digital forensic investigation. In: Proceedings of the 15th International Conference on Availability, Reliability and Security, ARES 2020. ACM, August 2020. https://doi.org/10.1145/3407023.3407068, ISBN: 9781450388337
2. Nguyen Thi, N., Cao, V.L., Le-Khac, N.-A.: One-class collective anomaly detection based on LSTM-RNNs. In: Hameurlain, A., Küng, J., Wagner, R., Dang, T.K., Thoai, N. (eds.) Transactions on Large-Scale Data- and Knowledge-Centered Systems XXXVI. LNCS, vol. 10720, pp. 73–85. Springer, Heidelberg (2017). https://doi.org/10.1007/978-3-662-56266-6_4
3. Moustafa, N., Hu, J., Slay, J.: A holistic review of network anomaly detection systems: a comprehensive survey. J. Netw. Comput. Appl. **128**, 33–55 (2019)
4. Othman, S., Alsohybe, N., Ba-Alwi, F., Zahar, A.: Survey on intrusion detection system. Int. J. Cyber-Secur. Digital Forensics (IJCSDF) (2018). ISSN: 2305–001
5. Buczak, A., Guven, E.: A survey of data mining and machine learning methods for cybersecurity intrusion detection. IEEE Commun. Surv. Tutor. **18**(2), 1153–1176 (2016). https://doi.org/10.1109/COMST.2015.2494502
6. Ahmed, M., Naser, A., Hu, J.: A survey of network anomaly detection techniques. J. Netw. Comput. Appl. **60**, 19–31 (2016). https://doi.org/10.1016/j.jnca.2015.11.016. ISSN: 1084–8045
7. Modi, U., Jain, A.: A survey of IDS classification using KDD cup 99 dataset in WEKA. Int. J. Sci. Eng. Res. **6**(11), 947–954 (2015). ISSN 2229–5518
8. Aljawarneh, S., Aldwairi, M., Yassein, M.: Anomaly-based intrusion detection system through feature selection analysis and building hybrid efficient model. J. Comput. Sci. **25**, 152–160 (2018). https://doi.org/10.1016/j.jocs.2017.03.006
9. Ambusaidi, M., He, X., Nanda, P., Tan, Z.: Building an intrusion detection system using a filter-based feature selection algorithm. IEEE Trans. Comput. **65**(10), 2986–2998 (2016). https://doi.org/10.1109/TC.2016.2519914
10. Hasan, M., Nasser, S., Ahmad, M., Molla, K.: Feature selection for intrusion detection using random forest. J. Inf. Secur. **7**, 129–140 (2016)
11. Elhag, S., Fernández, A., Alshomrani, S., Herrera, F.: Evolutionary fuzzy systems: a case study for intrusion detection systems. In: Bansal, J.C., Singh, P.K., Pal, N.R. (eds.) Evolutionary and Swarm Intelligence Algorithms. SCI, vol. 779, pp. 169–190. Springer, Cham (2019). https://doi.org/10.1007/978-3-319-91341-4_9
12. Denning, D.: An intrusion-detection model. In IEEE Trans. Softw. Eng., Piscataway, NJ, USA, vol. 13, pp. 222–232. IEEE Press, February 1987. https://doi.org/10.1109/TSE.1987.232894
13. Scarfone, K., Mell, P.: 800–94 rev-1. NIST Guide to Intrusion Detection and Prevention Systems (IDPS) Revision, vol. 1 (2012)

14. Stolfo, S., Lee, W., Chan, P., Fan, W., Eskin, E.: Data mining-based intrusion detectors: an overview of the Columbia ids project. ACM SIGMOD Rec. **30**(4), 5–14 (2001)

15. Gharib, A., Sharafaldin, I., Lashkari, A., Ghorbani, A.: An evaluation framework for intrusion detection dataset. In: 2016 International Conference on Information Science and Security (ICISS), pp. 1–6, December 2016. https://doi.org/10.1109/ICISSEC.2016.7885840

16. Sharafaldin, I., Lashkari, A., Ghorbani, A.: Toward generating a new intrusion detection dataset and intrusion traffic characterization. In: Proceedings of the 4th International Conference on Information Systems Security and Privacy - Volume 1: ICISSP, pp. 108–116. INSTICC, SciTePress (2018). https://doi.org/10.5220/0006639801080116, ISBN: 978-989-758-282-0

17. Lin, P., Ye, K., Xu, C.-Z.: Dynamic network anomaly detection system by using deep learning techniques. In: Da Silva, D., Wang, Q., Zhang, L.-J. (eds.) CLOUD 2019. LNCS, vol. 11513, pp. 161–176. Springer, Cham (2019). https://doi.org/10.1007/978-3-030-23502-4_12

18. Aksu, D., Aydin, M.: Detecting port scan attempts with comparative analysis of deep learning and support vector machine algorithms. In: 2018 International Congress on Big Data, Deep Learning and Fighting Cyber Terrorism (IBIGDELFT), pp. 77–80, December 2018. https://doi.org/10.1109/IBIGDELFT.2018.8625370

19. Aksu, D., Üstebay, S., Aydin, M.A., Atmaca, T.: Intrusion detection with comparative analysis of supervised learning techniques and fisher score feature selection algorithm. In: Czachórski, T., Gelenbe, E., Grochla, K., Lent, R. (eds.) ISCIS 2018. CCIS, vol. 935, pp. 141–149. Springer, Cham (2018). https://doi.org/10.1007/978-3-030-00840-6_16

20. Saber, M., El Farissi, I., Chadli, S., Emharraf, M.,Belkasmi, M.: Performance analysis of an intrusion detection systems based of artificial neural network. In: Europe and MENA Cooperation Advances in Information and Communication Technologies, pp. 511–521. Springer International Publishing, Cham (2017). https://doi.org/10.1007/978-3-319-46568-5_52, ISBN: 978-3-319-46568-5

21. Hodo, E., Bellekens, X., Hamilton, A., Tachtatzis, C., Atkinson, R.: Shallow and deep networks intrusion detection system: a taxonomy and survey. CoRR, abs/1701.02145, 2017. http://arxiv.org/abs/1701.02145

22. Papamartzivanos, D., Gómez Mármol, D., Kambourakis, G.: Introducing deep learning self-adaptive misuse network intrusion detection systems. IEEE Access **7**, 13546–13560 (2019). https://doi.org/10.1109/ACCESS.2019.2893871. ISSN: 2169-3536

23. Karatas, G., Demir, O., Koray Sahingoz, O.: Deep learning in intrusion detection systems. In: 2018 International Congress on Big Data, Deep Learning and Fighting Cyber Terrorism (IBIGDELFT), pp. 113–116, December 2018. https://doi.org/10.1109/IBIGDELFT.2018.8625278

24. Yang, K., Liu, J., Zhang, C., Fang, Y.: Adversarial examples against the deep learning based network intrusion detection systems. In: MILCOM 2018–2018 IEEE Military Communications Conference (MILCOM), pp. 559–564, October 2018. https://doi.org/10.1109/MILCOM.2018.8599759

25. Gurung, S., Ghose, M., Subedi, A.: Deep learning approach on network intrusion detection system using NSL-KDD dataset. Int. J. Comput. Netw. Inf. Secur. **11**(3), 8 (2019). https://ucd.idm.oclc.org/login?url=search-proquest-com.ucd.idm.oclc.org/docview/2193195455?accountid=14507

26. McHugh, J.: Testing intrusion detection systems: a critique of the 1998 and 1999 darpa intrusion detection system evaluations as performed by lincoln laboratory. ACM Trans. Inf. Syst. Secur. **3**(4), 262–294 (2000)

27. Vinayakumar, R., Alazab, M., Soman, K., Poornachandran, P., Al-Nemrat, A., Venkatraman, S.: Deep learning approach for intelligent intrusion detection system. IEEE Access, 41525–41550 (2019). https://doi.org/10.1109/ACCESS.2019.2895334, ISSN: 2169–3536

28. Ustebay, S., Turgut, Z., Aydin, M.: Intrusion detection system with recursive feature elimination by using random forest and deep learning classifier. In: 2018 International Congress on Big Data, Deep Learning and Fighting Cyber Terrorism (IBIGDELFT), pp. 71–76, December 2018. https://doi.org/10.1109/IBIGDELFT.2018.8625318

29. Han, J., Kamber, M., Pei, J.: Data Mining: Concepts and Techniques, 3rd edn. Morgan Kaufmann Publishers Inc., Burlington (2011). ISBN 0123814790, 9780123814791

30. Dunham, M.: Data Mining: Introductory and Advanced Topics. Prentice Hall PTR, Upper Saddle River (2002). ISBN 0130888923

31. Shone, N., Ngoc, T.N., Phai, V.D., Shi, Q.: A deep learning approach to network intrusion detection. IEEE Trans. Emerg. Top. Comput. Intell. **2**(1), 41–50 (2018). https://doi.org/10.1109/TETCI.2017.2772792

32. Witten, I., Frank, E., Hall, M.: Data Mining: Practical Machine Learning Tools and Techniques. Morgan Kaufmann Publishers Inc., Burlington (2011). ISBN 0123748569

33. Suh, S.: Practical Applications of Data Mining. Jones & Bartlett Learning, January 2011. ISBN 9780763785871

34. Benkhelifa, E., Welsh, T., Amouda, W.: A critical review of practices and challenges in intrusion detection systems for IoT: towards universal and resilient systems. IEEE Commun. Surv. Tutor. **20**(4), 1–15 (2018)

35. Pajouh, H., Javidan, R., Khayami, R., Ali, D., Choo, K.-K.R.: A two-layer dimension reduction and two-tier classification model for anomaly-based intrusion detection in IoT backbone networks. IEEE Trans. Emerg. Top. Comput. **7**, 1–11 (2016)

36. Moustafa, N., Adi, E., Turnbull, B., Hu, J.: A new threat intelligence scheme for safeguarding industry 4.0 systems. IEEE Access **6**, 32910–32924 (2018)

37. Elrawy, M., Awad, A. and Hamed, H.: Intrusion detection systems for IoT-based smart environments: a survey. J. Cloud Comput. (2018). ISSN 2192–113X 10.1186/s13677-018-0123-6

38. Deng, L., Li, D., Yao, X., Cox, D., Wang, H.: Mobile network intrusion detection for IoT system based on transfer learning algorithm. Cluster Comput. **22**(4), 9889–9904 (2018). https://doi.org/10.1007/s10586-018-1847-2

39. Amouri, A., Alaparthy, V., and Morgera, S.: Cross layer-based intrusion detection based on network behavior for IoT. In 2018 IEEE 19th Wireless and Microwave Technology Conference (WAMICON), pp. 1–4, April 2018. https://doi.org/10.1109/WAMICON.2018.8363921

40. Liu, L., Xu, B., Zhang, X., Wu, X.: An intrusion detection method for internet of things based on suppressed fuzzy clustering. EURASIP J. Wirel. Commun. Netw. **2018**(1), 1–7 (2018). https://doi.org/10.1186/s13638-018-1128-z

41. Colom, J., Gil, D., Mora, H., Volckaert, B., Jimeno, A.: Scheduling framework for distributed intrusion detection systems over heterogeneous network architectures. J. Netw. Comput. Appl. **108**, 76–86 (2018). https://doi.org/10.1016/j.jnca.2018.02.004. ISSN 1084-8045

42. Roman, R., Lopez, J., Mambo, M., et al.: Mobile edge computing, fog: a survey and analysis of security threats and challenges. Future Gener. Comput. Syst. **78**, 680–698 (2018). https://doi.org/10.1016/j.future.2016.11.009. ISSN 0167-739X
43. Fernandez, G.: Deep Learning Approaches for Network Intrusion Detection, MSc Thesis Presented to the Graduate Faculty of The University of Texas at San Antonio, May 2019
44. Manimurugan, S., Al-Mutairi, S., Aborokbah, M., Chilamkurti, N., Ganesan, S., Patan, R.: Effective attack detection in internet of medical things smart environment using a deep belief neural network. IEEE Access **8**, 77396–77404 (2020). https://doi.org/10.1109/ACCESS.2020.2986013
45. Pelletier, Z., Abualkibash, M.: Evaluating the CIC IDS-2017 dataset using machine learning methods and creating multiple predictive models in the statistical computing language R. Int. Res. J. Adv. Eng. Sci. **5**(2), 187–191 (2020)

Efficient Fingerprint Matching for Forensic Event Reconstruction

Tobias Latzo[(✉)]

Department of Computer Science,
Friedrich-Alexander-Universität Erlangen-Nürnberg (FAU),
Erlangen, Germany
`tobias.latzo@fau.de`

Abstract. Forensic investigations usually utilize log files to reconstruct previous events on computing systems. Using standard log files as well as traces of system calls, we analyze what traces are left by different events on a GNU/Linux server that runs different common services like an SSH server, Wordpress, Nextcloud and Docker containers. Based on these traces, we calculate characteristic fingerprints of these events that can later be matched to other log files to detect them. We develop a matching algorithm and examine the different parameters that influence its performance both in terms of event detectability and detection time. We also examine the effect of using different subsets of system calls to improve matching efficiency.

Keywords: Forensic event reconstruction · Linux logs · System call tracing · SIEM

1   Introduction

One of the main tasks of forensic analysts is to reconstruct what happened on a system in the past. To do so, they examine traces that are generated by actions or events that were executed on the system. One of the most prominent example of such traces are log messages in system or application log files [7]. Well-known examples in GNU/Linux systems are the `syslog` file and the file `auth.log`. On Windows, the central logging mechanism is the Windows Event Log [18]. Typically, these log files may contain a lot of log data giving insight into many different events from the past. However, there are also many events that do not appear in the common system logs, e.g., removing a file by a user with the proper access rights, connecting to a remote server, or shredding a file [14].

Security Information and Event Management (SIEM) systems aim at collecting (security relevant) information from log files, extract information from them and correlate this information with data from different computer systems with the goal to detect security relevant activities like incidents. However, these systems also struggle with imprecise and incomplete information if they depend

S. Goel et al. (Eds.): ICDF2C 2020, LNICST 351, pp. 98–120, 2021.
https://doi.org/10.1007/978-3-030-68734-2_6

on log files alone [17] and so other sources of information are used as well. One such source are the sequence of system calls that are executed on a particular system. It is well-known that system call traces help in detecting malicious and benign system activities [14,20]. However, it is also well-known that in terms of performance it is unrealistic to trace *all* system calls in a computing system. The resulting research question that underlies this paper is how system call traces can be used together with common system logs in a meaningful and efficient way to enable forensic event reconstruction?

1.1   Related Work

There is a lot of research in the field of incident detection based on log files. Most often these works focus on definitely malicious events. Examples of this stream of work are UCLog [15] (Unified Correlated LOGging architecture for intrusion detection) and its successor UCLog+ [25]. These tools correlate logging information from different sources like kernel API loggers (i.e., system calls), network loggers, file system loggers, etc., and generate an alarm in a suspected case. There also many approaches that utilize system call sequences to classify malware [12,13].

Another approach called "computer profiling" [16] infers events from cause-effect rules that are specified by an examiner. Thus, this approach is only partially automatable. Also similar is the approach of Kahn et al. [11] who make use of a neural-network to learn signatures based on file system metadata. Since neural networks need a huge amount of training data, this approach does not scale, too. Other research uses hidden Markov models [19,24]. Furthermore, there is an ontology-based approach for Windows systems [4] that generates timelines based on log files.

Gladyshev and Patel [9] pioneered the areas of formalizing event reconstruction using finite state machine representations of computing systems and applying formal logic to detect events [8]. Based on this research, there exists a slightly more practical approach that computes signatures of system events [10]. The resulting signatures are quite complex and probabilistic and were not applied to the reconstruction based on log files.

In this paper, we make use of the theory of forensic event reconstruction by Dewald [5]. This work was used by Latzo and Freiling [14] who examined the value of logging information for forensic event reconstruction. The work reveals that many events do not leave any traces in system log files. For enhancing event reconstruction, they utilized system call traces as an additional log source. The size of characteristic fingerprints (see also Sect. 2.2) is regarded as a quality criteria for forensic fingerprints. These sizes are examined for different feature sets and log sources. It turns out that using system call traces as log data is very beneficial in terms of the quality of characteristic fingerprints. It is obvious that tracing all system calls is expensive in terms of performance and the corresponding system cannot be used as a productive system anymore. In this paper, we want to calculate the characteristic fingerprints with a bigger event set, analyze how matching performs with that approach and show how to make matching more efficient.

1.2   Contribution

In this paper, we systematically analyze what and where traces are left by different events and how to utilize them for forensic event reconstruction by calculating characteristic fingerprints. We further study how these characteristic fingerprints perform in matching those events. We also utilize system call traces as an additional log source. Since tracing all system calls is extremely expensive in terms of performance, we show how to systematically reduce tracing overhead but still being able to detect events.

We make use of Dewald's theory of forensic event reconstruction [5] that was also applied by Latzo and Freiling [14] to log files. We build upon their research and calculate characteristic fingerprints on a larger event set. We additionally evaluate matching performance and the role of system calls in forensic event reconstruction and how to do that efficiently.

The main insights of our experiments are as follows:

1. Basically, we are able to reproduce the work of Latzo and Freiling [14] and show that our characteristic fingerprints are quite similar. Furthermore, we extended their event set by 30 events.
2. We show that characteristic fingerprints are actually applicable for forensic event reconstruction. The matching results are quite good. Overall, the sensitivity for our complete event set is about 88% and reaches 100% if only detectable events are considered.
3. We show how to systematically use system calls for forensic event reconstruction. Furthermore, we reveal what system calls are discriminative and how expensive these are in terms of performance.

1.3   Outline

The paper is structured as follows: First, in Sect. 2 we give some background information on system call tracing and the theory of forensic fingerprint calculation. In Sect. 3 we give insights into the experimental setup we used for our measurements. Further in Sect. 4 we calculate (characteristic) fingerprints for a large event set. Performance of the matching is analyzed in Sect. 5. Eventually, in Sect. 6 we investigate the role of system calls for forensic event reconstruction and how to use them efficiently.

2   Background

2.1   System Call Tracing

Operating systems offer an interface—the *system calls*—for user applications (and libraries) to perform specific actions usually on shared resources. Examples for GNU/Linux are: open, read or write a file or execve to spawn a new process, etc. Basically all interaction with a user or the machine, i.e., writing to a terminal or file, displaying something on the screen, sending a network package, etc. can only be performed using system calls.

Hence, system call traces disclose a lot about the behavior of a program. And so system call traces are a huge research topic and there are multiple ways to get those. One traditional approach is to run an application in a sandbox [23] which is used for dynamic analysis. In this approach, only system calls of a process (can have multiple threads) are monitored, though. Using virtual machine introspection allows to monitor all system calls on a system. This means that one does not need to know in advance what process or thread shall be monitored. One example is libvmtrace [21] that we used for our measurements. This software also allows to trace only a defined set of system calls which can be very beneficial in terms of performance. Basically, tracing *all* system calls cannot be used in practice for performance reasons.

2.2   Forensic Fingerprint Calculation

User actions—henceforth called *events*—on a computer system leave specific patterns. These patterns can be used as *forensic fingerprints* as they can help an analyst to determine if an event happened on a system, or not. In this paper, we make use of Dewald's [5] definitions of forensic fingerprints. In the following we want to explain briefly the adaption of this definitions for log messages.

Basically, a log message can be described by a set of features, i.e., a *feature vector*. In the following there are a few examples of possible features:

- source: the source, form where the log message comes from
- type_id: describes the kind of log message (e.g., a user login),
- time: a time stamp of the event,
- user: the login name (i.e., who is affected?),
- path: a path that is associated with the event,
- etc.

There are many features that are not very useful for fingerprint generation, e.g., the time stamp or the user. Otherwise, it would only be possible to detect an event of a specific user at a specific time. However, there is a set of *relevant features F*. Finally, V is defined as the set of all possible feature vectors over F.

An event that occurs may trigger entries in log files. Thus, an event can also be regarded as a generator of log files, i.e., of feature vectors. Σ is defined as a set of all events that may happen in a computer system. A single event $\sigma \in \Sigma$ generates a set of feature vectors. This feature vectors generated by σ can be regarded as the trace left by σ. The *Evidence Set $E(\sigma)$* [5] is defined as the set of all subsets of feature vectors in V generated by σ. Partial evidence is also evidence, so formally $E(\sigma)$ must be closed under subsets (which is also a technical requirement for calculations).

Overall, $E(\sigma)$ contains *all* feature vectors that σ generates. So it is clear, that evidence sets of different events are overlapping. Especially during a forensic analysis, it is important to determine whether an event σ happened or did not happen, though. This means, one needs to know which feature vectors are caused by σ and not by any other event. For this reason, *characteristic fingerprints* are calculated. The characteristic fingerprint $CE(\sigma)$ of $\sigma \in \Sigma$ is defined with respect to a *reference set* of other events $\Sigma' \subseteq \Sigma$:

$$\text{CE}(\sigma, \Sigma') = E(\sigma) \setminus \bigcup_{\sigma' \in \Sigma'} E(\sigma')$$

The characteristic fingerprint $\text{CE}(\sigma, \Sigma')$ can be regarded as the set of feature vectors of the evidence set $E(\sigma)$ that remains when one subtracts all feature vectors that are also part in any other evidence set $E(\sigma')$ with $\sigma' \in \Sigma'$. For forensically-sound evidence it is necessary that $|\text{CE}(\sigma, \Sigma')|$ (henceforth also called *size*) and $|\Sigma'|$ are sufficiently large. Then one can assume that σ happened and not any other event of the reference set $\sigma' \in \Sigma$. $\text{CE}(\sigma, \Sigma')$ may also have not have any feature vector. This means, σ cannot be detected reliably with the given feature vectors F. In this paper, the sizes of a bigger event set are investigated. Furthermore, this paper gives researches the matchability of characteristic fingerprints and how to make it efficient.

3   Experimental Setup

We now briefly describe the setup and architecture that was used for the measurements in this paper. In principle, we use a similar setup as Latzo and Freiling [3] while our software also comes with a Matching Engine.

3.1   Scenario and Attacker Model

Our setup consists of a GNU/Linux server running Ubuntu 16.04 with several services enabled: a Wordpress instance, an SSH-server, Docker containers and a Nextcloud instance. We assume that is may be a typical infrastructure in small and medium-sized enterprises. There such servers are a valuable asset and might be interesting for attacks as well as forensic analysis.

We assume a high-privileged attacker with root privileges that he or she might have gained by being either being the system administrator or via a privilege escalation attack. This makes it easy for the attacker to manipulate log messages and cover his or her traces after compromising.

3.2   Architecture and Implementation

In Fig. 1 one can see a simplified schema of the architecture of our experimental setup. The target system (Ubuntu 16.04) runs virtualized as a Xen guest on an x86-64 CPU and two GiB of RAM. System log files are drained via Filebeat [6]. A monitor VM using `libvmtrace` [21] instruments the target system and traces all requested system calls. Note, tracing of system calls happens on another virtual machine, so basically it is not possible for an attacker with root privileges on the target system to disable system call tracing. By default, we trace *all* system calls. Note, this highly impacts performance which is treated later. The system

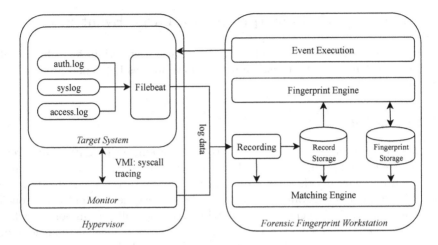

Fig. 1. Architecture of our experimental setup.

log files and the system calls are sent via Apache's Kafka [22] to the Forensic Fingerprint Workstation.

To calculate a new fingerprint for an event σ, the event is executed automatically multiple times from the Forensic Fingerprint Workstation. Most events can be executed via an open SSH session. The Recording module receives all logs (including system call traces) via Kafka and stores them in a unified log format as JSON files. To get the data in a uniform format, the log messages are parsed using regular expressions into the uniform log format—a feature vectore. Afterwards, the corresponding fingerprint can be calculated by the Fingerprint Engine as described in Sect. 2.2.

After calculating multiple fingerprints (in our case all), one can calculate characteristic fingerprints (also described in Sect. 2.2). All resulting characteristic fingerprints are also stored as JSON files.

There are two ways to start matching. First, it is possible to perform live matching. This means that all incoming logs (and system call traces) are processed directly by the Matching Engine. We assume that the feature vectors of any event all happen within at most Δ time units. For each enabled (characteristic) fingerprint the Matching Engine checks how many feature vectors of the fingerprint do match with the incoming log vectors within a time of 2Δ (in order to not miss an event that occurs between two such time slots). The second possibility is to match on recorded logs. In this case, the Matching Engine calculates the percentage of equal feature vectors in the characteristic fingerprint and the stored log. This is the way we use the Matching Engine in this paper and allows reproducibility.

In our evaluation, we only use a single target system. Log entries only need to be sent via Kafka. Thus, it is basically also possible to have multiple target systems.

4   Characteristic Fingerprints of a Large Event Set

In this section, we want to calculate characteristic fingerprints for a big event set, i.e., we calculate characteristic fingerprints similar as Latzo and Freiling [14] but for 45 events.

4.1   Event Set

To make the results comparable with the measurements of Latzo and Freiling [14], we extended the event set they use with "similar" events. This means, we also evaluate events that are usually performed by server administrators via the Linux command line. Since we want to analyze the genericity of the approach of forensic fingerprint generation and matching, it is actually not important what events are used and what an event does, i.e., if an event itself is malicious or not. In general, it is not possible to state whether an administrator's user input is malicious or not. Basically, all events can be also used in a malicious context, be it information retrieval, removal of traces, etc. Thus, we assume all events are potentially interesting for a forensic analyst.

All events are executed (and therefore recorded) 40 times (training set). Then for each event a fingerprint is calculated. For this purpose, we used the threshold of 0.8, i.e., features had to occur in the data of 80% of the 40 runs. The work of Latzo and Freiling [14] revealed that the more features are in F, the bigger the corresponding characteristic fingerprints. A possible drawback of using *too* many features for the (characteristic) fingerprints is that the feature vectors may become too specific and only work in a certain context, e.g., with a dedicated user. We decided to use the maximum feature set of [14]:

- source: from what file does the log come from,
- type_id: the type of the log message,
- path: a path that is related with the log message and
- misc: a miscellaneous field that may contain different information, e.g., a network adapter.

We assume that in our events, this feature set should not be too specific. All calculations of (characteristic) fingerprints are performed using this feature set. Table 2 shows the total amount of feature vectors in the fingerprints by origin. It is striking that system calls are clearly dominating the feature vectors in a fingerprint. Furthermore, depending on the class, an event typically leaves traces in other logs [14]. Note, the way we record events is rather error-prone. Tracing all system calls makes it hard to determine a good Δ since the actual duration of an event may vary. Especially for common log messages, it is possible that these do not become part of a fingerprint, when the variation is so big that they do not occur in 80% of the rounds.

Figure 2 gives an impression of the similarity of event fingerprints. The heatmap indicates what percentage of Fingerprint F_1 is overlapped by F_2. An "X" stands for a full overlap. Events with a larger Δ usually other events more

Table 1. List of events that is used for the evaluation. The corresponding event is recorded for Δ seconds.

Class	Name	Description	Δt
CLI	ls	Lists files	5
	cp	Copies file	5
	mv	Moves file	5
	cat	Cats file	5
	vmstat	Virtual memory statistics	5
	netstat	Network statistics	5
	tar	Creates compressed tar archive	5
	rm	Removes file	5
	shred	Shreds file	5
	curl	Downloads file	5
CLI root	tailShadow	Reads /etc/shadow	10
	vimHosts	Opens /etc/hosts in Vim	10
	rmSudo	Removes file with sudo	10
	shredSudo	Shreds file with sudo	10
Web	wordpressLogin	Wordpress Login	20
	wordpressSearch	Wordpress Search	20
	wordpressOpen	Opens Wordpress website	20
Service	sshLogin	SSH login (server side)	30
	apacheStop	Stops apache web server	110
	mysqlWp	Login into Wordpress DB via command line	20
Kernel modules	lsmod	Lists loaded kernel modules	10
	insmod	Loads kernel module	5
	rmmod	Unloads kernel module	5
Docker	dockerHelloWorld	Starts docker hello world example	105
	dockerUbuntuLog	Starts docker ubuntu and show log	110
	dockerImages	Lists all docker images	10
	dockerPs	Lists all running dockers	10
	dockerPSA	Lists all dockers container	10
	dockerUbuntuSleep	Starts docker in background	100
	dockerRm	Removes all docker containers	15
	dockerNginx	Runs nginx docker and curl it	80
	dockerUbuntuBash	Attaches bash of container	15
	dockerPrune	Removes unused container	60
	dockerPruneVolumes	Removes unused objects and volumes	60
	dockerRmImages	Removes all images	60
	dockerUbuntuBashCp	Attaches container and runs cp	95
	dockerUbuntuBashMv	Attaches container and runs mv	95
	dockerUbuntuBashRm	Attaches container and runs rm	95
	dockerUbuntuBashCat	Attaches container and runs cat	95
Nextcloud	nextcloudStatus	Shows Nextcloud status	35
	nextcloudAppList	Lists Nextcloud apps	40
	nextcloudUserList	Lists Nextcloud user	40
	nextcloudUserAdd	Adds new Nextcloud user	65
	nextcloudGroupList	List Nextcloud groups	40

than events with small Δ. Fingerprints usually contain a lot of feature vectors that are related to other events that are running simultaneously in background. We treat those feature vectors as *noise*. Usually, most overlapping feature vectors are related to noise. Fingerprints of events with very small Δ, e.g., events from the class CLI are overlapped with rather bigger proportions. It is also striking that fingerprints within a class do have higher overlapping rates, e.g., some Docker fingerprints even fully overlap some other docker fingerprints.

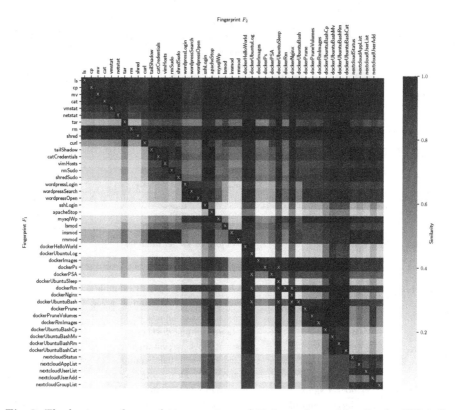

Fig. 2. The heatmap shows what percentage of F_1 is overlapped by F_2. An "X" indicates that F_2 fully overlaps F_1.

4.2 Results

Table 3 shows the number of feature vectors of characteristic fingerprints by their origin. The reference set (see also Sect. 2.2) is always the set of all other events.

It is noteworthy that the system calls clearly dominate the characteristic fingerprints. While there are several entries in the corresponding fingerprints from other log sources (see also Table 2), these vectors are no longer part of the characteristic fingerprints. If one compares the results with Latzo and Freiling [14], one can see that the sizes of characteristic fingerprints are in the same order of magnitude than ours while our event set is about three times as big. So, the characteristic fingerprints are considerably more *stable* regarding our reference set.

There are also seven zero entries. This means that for these event, it was not possible to calculate a characteristic fingerprint with all other entries in the reference set. Since now the event set is bigger, it is more likely that some events are fully overlapped by other events (see also Fig. 2).

While Latzo and Freiling [14] observed a relation between the size of an event (with respect to Δ) and the size of the corresponding characteristic fingerprint, with our larger event set we can not fully confirm this. Docker events are quite large and also do have rather large fingerprints. However, the size of the characteristic fingerprints is not in the same order of magnitude as for example the service events. So we assume that the duration of the event has not such a big impact as expected.

The last column of Table 3 contains the costs of the characteristic fingerprints. How these costs are calculated is shown later in Sect. 6.

5   Matching

We could show that it is possible to calculate characteristic fingerprints for most events for even a bigger reference set Σ'. In this section we want to analyze how the characteristic fingerprints perform in terms of event reconstruction by matching on event traces.

5.1   Methodology

To evaluate matching with characteristic fingerprints, we executed each event ten times (test set) and saved the corresponding traces as described in Sect. 3. Then, the Matching Engine calculates for all traces a score. Let $T(\sigma')$ be the trace of the event σ', then the score is calculated as follows:

$$\text{score}(\text{CE}(\sigma, \Sigma'), T(\sigma')) = \frac{|\text{CE}(\sigma, \Sigma') \cap T(\sigma')|}{|\text{CE}(\sigma, \Sigma')|}$$

This means that the score of a characteristic fingerprint $\text{CE}(\sigma, \Sigma')$ is the proportion of matched feature vectors of $T(\sigma')$ in the characteristic fingerprint. The term *matched* means that all relevant Features F that were used for calculating the fingerprint are the same in the trace vector and in the fingerprint vector. Ideally, $\text{score}(\text{CE}(\sigma, \Sigma'), T(\sigma)) = 1$ while $\text{score}(\text{CE}(\sigma, \Sigma'), T(\sigma')) = 0$ for $\sigma' \neq \sigma$.

5.2   Matching Results

Figure 3 shows the results of our matching experiment. The heatmap shows the average scores (formula is shown above for one execution) for ten executions of the event. The higher the average matching score, the darker the cell. Basically,

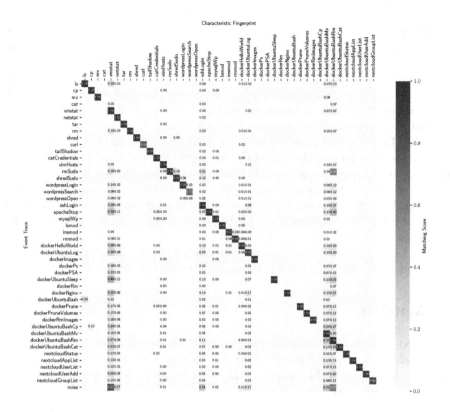

Fig. 3. The heatmap shows a matching matrix before subtracting noise from the characteristic fingerprints. On the y-axis, the ground truth, i.e., the actual event traces are listed while on the x-axis are the corresponding characteristic fingerprints. The average matching scores of ten traces is represented by the darker coloring and average score.

the matching results in Fig. 3 look considerably decent. For all existing characteristic fingerprints, the average matching score is rather high while overall the matching scores of the false events are almost everywhere below 0.1. The last line in the matrix shows the matching of one hour of noise, i.e., in this hour no user interaction with the system happened but only standard background tasks are running. There, the matching scores are also very low with one exception (vmstat). Optimally, the matrix would only have a one-diagonal while the rest are zero entries. Since we use *characteristic* fingerprints for matching, a similar graph is expected.

Figure 3 also shows that only some characteristic fingerprints produce false matches (even if the score is usually quite low). However, these characteristic fingerprints usually also do match noise (also with usually rather low scores). By researching the false matches, it is noticeable that matching feature vectors in these cases come from still present noise in the corresponding characteristic fingerprints. For example, there are some system calls related to the Filebeat [6] (the software we use to drain log files) and to Xymon [1] (a system monitoring software).

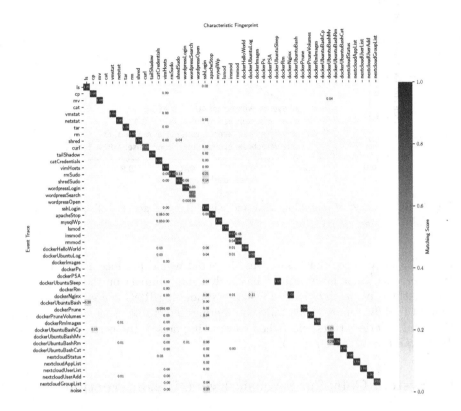

Fig. 4. The heatmap shows a matching matrix after subtracting noise from the characteristic fingerprints. On the y-axis, the ground truth, i.e., the actual event traces are listed while on the x-axis are the corresponding characteristic fingerprints. The average matching scores of ten traces is represented by the darker coloring and average score.

To get rid of the matching noise in the characteristic fingerprints, we subtract the noise from the characteristic fingerprints and perform matching again. The results can be seen in Fig. 4. There are much fewer false matching entries and the corresponding matching scores are also much lower. Thus, subtracting noise from characteristic fingerprints has turned out to be beneficial. Only `vimHots` and `sshLogin` still seem to contain some noise.

Figure 5 shows the corresponding *Receiver Operating Characteristic curves* (ROC). The ROC curves compare the true positive rate—also called *sensitivity*—with the false positive rate while varying the matching threshold. This value says above which threshold a matching score is interpreted as a match. Especially, using Fig. 4, it is easily possible to determine a perfect threshold (sensitivity of 1) and false positive rate of 0. An example of such a threshold would be 0.7.

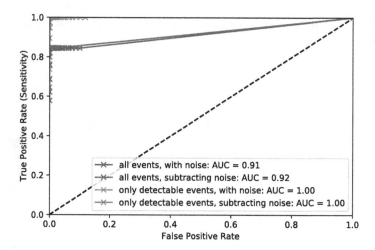

Fig. 5. ROC curves of matching with and without noise and for all events and only detectable events.

In Fig. 3, one can see that using this threshold would produce a false positive. However, this single false positive has such a small impact on the false positive rate that it is not really visible in the corresponding ROC curves. Figure 5 also shows the ROC curves when only considering detectable events. Since we can then find a perfect threshold (when subtracting noise), the corresponding *Area Under the Curve* (AUC) is 1.0.

6   System Calls for Forensic Event Reconstruction

The results in the previous sections show that system calls are dominating characteristic fingerprints so also play an important role for forensic event reconstruction. Many events could not be detected using common system log sources. The Δ values in Table 1 indicate that tracing all system calls makes the system nearly unusable, though. In this section, we want to give an overview of the distribution of system calls occuring on a system. Based on this distribution, we define a cost function for system calls that allows to make a statement about the *costs* of a characteristic fingerprint. Furthermore, this section shows what set of system calls is discriminatory, i.e., is useful for forensic event reconstruction.

6.1   System Call Distribution in System Activity and in Characteristic Fingerprints

To get the distribution of system calls occurrences, we record one hour of noise in the system. So, all system calls are traced for an hour while no user interaction is happening. Then, all records of the events (40 rounds per event) and the noise recording are merged together to get a representative list of system calls occurring on the system A. This list contains more than 41 million system calls.

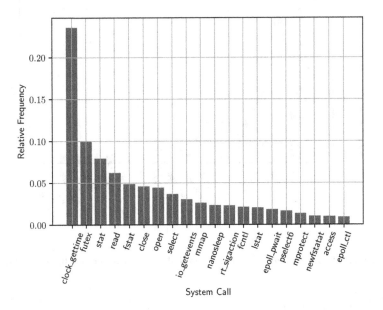

Fig. 6. Typical distribution of system calls in a system (using reference set A).

Figure 6 shows a histogram of the 20 most frequent system calls in our set of system calls. The most frequent system call (24%) is clock_gettime which—as the name suggests—is responsible for returning the current time. futex is used for synchronisation while the next next system calls read, fstat, close and open are all related to basic file operations. Since Linux is a file-based system, it is no surprise that these kind of system calls are quite frequent.

The histogram in Fig. 7 shows the absolute numbers of system calls in characteristic fingerprints. Here, we also see that file-related system calls like open and stat are also important in characteristic fingerprints. Table 4 lists these system calls and describes their purpose in more detail. Basically, one can say that file-related system calls are quite generic and occur in many characteristic fingerprints. Other system calls in this list are used more for special purpose like finit_module and delete_module that are used for loading and unloading Linux kernel modules and so clearly belong to the corresponding events (see also Table 1).

In the following section, we want to show how to make the system call tracing more efficient by tracing fewer system calls based on the knowledge of the distributions of system calls in the system and in characteristic fingerprints.

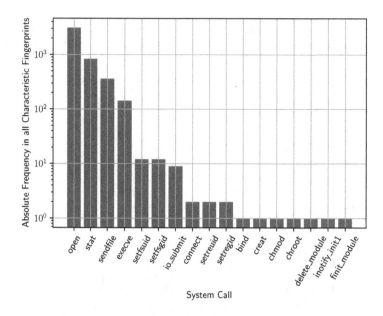

Fig. 7. Absolute occurences of system calls in characteristic fingerprints.

6.2 The Cost Function

In this section we want to develop a cost function for characteristic fingerprints. This function shall be used to assess how expensive it is to trace all system calls that are used in a characteristic fingerprint.

Basically, `libvmtrace` [21] (the software we use for system call tracing) allows to trace a defined set of system calls. For example, only for a specific set of system calls, there is a trap into the hypervisor. Traps into the hypervisor are quite expensive and so if one traces a lot of system calls, there are a lot of traps and context switches which strongly decreases the performance. We assume every trace of a system call has the same constant costs as the most expensive part is trapping into the hypervisor that is the same for every system call.

Let s be a system call that should be traced and A be a representative list of system calls that happen over a long period of time in the system. Then we define the costs c of s as the relative frequency of the system call in the representative system activity A, i.e., the number of times that s occurs in A over the total length of the list. Overall, we traced about 320 different system calls.

Table 4 lists the system calls that appear in characteristic fingerprints, describes their purpose and shows the (rounded) costs of the system calls that appear in characteristic fingerprints. It is striking that most system calls that are part of characteristic fingerprints should not have an impact on performance. The two most frequent system calls in characteristic fingerprints (**open** and **stat**) are the most expensive in this table, though. However, the table shows that tracing most system calls is not necessary.

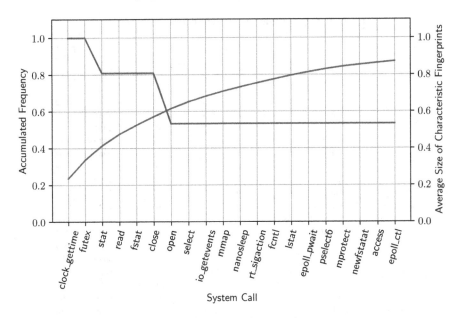

Fig. 8. The accumulated frequency of system calls occurrences (in blue) and the factor of reduction of the size of characteristic fingerprints when successively tracing fewer system calls. (Color figure online)

Based on the formula above, we can define a cost function for characteristic fingerprints. Let $CE(\sigma, \Sigma')$ be a characteristic fingerprint, then the cost of a characteristic fingerprint is defined as follows:

$$c(CE(\sigma, \Sigma')) = \sum_{s \in CE(\sigma, \Sigma')} c(s)$$

So, the costs of a characteristic fingerprint $CE(\sigma, \Sigma')$ is the sum of the relative frequencies of system calls that are part of the characteristic fingerprint. In the last column of Table 3 are the cost of each characteristic fingerprint when tracing all possible system calls. It shows that the maximum costs of a characteristic fingerprint is only about 0.125. Nearly 88% of all system calls do not need to be traced which would increase performance a lot. However, 12.5% of the performance overhead is a lot (see also Table 1). The following shows how to reduce further the costs of characteristic fingerprints and the impact on the size of the characteristic fingerprints.

6.3   Greedy Elimination of Expensive System Calls

About 88% of occurring system calls do not need to be traced since they are not part of any characteristic fingerprint, anyway. Obviously this should increase performance already a lot. However, even 12.5% of the performance overhead is

Table 2. Sizes of fingerprint sets classified by origin.

Class	Name	Source				Total
		syslog	auth.log	access.log	syscalls	
CLI	ls	0	0	0	1386	1386
	cp	0	0	0	1401	1401
	mv	0	0	0	1382	1382
	cat	0	0	0	1315	1315
	vmstat	0	0	0	1457	1457
	netstat	0	0	0	1614	1614
	tar	0	0	0	3367	3367
	rm	0	0	0	1308	1308
	shred	0	0	0	1372	1372
	curl	0	0	0	3173	3173
CLI Root	tailShadow	0	4	0	2944	2948
	catCredentials	0	4	0	3032	3036
	vimHosts	0	1	0	3100	3101
	rmSudo	0	1	0	2932	2933
	shredSudo	0	1	0	2649	2650
Web	wordpressLogin	0	0	19	9596	9615
	wordpressSearch	0	0	10	8250	8260
	wordpressOpen	0	0	10	8096	8106
Service	sshLogin	1	4	0	32380	32385
	apacheStop	0	4	0	45984	45988
	mysqlWp	0	0	0	4644	4644
Kernel Modules	lsmod	0	0	0	3776	3776
	insmod	1	2	0	3485	3488
	rmmod	1	1	0	3474	3476
Docker	dockerHelloWorld	7	0	0	60928	60935
	dockerUbuntuLog	0	0	0	57208	57208
	dockerImages	0	0	0	3345	3345
	dockerPs	0	0	0	5107	5107
	dockerPSA	0	0	0	8057	8057
	dockerUbuntuSleep	4	0	0	61405	61409
	dockerRm	0	0	0	5992	5992
	dockerNginx	0	0	0	44231	44231
	dockerUbuntuBash	0	0	0	5051	5051
	dockerPrune	0	0	0	21802	21802
	dockerPruneVolumes	0	0	0	21622	21622
	dockerRmImages	0	0	0	4194	4194
	dockerUbuntuBashCp	4	0	0	73529	73533
	dockerUbuntuBashMv	4	0	0	53373	53377
	dockerUbuntuBashRm	4	0	0	57698	57702
	dockerUbuntuBashCat	4	0	0	73032	73036
Nextcloud	nextcloudStatus	0	4	0	24768	24772
	nextcloudAppList	0	4	0	26830	26834
	nextcloudUserList	0	4	0	24936	24940
	nextcloudUserAdd	0	4	0	30966	30970
	nextcloudGroupList	0	4	0	21764	21768

a lot (see also Table 1). In the following we show how to reduce further the costs of characteristic fingerprints and the impact on the size of the characteristic fingerprints.

Table 3. Sizes and costs of characteristic fingerprints.

Class	Name	Source				Total	$c(\mathrm{CE}(\sigma, \Sigma'))$
		syslog	auth.log	access.log	syscalls		
CLI	ls	0	0	0	1	1	0.001
	cp	0	0	0	4	4	0.124
	mv	0	0	0	2	2	0.08
	cat	0	0	0	0	0	0
	vmstat	0	0	0	6	6	0.045
	netstat	0	0	0	15	15	0.045
	tar	0	0	0	5	5	0.08
	rm	0	0	0	1	1	0.001
	shred	0	0	0	2	2	0.045
	curl	0	0	0	1	1	0.044
CLI Root	tailShadow	0	1	0	6	7	0.08
	catCredentials	0	1	0	3	4	0.045
	vimHosts	0	1	0	219	220	0.124
	rmSudo	0	0	0	2	2	0.001
	shredSudo	0	2	0	7	9	0.124
Web	wordpressLogin	0	0	7	56	63	0.123
	wordpressSearch	0	0	1	2	3	0.123
	wordpressOpen	0	0	0	0	0	0
Service	sshLogin	1	3	0	2215	2219	0.125
	apacheStop	0	1	0	1711	1712	0.124
	mysqlWp	0	0	0	47	47	0.125
Kernel Modules	lsmod	0	0	0	251	251	0.045
	insmod	0	0	0	10	10	0.124
	rmmod	0	0	0	12	12	0.124
Docker	dockerHelloWorld	0	0	0	28	28	0.045
	dockerUbuntuLog	0	0	0	23	23	0.124
	dockerImages	0	0	0	1	1	0.001
	dockerPs	0	0	0	0	0	0
	dockerPSA	0	0	0	0	0	0
	dockerUbuntuSleep	0	0	0	2	2	0.001
	dockerRm	0	0	0	0	0	0
	dockerNginx	0	0	0	65	65	0.124
	dockerUbuntuBash	0	0	0	0	0	0
	dockerPrune	0	0	0	1	1	0.001
	dockerPruneVolumes	0	0	0	1	1	0.001
	dockerRmImages	0	0	0	2	2	0.001
	dockerUbuntuBashCp	0	0	0	0	0	0
	dockerUbuntuBashMv	0	0	0	18	18	0.124
	dockerUbuntuBashRm	0	0	0	3	3	0.08
	dockerUbuntuBashCat	0	0	0	24	24	0.044
Nextcloud	nextcloudStatus	0	1	0	2	3	0.001
	nextcloudAppList	0	1	0	43	44	0.124
	nextcloudUserList	0	1	0	2	3	0.001
	nextcloudUserAdd	0	1	0	102	103	0.045
	nextcloudGroupList	0	1	0	4	5	0.045

The blue line in Fig. 7 shows the accumulated frequency of the 20 most frequent system calls in our representative system call set. It can be seen that these 20 system calls make together nearly 90% of all system call calls. The

Table 4. Costs to trace system calls that are part of characteristic fingerprints ordered by the frequency in characteristic fingerprints. The descriptions are taken from the Linux Programmer's Manual [2].

System call	Description	Costs
open	Opens a file for reading or writing	0.0442
stat	Retrieves a files status	0.0791
sendfile	Transfers data between file descriptors	0.0003
execve	Executes a program	0.0009
setfsuid	Sets user identity used for filesystem checks	0.0000
setfsgid	Sets group identity used for filesystem checks	0.0000
io_submit	Submits asynchronous I/O blocks for processing	0.0000
connect	Initiates a connection on a socket	0.0007
setreuid	Sets a real and/or effective user or group ID	0.0000
setregid	Sets a real and/or effective user or group ID	0.0000
bind	Binds a name to a socket	0.0002
creat	Opens and possibly creates a file	0.0000
chmod	Changes permissions of a file	0.0000
chroot	Changes root directory	0.0000
delete_module	Unloads a kernel module	0.0000
inotify_init1	Initializes an inotify instance	0.0000
finit_module	Loads a kernel module	0.0000

red line shows the average characteristic fingerprint size when successively the system calls are removed from the characteristic fingerprints. One can spot two steps in the graph. One, when stat is not traced and one bigger when open is not traced. This is in accordance with Table 4 that shows only these two system calls are the "expensive". The average size of characteristic fingerprints shrinks by the factor 0.57.

Now we want to investigate in more detail how the sizes of characteristic fingerprints decreases when not tracing stat and open. Table 5 shows the size of characteristic fingerprints when tracing all system calls, all but not stat, all but not open and all but not stat and open. The table shows (as Fig. 7) that not tracing stat shrinks the size of characteristic fingerprints with an overage of about 20%. The same applies for open with about 27%. However, even though the table reveals quite large reduction rates are for some fingerprints, only two events have no vectors after the removal of stat and open from the characteristic fingerprints (Fig. 8).

The costs in Table 4 also show that not tracing stat and open should increase performance a lot. Table 6 gives an impression of the benefits in terms of performance of tracing fewer system calls. There, for three events the average overheads are calculated for different sets of traced system calls. Note, the "No Tracing"

Table 5. Loss of vectors in characteristic fingerprints when not tracing `stat` or `open` or both.

Class	Name	Before	w/o stat	w/o open	w/o stat,open
CLI	ls	1	1 (−0.00)	1 (−0.00)	1 (−0.00)
	cp	4	2 (−0.50)	3 (−0.25)	1 (−0.75)
	mv	2	1 (−0.50)	2 (−0.00)	1 (−0.50)
	cat	0	0 (−0.00)	0 (−0.00)	0 (−0.00)
	vmstat	6	6 (−0.00)	1 (−0.83)	1 (−0.83)
	netstat	15	15 (−0.00)	1 (−0.93)	1 (−0.93)
	tar	5	4 (−0.20)	5 (−0.00)	4 (−0.20)
	rm	1	1 (−0.00)	1 (−0.00)	1 (−0.00)
	shred	2	2 (−0.00)	1 (−0.50)	1 (−0.50)
	curl	1	1 (−0.00)	0 (−1.00)	0 (−1.00)
CLI Root	tailShadow	7	3 (−0.57)	7 (−0.00)	3 (−0.57)
	catCredentials	4	4 (−0.00)	3 (−0.25)	3 (−0.25)
	vimHosts	220	97 (−0.56)	127 (−0.42)	4 (−0.98)
	rmSudo	2	2 (−0.00)	2 (−0.00)	2 (−0.00)
	shredSudo	9	5 (−0.44)	8 (−0.11)	4 (−0.56)
Web	wordpressLogin	63	38 (−0.40)	41 (−0.35)	16 (−0.75)
	wordpressSearch	3	2 (−0.33)	2 (−0.33)	1 (−0.67)
	wordpressOpen	0	0 (−0.00)	0 (−0.00)	0 (−0.00)
Service	sshLogin	2219	1381 (−0.38)	1305 (−0.41)	467 (−0.79)
	apacheStop	1712	1697 (−0.01)	31 (−0.98)	16 (−0.99)
	mysqlWp	47	14 (−0.70)	35 (−0.26)	2 (−0.96)
Kernel Modules	lsmod	251	251 (−0.00)	1 (−1.00)	1 (−1.00)
	insmod	10	5 (−0.50)	8 (−0.20)	3 (−0.70)
	rmmod	12	6 (−0.50)	9 (−0.25)	3 (−0.75)
Docker	dockerHelloWorld	28	28 (−0.00)	3 (−0.89)	3 (−0.89)
	dockerUbuntuLog	23	12 (−0.48)	16 (−0.30)	5 (−0.78)
	dockerImages	1	1 (−0.00)	1 (−0.00)	1 (−0.00)
	dockerPs	0	0 (−0.00)	0 (−0.00)	0 (−0.00)
	dockerPSA	0	0 (−0.00)	0 (−0.00)	0 (−0.00)
	dockerUbuntuSleep	2	2 (−0.00)	2 (−0.00)	2 (−0.00)
	dockerRm	0	0 (−0.00)	0 (−0.00)	0 (−0.00)
	dockerNginx	65	45 (−0.31)	29 (−0.55)	9 (−0.86)
	dockerUbuntuBash	0	0 (−0.00)	0 (−0.00)	0 (−0.00)
	dockerPrune	1	1 (−0.00)	1 (−0.00)	1 (−0.00)
	dockerPruneVolumes	1	1 (−0.00)	1 (−0.00)	1 (−0.00)
	dockerRmImages	2	2 (−0.00)	2 (−0.00)	2 (−0.00)
	dockerUbuntuBashCp	0	0 (−0.00)	0 (−0.00)	0 (−0.00)
	dockerUbuntuBashMv	18	6 (−0.67)	13 (−0.28)	1 (−0.94)
	dockerUbuntuBashRm	3	1 (−0.67)	3 (−0.00)	1 (−0.67)
	dockerUbuntuBashCat	24	24 (−0.00)	0 (−1.00)	0 (−1.00)
Nextcloud	nextcloudStatus	3	3 (−0.00)	3 (−0.00)	3 (−0.00)
	nextcloudAppList	44	4 (−0.91)	43 (−0.02)	3 (−0.93)
	nextcloudUserList	3	3 (−0.00)	3 (−0.00)	3 (−0.00)
	nextcloudUserAdd	103	103 (−0.00)	17 (−0.83)	17 (−0.83)
	nextcloudGroupList	5	5 (−0.00)	3 (−0.40)	3 (−0.40)
Average		109	83 (−0.19)	38 (−0.27)	13 (−0.47)

may differ from the corresponding Δ values since Δ values were determined more pessimistically. While tracing all system calls can have an overhead of 90 which makes interactive usage nearly impossible, the overheads when only

Table 6. Average overhead of system call tracing.

Event name	No tracing	All syscalls	Only occurring	w/o open	w/o stat	w/o open, stat
tar	0.05 s	4.5 s (90)	0.2 s (4)	0.1 s (2)	0.18 s (3.6)	0.08 s (1.6)
sshLogin	0.5 s	21 s (42)	1.0 s (2)	0.6 s (1.2)	0.8 s (1.6)	0.6 s (1.2)
dockerHelloWorld	0.9 s	70 s (78)	8 s (8.9)	4 s (4.4)	6.5 s (7)	1.5 s (1.6)

tracing system calls that appear in characteristic fingerprints are a lot better. Removing `stat` and `open` from tracing has a huge impact. When not tracing `stat` and `open` the worst performance overhead we measure is 1.6.

7   Conclusion and Future Work

In this work we firstly were basically able to reproduce recent research [14] and could show that their kind of characteristic fingerprint calculation is also applicable for an even larger event set. We secondly showed that these characteristic fingerprints can be used to perform matching and so to actually reconstruct events based on log files (including system call traces). Thirdly we analyzed the possibilities and impact of system calls in characteristic fingerprints and show how to systematically reduce overhead by tracing only necessary system calls. We furthermore named discriminating system calls where future work can build upon.

Our measurements also revealed that with more events and so a bigger reference set there is more overlap between feature sets though. So, for some events we could not calculate a characteristic fingerprint. To calculate characteristic fingerprints it would be necessary to make the events more characteristic. This can be done by increasing the feature set or log source set. It would also be interesting how these characteristic fingerprints perform in term of unknown events. Future work should consider the false positive rate of unknown events.

Acknowledgements. We want to thank Felix Freiling for his valuable advice and feedback on this paper. This research was supported by the Federal Ministry of Education and Research, Germany, as part of the BMBF DINGfest project (https://dingfest. ur.de) and by Deutsche Forschungsgemeinschaft (DFG, German Research Foundation) as part of the Research and Training Group 2475 "Cybercrime and Forensic Computing" (grant number 393541319/GRK2475/1-2019).

References

1. The xymon monitor. https://xymon.sourceforge.io/
2. Linux programmer's manual (2018). http://man7.org/linux/man-pages/dir_section_2.html
3. 18th IEEE International Conference On Trust, Security And Privacy In Computing And Communications/13th IEEE International Conference On Big Data Science And Engineering, TrustCom/BigDataSE 2019, Rotorua, New Zealand, 5–8 August 2019. IEEE (2019). https://ieeexplore.ieee.org/xpl/conhome/8883860/proceeding

4. Chabot, Y., Bertaux, A., Nicolle, C., Kechadi, T.: An ontology-based approach for the reconstruction and analysis of digital incidents timelines. Digit. Invest. **15**, 83–100 (2015)

5. Dewald, A.: Characteristic evidence, counter evidence and reconstruction problems in forensic computing. IT - Inf. Technol. **57**(6), 339–346 (2015). http://www. degruyter.com/view/j/itit.2015.57.issue-6/itit-2015-0017/itit-2015-0017.xml

6. Elasticsearch B.V.: Filebeat - lightweight shipper for logs (2020). https://www. elastic.co/products/beats/filebeat

7. Gerhards, R.: The syslog protocol. Technical report (2009)

8. Gladyshev, P., Enbacka, A.: Rigorous development of automated inconsistency checks for digital evidence using the B method. IJDE **6**(2) (2007). http://www. utica.edu/academic/institutes/ecii/publications/articles/1C35450B-E896-6876- 9E80DA0F9FEEF98B.pdf

9. Gladyshev, P., Patel, A.: Finite state machine approach to digital eventreconstruction. Digit. Invest. **1**(2), 130–149 (2004). https://doi.org/10.1016/j.diin.2004. 03.001

10. James, J.I., Gladyshev, P.: Automated inference of past action instances indigital investigations. Int. J. Inf. Sec. **14**(3), 249–261 (2015). https://doi.org/10.1007/ s10207-014-0249-6

11. Khan, M.N.A., Chatwin, C.R., Young, R.C.D.: A framework for post-event timelinereconstruction using neural networks. Digit. Invest. **4**(3–4), 146–157 (2007). https://doi.org/10.1016/j.diin.2007.11.001

12. Kolosnjaji, B., Zarras, A., Webster, G., Eckert, C.: Deep learning for classification of malware system call sequences. In: Kang, B.H., Bai, Q. (eds.) AI 2016. LNCS (LNAI), vol. 9992, pp. 137–149. Springer, Cham (2016). https://doi.org/10.1007/ 978-3-319-50127-7_11

13. Kruegel, C., Mutz, D., Valeur, F., Vigna, G.: On the detection of anomalous system call arguments. In: Snekkenes, E., Gollmann, D. (eds.) ESORICS 2003. LNCS, vol. 2808, pp. 326–343. Springer, Heidelberg (2003). https://doi.org/10.1007/978- 3-540-39650-5_19

14. Latzo, T., Freiling, F.C.: Characterizing the limitations of forensic event reconstruction based on log files. In: 18th IEEE International Conference on Trust, Security and Privacy in Computing and Communications/13th IEEE International Conference on Big Data Science and Engineering, TrustCom/BigDataSE 2019, Rotorua, New Zealand, 5–8 August 2019 [3], pp. 466–475 (2019). https://doi.org/ 10.1109/TrustCom/BigDataSE.2019.00069

15. Li, Z., et al.: UCLog: a unified, correlated logging architecture for intrusion detection. In: the 12th International Conference on Telecommunication Systems-Modeling and Analysis (ICTSM) (2004)

16. Marrington, A., Mohay, G.M., Morarji, H., Clark, A.J.: A model for computer profiling. In: ARES 2010, Fifth International Conference on Availability, Reliability and Security, 15–18 February 2010, Krakow, Poland, pp. 635–640 (2010). https:// doi.org/10.1109/ARES.2010.95

17. Menges, F., et al.: Introducing DINGfest: an architecture for next generation SIEM systems. In: Langweg, H., Meier, M., Witt, B.C., Reinhardt, D. (eds.) Sicherheit 2018, Beiträge der 9. Jahrestagung des Fachbereichs Sicherheit der Gesellschaft für Informatik e.V. (GI), 25–27 April 2018, Konstanz. LNI, vol. P-281, pp. 257–260. Gesellschaft für Informatik e.V. (2018). https://doi.org/10.18420/ sicherheit2018_21

18. Microsoft Corporation: Event logging (2019). https://docs.microsoft.com/en-us/ windows/desktop/msi/event-logging

19. Ravi, S., Balakrishnan, N., Venkatesh, B.: Behavior-based malware analysis using profile hidden Markov models. In: 2013 International Conference on Security and Cryptography (SECRYPT), pp. 1–12. IEEE (2013)
20. Rieck, K., Trinius, P., Willems, C., Holz, T.: Automatic analysis of malwarebehavior using machine learning. J. Comput. Secur. **19**(4), 639–668 (2011). https://doi.org/10.3233/JCS-2010-0410
21. Taubmann, B., Kolosnjaji, B.: Architecture for resource-aware VMI-based cloud malware analysis. In: Proceedings of the 4th Workshop on Security in Highly Connected IT Systems, SHCIS@DAIS 2017, Neuchâtel, Switzerland, 21–22 June 2017, pp. 43–48 (2017). https://doi.org/10.1145/3099012.3099015
22. The Apache Software Foundation: Apache kafka - a distributed streaming platform (2020). https://kafka.apache.org/
23. Willems, C., Holz, T., Freiling, F.C.: Toward automated dynamic malware analysis using CWSandbox. IEEE Secur. Priv. **5**(2), 32–39 (2007). https://doi.org/10.1109/MSP.2007.45
24. Yadwadkar, N.J., Bhattacharyya, C., Gopinath, K., Niranjan, T., Susarla, S.: Discovery of application workloads from network file traces. In: FAST, pp. 183–196 (2010)
25. Yurcik, W., Abad, C., Hasan, R., Saleem, M., Sridharan, S.: UCLog+: a security data management system for correlating alerts, incidents, and raw data from remote logs. arXiv preprint cs/0607111 (2006)

Modelling GOP Structure Effects on ENF-Based Video Forensics

Pasquale Ferrara$^{(\boxtimes)}$, Gerard Draper-Gil, Ignacio Sanchez,
Henrik Junklewitz, and Laurent Beslay

European Commission – DG Joint Research Centre, Ispra, Italy
pasquale.ferrara@ec.europa.eu

Abstract. Electricity is transported through the network as alternate current, usually at a carrier frequency (50/60 Hz) which is known as Electric Network Frequency (ENF). In practice, ENF fluctuates around the nominal value because of changes in the supply and demand of power over time. These fluctuations are conveyed by the light that is emitted by sources connected to the power grid. Captured by video recordings, such localized variations can be exploited as digital watermarks in order to determine the position of a video in time (e.g. timestamping) and space, as well as to verify its integrity. However, the encoded formats of acquired videos alter the shape of ENF extracted from video frames. This paper provides an analytical model for characterizing the effects of group of pictures (GOP) structure adopted by the most widespread video encoders. The model is assessed through an experimental evaluation campaign, by analyzing different working conditions and by showing how the information from the GOP can contribute to the extraction of ENF from video frames.

Keywords: Electric network frequency · Video · Compression · GOP · Signal processing · Forensics

1 Introduction

As a result of the recent major digital transformation of the society, forensic analysis of multimedia evidence has acquired a growing importance in the investigation of crimes. Law enforcement investigation and prosecution have to face the growing misuse of new information technologies by criminals. Examples of such misuse include networks anonymization or data encryption, which defeat the efforts of the investigation process aiming to identify victims and perpetrators, to characterize the nature of the criminal activity and to localize the crime. In this context, multimedia forensics constitutes an increasingly central factor in criminal investigations. Audio and video forensic techniques [1] such as source camera identification or microphone forensics can enable law-enforcement to overcome the growing limitations posed of more classical forensic methodologies.

© ICST Institute for Computer Sciences, Social Informatics and Telecommunications Engineering 2021
Published by Springer Nature Switzerland AG 2021. All Rights Reserved
S. Goel et al. (Eds.): ICDF2C 2020, LNICST 351, pp. 121–138, 2021.
https://doi.org/10.1007/978-3-030-68734-2_7

Electric Network Frequency (ENF) analysis is another multimedia forensic technique that has demonstrated a strong potential to support forensic investigations[1]. When an electric device (computers, microphones, camcorders, surveillance cameras etc.) is plugged to the electric network, it captures not only a scene or a speech, but also the unique pattern of the 50/60 Hz electric network carrier frequency. ENF is not constant but it fluctuates around its nominal value because of the variations of power production and consumption. Such variations can be exploited as a digital watermark complementing the more classical forensic techniques used for timestamping and localization of multimedia recordings, and even overcome their limitations. These classical approaches rely on the analysis of content information which can be more and more subject to manipulation (spoofing, deep-fake, etc.). Metadata that might be present in the multimedia evidence (such as geo-tags or EXIF) could also contribute to the forensic analysis but they can be easily removed or tampered with by the perpetrators.

In 2010, ENF was considered as the "most significant development in audio forensics since Watergate"[2]. Indeed, ENF has been successfully used to extract forensic evidences from audio files that have been instrumental in court [2]. In particular, ENF forensics has proven to be effective with the following tasks:

- **Timestamping of the recording:** by matching the extracted ENF signal against a reference database of network frequencies of known electricity grids, it is possible to determine the precise point in time when the recording took place.
- **Localization of the recording:** it is possible to determine unique geographical constraints linked to the specific location, where the recording took place. This becomes possible by either analyzing specific features of the signal and comparing them statistically with intrinsic features present in each electric network or, by directly matching patterns extracted from recordings against a reference database of measurements of multiple registered electric networks from different geographical zones.
- **Integrity verification:** by analyzing the ENF signal extracted from the multimedia recording it is possible to identify fragments that have been edited, removed or inserted.

Most of the research ENF forensics has been focused on audio signals, where the ENF signal is included in the data stream due to the specific recording media used (e.g. audio recording in magnetic tapes) or electric induction over the power supply or other nearby strong magnetic fields.

More recently, researchers have demonstrated that the ENF signal can also be reconstructed from video recordings taken under artificial light, by exploiting the light fluctuations captured in the video [3]. The extraction of ENF from video frames is a new promising approach that, so far, has not yet been explored to its full potential. Among the factors that affects ENF-based video forensics [4], such as type of artificial light or time recording, there is still a lack of understanding on the role of video

---

[1] https://enfsi.eu/wp-content/uploads/2016/09/forensic_speech_and_audio_analysis_wg_-_best_practice_guidelines_for_enf_analysis_in_forensic_authentication_of_digital_evidence_0.pdf.

[2] https://www.theregister.co.uk/2010/06/01/enf_met_police/.

compression for the ENF captured in video frames. This aspect plays a key role as widely used smart devices provide only encoded videos. To the best of our knowledge, this work represents the first attempt to model the effects of group of pictures (GOP) structures, typical of the most common compression standard on the market such as H.262/MPEG-2, H.263, or newer ones such as H.264/MPEG-4 AVC and HEVC.

The rest of the paper is organized as follows: in Sect. 2 we provide an overview of the state-of-the-art on ENF-based media forensics. In Sect. 3, we focus on the extraction of ENF signal from video frames, while in Sect. 4 we explain the model that we propose to tackle with video compression. Then, we present our experimental results in Sect. 5, while we draw the conclusions in Sect. 6.

2 Related Works

The use of ENF in digital media forensics has gained large attention in the last decade due to its potential applications. Initial works focused on its application to digital audio forensics [5, 6], defining the "ENF criterion" as the reference procedure for the application of ENF in timestamping digital recordings. The ENF criterion procedure is based on three steps:

- ENF reference signal extraction (from the electricity grid);
- ENF audio signal extraction;
- ENF matching.

More recently, it has been demonstrated that ENF signals can also be extracted from video frames [3, 7] using the "light-flickering" effect, fluctuations of light intensity produced when illumination systems are connected to the power grid.

ENF reference signal extraction and matching are processing challenges independent of the source signal (i.e. audio or video frames). Most authors [8–10] assume that obtaining the ENF reference signal is a straightforward process, although the authors in [11] argued that ENF extraction from the electric grid is prone to errors if obtained from only one source.

Initially, ENF matching was done using visual inspection or Minimum Mean Square Error (MMSE) criteria [8, 12]. In the latest years, this process has captured the attention of several authors [13, 14], including proposals based on machine learning and more advanced statistical properties of ENF signals [15, 16].

There are many proposals for ENF extraction from audio signals [17–19], although according to [10], the improvements proposed in these works have a marginal effect on the overall result. Moreover, since most efforts address the problem of ENF extraction, other problems like ENF signal detection or audio tampering detection remain open.

Previous works on ENF extraction from video frames have followed two different approaches, those working with CCD [3, 7, 20] cameras and those working with CMOS [21–23] cameras. CCD sensor cameras adopt a global shutter system that capture all pixels at the same time, whereas CMOS sensor cameras use a rolling shutter sampling mechanism, capturing each pixel-row at different time instants. Moreover, other factors that can affect the quality of ENF signal are compression and light source.

The effects of rolling shutter have been studied in [3, 21, 23] with a comprehensive analysis done by the authors of [22]. The influence of the light source has also been addressed in [4]. Although, there are some papers addressing compression [3, 4], none of them offers a detailed explanation of its effects. Furthermore, none of the papers addressing compression envisage to take advantage of its effects and exploit them forensically.

3   ENF-Based Video Forensics

The voltage measured from the plug varies over time as:

$$V(t) = A_0 cos(2\pi(f_0 + \varepsilon(t))t) \tag{1}$$

where f_0 is the nominal electrical network frequency (50 or 60 Hz, depending on the region) and $\varepsilon(t)$ models the fluctuation of the ENF over the time. Even though $\varepsilon(t)$ exhibits pseudo-periodic behavior due to the load control mechanism of the electricity grids [24], it can be considered as a unique pattern that allows localizing a given recording in time and space. In [7], authors demonstrated that ENF, defined as $f_0 + \varepsilon(t)$, impacts on most light sources by slightly changing the intensity of the emitted light. Being light intensity and electric voltage related to each other by a power law, light oscillations are at double frequency (100 or 120 Hz). It is also demonstrated that camera sensors can capture such variations during a video recording.

It is worth to note, however, that cameras usually acquire a video at a frame rate (25 or 30 frame per second) which is lower than light fluctuation (100 or 120 Hz). This implies that the ENF signal conveyed by the light is acquired at a sampling rate which is lower than the signal frequency, causing aliasing. This means that the ENF appears around a different frequency, which can be derived from the Nyquist theorem as:

$$f_a(t) = |f_x(t) - m \cdot f_s| \tag{2}$$

where $f_a(t)$, f_s and $f_x(t)$ are, respectively, the aliased frequency, the sampling frequency and the signal frequency; m is a positive integer such that $f_a(t) < f_s/2$. Assuming that $f_s = 30$ fps and $f_x(t) = 100 + \varepsilon(t)$ Hz, then $f_a(t) = |m \cdot 30 - 100 \cdot \varepsilon(t)| = 10$ Hz for $m = 3$.

Finally, modern cameras are equipped with camera sensors of different technologies, which employ different shutter technologies. CCD sensors are usually associated with a global shutter, meaning all pixels are illuminated at the same global time. CMOS sensors typically use a rolling shutter, so that not all pixels are acquired in the same time, but only each row. The latter could theoretically lead to a much higher sampling rate. However, in the rest of the paper we will consider only the global shutter approach, so that the ENF related signal $2f_0 + 2\varepsilon(t)$ is extracted by averaging all pixel intensities $I(i, j; t)$ for each video frame of size $M \times N$ as:

$$I(t) = \frac{1}{MN} \sum_{i,j=1}^{M,N} I(i,j;t).$$

(3)

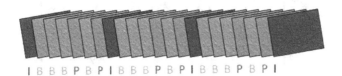

I B B B P B P I B B B P B P I B B B P B P I

Fig. 1. Sequence of video frames whose GOP size is 7.

4 GOP Structure Effects on ENF Signal

We first recall some basics of video coding that are useful in order to comprehend the approach we propose for modelling the effects of compression when ENF is extracted from encoded videos.

4.1 Basics of Video Coding

By nature, every digital video is essentially a temporal sequence of pictures (i.e. frames) acquired at a given rate (e.g. 30 frames per second, in most of commercial devices). Such data stream can be properly compressed to save storage or transmission bandwidth by taking advantage of the redundancies that are present in the spatial (i.e. within each frame) and in the temporal (i.e. between two or more adjacent frames) domains and, at the same time, by exploiting the characteristics of the Human Vision System (HVS) to minimize visual degradation. To achieve this goal, the most common video compression standards such as MPEG-4 [25] and Advanced Video Coding (also known as MPEG-4 AVC or H.264) [26] employ a block-oriented and motion-compensated video coding approach. Briefly, such coding schemes divide frames into two different types: intra-coded frames, also referred as I-frames, and predictive-coded frames, which can in turn be divided in subtypes such as predicted (P) and bi-predicted (B) frames. During the encoding process, frames are grouped in GOPs (group of pictures) according to a structure that always begins with an I-frame and then present a certain number of predictive frames, as shown in Fig. 1. Encountering a new GOP in a stream means that the decoder does not need any previous frames to decode the next ones. The number of frames composing a group of pictures is called GOP size, and it might be constant or variable depending on the specific implementation.

When a frame is compressed, the encoder divides it in macroblocks (MBs) and encodes each MB individually: MBs belonging to I-frames are always encoded as they are, without referring to other frames, by means of a DCT quantization strategy. At the same time, MBs belonging to predictive-coded frames may be encoded referring to previous frames (this is the only possibility in P-frames) or even referring following frames (allowed in B-frames). Besides predicted MBs, the encoder embeds the motion vectors MVs associated to each MB. Finally, the encoder has also the possibility to skip a MB in a predictive-coded frame, if this MB can be directly copied from a previous

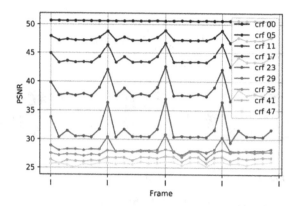

Fig. 2. PSNR between each raw frame and its corresponding encoded frame for different bitrates and a GOP size forced to 7.

frame (for instance, in presence of a static content). A more detailed description of video compression can be found in [27].

4.2 Modelling Compression Artifacts

We underline that, given their definitions in the last subsection, only I-frames certainly contain the information about pixels intensities of the original uncompressed frames, whereas in case of P and B-frames this information is borrowed from previous or neighboring frames.

In Fig. 2 we qualitatively illustrate the rationale of this assumption. We show the Peak Signal-to-Noise Ratio (PSNR) obtained between the uncompressed frames of a static video and their corresponding frames encoded for different constant rate factors (CRF). In this example, we forced the encoder to keep a GOP size equal to 7. For CRF = 0, the encoder codifies all frames as intra-coded at their maximum quality, so that to produce the average highest PSNR and no significant difference are visible among frames. Once the CRF increases, we observe that the fidelity of I-frames is systematically higher than the other predictive-encoded frames, which are more and mostly affected by the motion compensation strategy. For CRF greater than 29 (in our example), such differences between intra-coded and predictive-coded frames become smaller, because quantization effects on macro-block DCT coefficients become significant.

Starting from this observation, we model the way in which GOP structure acts on the video stream as a down-sampling operation. To simplify our analysis, we assume that a generic video is encoded by using a constant GOP size L, meaning that our intensity signal is subsampled of a factor L. From the Nyquist-Shannon theorem, we know that a band-limited signal can be reconstructed without *aliasing* if $F_S \geq 2B$, where F_S is the sampling frequency and B is the maximum frequency of the sampled signal. In our case, we can rewrite the Nyquist-Shannon inequality in function of the ENF frequency $F_X = 2f_0 + 2\varepsilon(t)$, the camera frame rate f_s and the GOP size L. First, we define the sampling rate after GOP encoding as:

$$F_S = \frac{1}{T_S^{GoP}} = \frac{1}{L \cdot \left(\frac{1}{f_s}\right)} = \frac{f_s}{L} \tag{4}$$

By substituting in the Nyquist-Shannon inequality, we obtain:

$$\frac{f_s}{L} \geq 2F_X \tag{5}$$

This means that aliasing due to the down-sampling operated by GOP structure does not appear if:

$$L \leq \frac{f_s}{2F_X} \tag{6}$$

As a numerical example, we consider the ENF extraction from a stand-still video using the global approach (Sect. 3) to obtain the signal $I(t)$. We assume that $f_0 = 50$ Hz and a camera frame rate $f_S = 30$ fps. Because the light flickering oscillates at a double frequency with respect the ENF, the aliased (see Sect. 3) ENF signal appears in the spectrum of the intensity signal at a frequency of $F_X = 10$ Hz. By applying these values to Eq. (6), we derive that the absence of the aliasing is guaranteed if and only if $L \leq 1.5$. On the contrary, for a GOP size $L \geq 2$, we observe aliasing in the spectrum of $I(t)$.

The assumption that the GOP size is constant can be relaxed by taking advantages of the generalization of the Nyquist-Shannon to nonuniform sampling [28], by considering the average sampling period, or GOP size in this specific application.

Finally, the Nyquist-Shannon theory also provides information about the positions of the alias ENF in the Fourier spectrum. By using the symmetry property of the Fourier transform of real signals, the location of aliased ENF signals is:

$$F_X^a = \begin{cases} F_X - k\dfrac{f_s}{L} & \text{if } 0 < F_X - k\dfrac{f_s}{L} < f_s/2 \\ \mod\left(f_s/2 - \left(F_X - k\dfrac{f_s}{L}\right), f_s/2\right) & \text{elsewhere} \end{cases}, \ k \in \mathbb{Z}. \tag{7}$$

It is worth to note that for $F_X - k\frac{f_s}{L} \notin (0, f_s/2)$, the alias spectrum is $I(-f) = -I(f)$. In the case of variable GOP size, the model still applies but with $\bar{L} = \frac{1}{N} \sum_{i=0}^{N-1} L_i$, where L_i are the GOP sizes of each group of pictures present in video.

5 Results and Discussions

This Section provides an experimental analysis validating the model we described in Sect. 4, in order to demonstrate its capability to predict the effects of video coding when extracting ENF signal from video frames.

5.1   Experimental Settings

We employed an Allied Vision[3] Manta GigaE 145BNIR camera to acquire uncompressed video frames of a white wall scene. The camera is equipped with a CCD sensor whose resolution is 347×259 pixels and adopting a global shutter system. We set the frame rate at 30 frame per second, constant shutter time and manual focus. Each frame is transferred to and stored into a laptop by means of a Gigabit Ethernet connection, in a bitmap format.

Two uncompressed videos of at least 3 min are acquired by using sunlight and indoor LED light powered by the electrical network. The nominal electric network frequency is 50 Hz. While acquiring the video with artificial light, we also recorded a reference ENF directly from the electric plug, in order to check whether any recorded signal extracted in the video is actually the real ENF or not.

From these two raw videos, we generated compressed videos by making use of FFMPEG[4], a well-known tool for video processing and coding. In terms of type compression, we divided our experiments into three stages: first, we analyze the case constant GOP size; then, we carried out our analysis for variable GOP size and, finally, we analyze the case of variable bitrates. In all cases, we applied different GOP sizes and/or different bitrates.

The analysis is carried on in the Fourier domain, by analyzing the periodograms and the spectrograms of the signal obtained as Eq. (3). For the periodogram based analysis, we used 512 FFT points and Hamming window. For the spectrogram-based analysis, we used 8192 FFT points, Hamming window, 30 s of frame time and 29/30 of overlap between frames in order to have a time resolution of 1 s.

5.2   Reference ENF Acquisition

We used an Arduino UNO with an emonTxShield[5] to sample the voltage from the electric grid at a sampling rate of 1 kHz. The raw voltage values are directly measured from the emonTxShield. In order to extract the ENF, the voltage measurements can be analyzed in the frequency (periodogram) and time-frequency (spectrogram) domains by means of Short-time Fourier transform (STFT).

The resulting reference ENF signal is shown Fig. 3. From the periodogram figure (first subplot), we observe that most of the energy is concentrated around the fundamental frequency $f_0 = 50$ Hz, while other peaks are visible at its integer multiples (harmonics). By looking at the spectrogram (second subplot in Fig. 3), centered at the fundamental frequency, we observe that the signal energy (yellow) is deviating from the nominal value over time. Finally, the network frequency at a given time can be estimated from the spectrogram by detecting the energy peak along frequencies axis, for instance by using quadratic interpolation [12]. The punctual ENF is show in the third subplot of Fig. 3.

---

[3] https://www.alliedvision.com/en/digital-industrial-camera-solutions.html.

[4] https://ffmpeg.org/.

[5] https://wiki.openenergymonitor.org/index.php/EmonTx_Arduino_Shield.

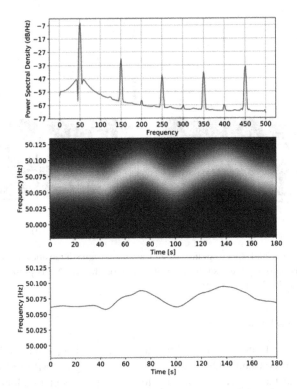

Fig. 3. Power spectral density, periodogram and punctual values of the reference ENF measured by an electric plug. (Color figure online)

5.3 ENF Extraction from Raw Frames

For each frame, the average pixels intensity is calculated as in Eq. (3), and the resulting 1-D signal is processed to extract ENF. As we have done for the reference ENF signal, we show the periodograms and the spectrograms of I(t) for the two uncompressed recordings that we have acquired with sunlight and artificial light illumination. The results are presented is Fig. 4. In the case of artificial light (a), we clearly see a prominent peak at 10 Hz in the periodogram because of the aliasing that raises with these experimental settings. Moreover, we can visually recognize the same ENF time-frequency behavior in the spectrogram between the refence ENF (Fig. 3) and the one extracted from the video (Fig. 4(a)). Conversely, for the signal extracted under sunlight condition (Fig. 4(b)), we do not observe any peak either in the periodogram (apart from the DC component) or in the spectrogram.

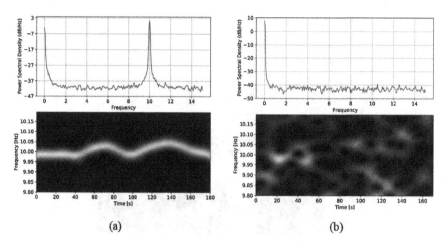

Fig. 4. Periodograms and spectrograms of the average frame intensities from uncompressed videos under LED indoor (a) and sunlight (b) illumination. In (a) ENF is present at the expected frequency, whereas in (b) it is not present.

5.4 Constant GOP Size

First, we compressed both raw recordings under artificial light and sunlight illumination with different constant GOP size L. We did it through FFMPEG by using H.264 coding, a chroma factor yuv420p and by forcing the encoder to adopt a fixed GOP size. We considered 8 GOP sizes L = {1, 7, 11, 15, 30, 60, 135, 222}. Then, we analyzed the signal I(t) for each video. For convenience, we split our analysis between $L < f_s$ and $L \geq f_s$.

In Fig. 5 we globally note that, despite different GOP sizes, the peak at the fundamental frequency 10 Hz is maintained for all GOP sizes, and that its SNR does not vary significantly. However, depending on L, we assist to the emergence of other small peaks at different positions in function of L, except for the case of L = 1. Such peaks can be explained by the aliasing effects due to the GOP structure. We confirm this

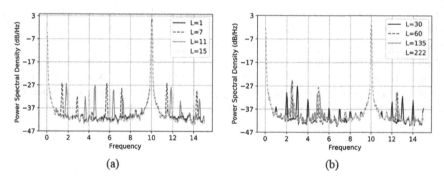

Fig. 5. Periodograms of I(t) extracted from videos encoded with constant GOP sizes, either if $L < f_s$ (a) or $L \geq f_s$ (b), with LED artificial light.

deduction in Fig. 6, wherein we plot the spectrograms of the signal for three different GOP sizes (11, 30, 135). To better visualize them, we cropped the complete spectrogram in correspondence of some expected alias frequencies. For instance, for L = 11 we should observe the aliased signal at $10-k\left(\frac{30}{11}\right) = 10-k \cdot 2.73$. This hypothesis is confirmed in Fig. 6(a), where we observe distinctive replicas of the same signal at

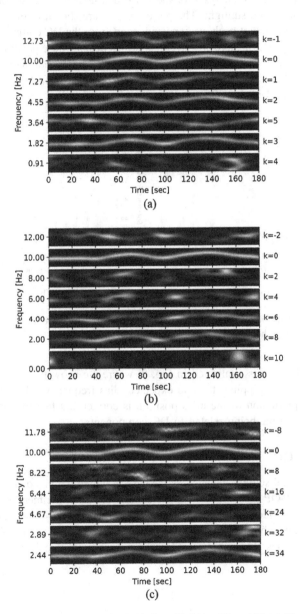

Fig. 6. Spectrograms for GOP size L = 11 (a), L = 30 (b) and L = 135 (c). For each subfigure, we cropped the fundamental component (k = 0) and the most significant aliased frequency.

4.55 Hz (k = 2) and 1.82 Hz (k = 4). Similar considerations can be drawn from the other spectrograms, where we observe temporally correlated energies at 2 Hz for L = 30 and 2.44 Hz for L = 135. It is also worth to note that the alias components do not have the same SNR. Moreover, some of them are in opposite phase with respect to the principal component (see the case k = 3 for L = 11).

We repeated the same analysis for the video that does not contain the ENF signal, since it is acquired with sunlight. The periodograms are shown in Fig. 7, and they do not present any prominent peak, as expected, apart from the DC component. However, we observe that for L > 1 there are several spurious peaks whose position changes with L. This phenomenon is still in agreement with our model, but with respect to the previous case, what is aliased now is the DC components. In fact, we can verify that every peak is spaced of d = 30/L starting from frequency 0.

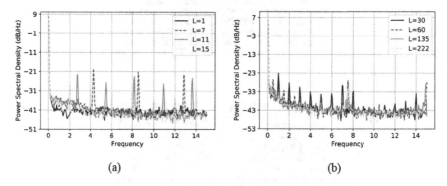

(a)

(b)

Fig. 7. Periodograms of average frame intensity signal extracted from videos encoded with constant GOP sizes, either if $L < f_s$ (a) or $L \geq f_s$ (b), with sunlight.

This consideration is confirmed in Fig. 8, where we show the spectrogram of the signal for L = 7 by cropping it at the expected alias frequency. Thus, we verify that effectively the prediction of the alias position is correct and that the signal is almost constant over the time being related to DC components.

5.5   Variable GOP Size

In this experimental setting, we address the case in which the video stream is encoded with a variable GOP size. To do that, we built up an experiment that consists of producing a set of videos at a fixed constant bitrate (CRF = 23 is the standard quality in FFMPEG7H.264) but forcing the encoder to adopt a GOP size variable but close to predetermined values. The parameters are summarized in Table 1.

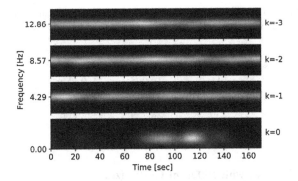

Fig. 8. Spectrogram obtained for L = 7 from the video acquired with sunlight.

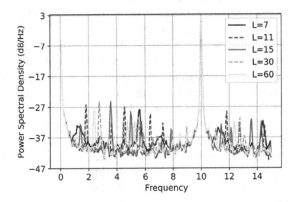

Fig. 9. Periodograms of I(t) extracted from videos encoded with variable GOP size.

We extracted the actual GOP structure from the video streams by means of the FFMPEG routine *ffprobe*. As in the previous set of experiments, we analyzed the effects of GOP structure by means of periodograms and spectrograms. In Fig. 9, we plotted the power density spectra of the intensity signals I(t), for each case study. In a similar way to the case of constant GOP size, several alias frequencies emerge in the periodogram. However, we registered the main differences in the spectrograms. In Fig. 10, we show the spectrograms for L close to 11, in subfigure (a), and for L close to 30, in subfigure (b), analogously to Fig. 6(a) and Fig. 6(b). By comparing Fig. 10(a) and Fig. 6(a), we observe that patterns are remarkably similar each other. At the same time, a similar conclusion cannot be drawn by observing Fig. 10(b) and Fig. 6(b). We can therefore conclude that the model has less predictive power in the case of variable GOP size, even though for some configurations it still applies satisfactorily.

Table 1. Parameters adopted in variable GOP size experiment. Nominal and real (average) GOP size are highlighted, as well as the bitrates of the resulting videos.

CRF	Nominal L	Average L	Bitrate
23	7	6.796	2383 kbps
23	11	10.995	2460 kbps
23	15	13.974	2408 kbps
23	30	28.759	2322 kbps
23	60	57.843	2246 kbps

5.6 Variable Bitrates with Different GOP Sizes

In this last test we analyze the case of different bit rates given a fixed GOP size. We forced the encoder to adopt two different GOP sizes, 7 and 30 and we varied the constant rate factor CRF = {0, 5, 11, 17, 23, 29, 35, 41, 47}. The periodograms of the signals extracted from each video are shown in Fig. 11. As we expected, aliased patterns appear also in this case, but we assist also to a lessening of the ENF SNR at 10 Hz when the bitrate decreases. The most interesting part of this analysis is provided in Fig. 12, where we show spectrograms cropped at the frequencies where the aliased peaks have the higher power spectral densities. For the sake of simplicity, we show them for CRF = 23 (standard compression in FFMPEG) and CRF = 47 (heavy compression). It can be noticed that for L = 7, the ENF signal energy is concentrated at 10 Hz and non-significant replicas are present, independently from the bitrate. Conversely, for L = 30, weak aliased signals are visible, especially at 11.04 Hz and the replicas become even more pronounced when the bitrate decrease (see bottom-right plot of Fig. 12). This behavior can be explained qualitatively as follows: at a given bitrate, we forced the encoder to have a certain number of I-frames, accordingly to the GOP size; because of the constraint on the total bitrate, the DCT coefficients quantization applied to the I-frames is strong for small GOP sizes (i.e. high number of I-frame for a given recording). This fact negatively affects the aliased frequencies making them not distinguishable, even at high bitrates. On the other hand, when the GOP size is larger, so that the number of I-frames encoded decreases, the DCT coefficients quantization becomes less severe. This means that I-frames have a higher PSNR compared to the case of small GOP size, so that the effects of GOP structure adhere more to the down-sampling model that we described in Subsect. 4.2.

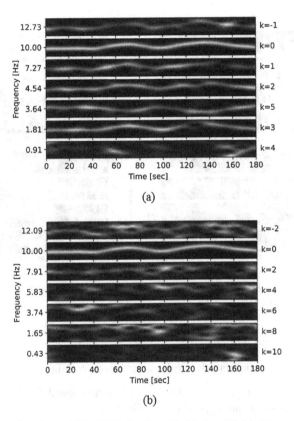

(a)

(b)

Fig. 10. Spectrograms for variable GOP size L = 11 (a), L = 30 (b). For each subfigure, we cropped the fundamental component (k = 0) and some aliased frequency for k ≠ 0.

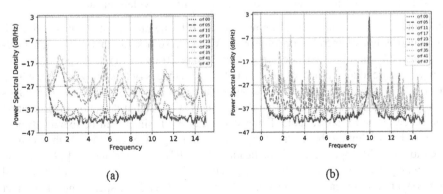

(a)   (b)

Fig. 11. Periodograms of I(t) extracted from videos encoded with L = 7 (a) and L = 30 (b) at different constant rate factors.

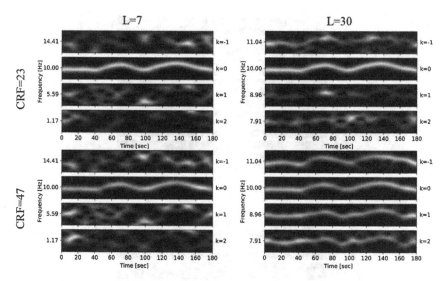

Fig. 12. Spectrograms of intensities signals for 4 combination of GOP sizes (7 and 30) and different CRF (23 and 47).

5.7 Discussions and Applications

The main findings of our analysis can be summarized as follows:

1. At a given bitrate and constant GOP size, the fundamental ENF is present and its position and SNR do not depend on the GOP size.
2. Alias ENF replicas appear in the spectrum in function of the GOP size with a lower SNR, matching out theoretical predictions within reasonable bounds.
3. The SNR of aliased ENFs decreases if the GOP size is variable and, generally, by increasing the GOP size.
4. The SNR of the fundamental ENF decrease with the video bit rate.

In a forensic setting, the analyst knows the video frame rate and its GOP structure, if the video is not re-encoded or tampered. We can also assume that the nominal frequency is known (only two cases are possible, 50 or 60 Hz). From these postulates, we can propose several approaches in order to take advantages of this analysis. As we have seen in our experiments, some GOP configurations make ENF emerge in other bands so that, by taking into consideration these effects, ENF signal detection or estimation can be easier and more reliable. For instance, the ENF signal can be extracted more reliably by combining those alias frequencies with a good SNR [18]. Or they can be used to target Multiple Signal Classification (MUSIC) based techniques [29], wherein the signal power spectrum is estimated by defining in advance the number of sinusoidal components (i.e. eigenspace signal decomposition). Therefore, specifying the correct number of sinusoidal components, that might be present within the signal because of compression effects, could lead to better spectral estimation. Finally, it can also help when the nominal ENF is a multiple integer of the frame rate and, therefore, ENF appears around the DC component.

6 Conclusions

In this paper, we modelled the effects of GOP structure on the ENF signal conveyed by the light and then captured by a video camera. We formalized the problem by making use of Nyquist-Shannon sampling theory and we showed how side information such as video frame rate, targeted ENF and GOP size allows to predict the spectrum of the signal containing ENF. As a new and determinant contribution for improving forensic procedure, our study demonstrated that the ENF signal is affected by the aliasing due to the GOP structure, with different degrees in function of the GOP size and if this last is constant or variable, as well as in function of the total bitrate. In future works, moving closer to videos processed in real investigations, we will take advantage of the outcomes presented in this work to design stronger ENF detection and extraction procedures, and apply this methodology to video time-stamping and geo-localization.

References

1. Ho, A.T.S., Li, S.: Handbook of Digital Forensics of Multimedia Data and Devices, 1st edn. Wiley – IEEE Press, Hoboken (2015)
2. Kajstura, M., Trawinska, A., Hebenstreit, J.: Application of the electrical network frequency (ENF) criterion: a case of a digital recording. Forensic Sci. Int. **155**(2), 165–171 (2005)
3. Garg, R., Varna, A.L., Hajj-Ahmad, A., Wu, M.: 'Seeing' ENF: power-signature-based timestamp for digital multimedia via optical sensing and signal processing. IEEE Trans. Inf. Forensics Secur. **8**(9), 1417–1432 (2013)
4. Vatansever, S., Dirik, A.E., Memon, N.: Factors affecting ENF Based time-of-recording estimation for video. In: IEEE International Conference on Acoustics, Speech, and Signal Processing, pp. 2497–2501. IEEE, Brighton (2019)
5. Grigoras, C.: Digital audio recording analysis: the electric network frequency (ENF) criterion. Int. J. Speech Lang. Law **12**(1), 63–76 (2005)
6. Grigoras, C.: Applications of ENF criterion in forensic audio, video, computer and telecommunication analysis. Forensic Sci. Int. **167**(2), 136–145 (2007)
7. Garg, R., Varna, A.L., Wu, M.: 'Seeing' ENF: natural time stamp for digital video via optical sensing and signal processing. In: Proceedings of the 19th ACM International Conference on Multimedia, pp. 23–32. Association for Computing Machinery, New York (2011)
8. Ojowu, O., Karlsson, J., Li, J., Liu, Y.: ENF extraction from digital recordings using adaptive techniques and frequency tracking. IEEE Trans. Inf. Forensics Secur. **7**(4), 1330–1338 (2012)
9. Hua, G., Goh, J., Thing, V.L.L.: A dynamic matching algorithm for audio timestamp identification using the ENF criterion. IEEE Trans. Inf. Forensics Secur. **9**(7), 1045–1055 (2014)
10. Hua, G., Bi, G., Thing, V.L.L.: On practical issues of ENF based audio forensics. IEEE Access **3536**, 20640–20651 (2017)
11. Elmesalawy, M.M., Eissa, M.M.: New forensic ENF reference database for media recording authentication based on harmony search technique using GIS and wide area frequency measurements. IEEE Trans. Inf. Forensics Secur. **9**(4), 633–644 (2014)
12. Cooper, A.: An automated approach to the electric network frequency (ENF) criterion: theory and practice. Int. J. Speech Lang. Law **16**(2), 193–218 (2009)

13. Hua, G.: Error analysis of forensic ENF matching. In: IEEE International Workshop on Information Forensics and Security, pp. 1–7. IEEE, Hong Jong (2018)
14. Zheng, L., Zhang, Y., Lee, C.E., Thing, V.L.L.: Time-of-recording estimation for audio recordings. Digit. Invest. **22**, S115–S126 (2017)
15. Hajj-Ahmad, A., Garg, R., Wu, M.: ENF-based region-of-recording identification for media signals. IEEE Trans. Inf. Forensics Secur. **10**(6), 1125–1136 (2015)
16. Cui, Y., Liu, Y., Fuhr, P., Morales-Rodriguez, M.: Exploiting spatial signatures of power ENF signal for measurement source authentication. In: IEEE International Symposium on Technologies for Homeland Security, pp. 1–6. IEEE, Woburn (2018)
17. Bykhovsky, D., Cohen, A.: Electrical network frequency (ENF) maximum-likelihood estimation via a multitone harmonic model. IEEE Trans. Inf. Forensics Secur. **8**(5), 744–753 (2013)
18. Hajj-Ahmad, A., Garg, R., Wu, M.: Spectrum combining for ENF signal estimation. IEEE Signal Process. Lett. **20**(9), 885–888 (2013)
19. Su, H, Hajj-Ahmad, A., Wong, C.-W., Garg, R., Wu, M.: ENF signal induced by power grid: a new modality for video synchronization. In Proceedings of the 2nd ACM International Workshop on Immersive Media Experiences. Association for Computing Machinery, New York, pp. 13–18 (2014)
20. Vatansever, S., Dirik, A.E., Memon, N.: Detecting the presence of ENF signal in digital videos: a superpixel-based approach. IEEE Signal Process. Lett. **24**(10), 1463–1467 (2017)
21. Vatansever, S., Dirik, A.E., Memon, N.: Analysis of rolling shutter effect on ENF-based video forensics. IEEE Trans. Inf. Forensics Secur. **14**(9), 2262–2275 (2019)
22. Su, H., Hajj-Ahmad, A., Garg, R., Wu, M.: Exploiting rolling shutter for ENF signal extraction from video. In 2014 IEEE International Conference on Image Processing, pp. 5367–5371. IEEE (2014)
23. Hajj-Ahmad, A., Berkovich, A., Wu, M.: Exploiting power signatures for camera forensics. IEEE Signal Process. Lett. **23**(5), 713–717 (2016)
24. Lin, X., Kang, X.: Supervised audio tampering detection using an autoregressive model. In IEEE International Conference on Acoustics, Speech and Signal Processing, pp. 2142–2146. IEEE, New Orleans (2017)
25. ISO: Information technology - coding of audio-visual objects-part 2: Visual. ISO/IEC IS 14496-2, International Organization for Standardization, Geneva (2009)
26. ISO: Information technology - coding of audio-visual objects - part 10: Advanced video coding (AVC). ISO/IEC IS 14496-10, International Organization for Standardization, Geneva (2010)
27. Bovik, A.C.: Handbook of Image and Video Processing, 2nd edn. Elsevier, Amsterdam (2005)
28. Marvasti, F.: Nonuniform Sampling, Theory and Practice. Springer, Kluwer Academic/Plenum Publishers, New York (2001)
29. Schmidt, R.: Multiple emitter location and signal parameter estimation. IEEE Trans. Antennas Propag. **34**(3), 276–280 (1986)

Android Dumpsys Analysis to Indicate Driver Distraction

Lukas Bortnik and Arturs Lavrenovs[(✉)]

NATO Cooperative Cyber Defence Centre of Excellence, Filtri Tee 12,
10132 Tallinn, Estonia
bortnik.lukas@gmail.com, arturs.lavrenovs@ccdcoe.org

Abstract. Police officers investigating car accidents have to consider the driver's interaction with a mobile device as a possible cause. The most common activities such as calling or texting can be identified directly via the user interface or from the traffic metadata acquired from the Internet Service Provider (ISP). However, 'offline activities', such as a simple home button touch to wake up the screen, are invisible to the ISP and leave no trace at the user interface. A possible way to detect this type of activity could be analysis of system level data. However, security countermeasures may limit the scope of the acquired artefacts.

This paper introduces a non-intrusive analysis method which will extend the range of known techniques to determine a possible cause of driver distraction. All Android *dumpsys* services are examined to identify the scope of evidence providers which can assist investigators in identifying the driver's intentional interaction with the smartphone. The study demonstrates that it is possible to identify a driver's activities without access to their personal content. The paper proposes a minimum set of requirements to construct a timeline of events which can clarify the accident circumstances. The analysis includes online activities such as interaction with social media, calling, texting, and offline activities such as user authentication, browsing the media, taking pictures, etc. The applicability of the method are demonstrated in a synthetic case study.

Keywords: Digital evidence · Mobile forensics · Car accident · Driver's distraction · Android *dumpsys*

1 Introduction

The scope of digital evidence is growing in parallel with minor improvements and newly added functionalities in mobile devices. In general, newly introduced operating system (OS) upgrades are targeted to improve the security and ergonomics of the mobile devices. While security upgrades challenge the investigator's ability to acquire detailed digital evidence, the opposite is the case when enhancing the usability of the system: an improved user environment requires integrating new hardware and software components, which results in new streams of evidence ready to be investigated by forensic practitioners.

In comparison to traditional host-based digital forensic techniques, mobile forensic solutions must consider a range of different mobile-device specific requirements.

© ICST Institute for Computer Sciences, Social Informatics and Telecommunications Engineering 2021
Published by Springer Nature Switzerland AG 2021. All Rights Reserved
S. Goel et al. (Eds.): ICDF2C 2020, LNICST 351, pp. 139–163, 2021.
https://doi.org/10.1007/978-3-030-68734-2_8

Firstly, mobile device data is highly volatile. Some evidence will simply not survive until the police arrive at the accident. Some can be intentionally or unintentionally and irreversibly destroyed by the user. Secondly, evidence acquisition is another challenge. Taking into consideration the usual methods of accident investigation, it is unclear how, if at all, the data from the mobile devices can be acquired. Depending on the brand, model, operating system, version and patch level, the scope to successfully acquire data varies significantly. The data available through the user interface (UI) might reveal the most common activities such as telephony or texting, but offline activities such as waking the screen would remain undetected. Even though data from lower architecture layers may deliver further clarity, current mobile phone forensic analysis solutions are simply not designed to reflect specific accident-related cases. For instance, login activities or an attempt to reply to an incoming message can easily lead to driver distraction, but whether this type of activity can be detected by current state-of-the-art solutions is questionable.

Android Operating System (AOS) devices are equipped with an interactive interface to observe user and system activities. Users and developers can inspect application and system behaviour through built-in functionalities such as a circular buffer log (*logcat*), the *dumpsys* tool or *bugreports*. These functionalities allow access to the portion of the data which is normally not visible from the standard UI. Although the ability to 'abuse' mobile phone diagnostic data for forensic purposes has been known for almost a decade, analysis of Android *dumpsys* diagnostic data seems to have been overlooked. In comparison to traditional smartphone digital forensic techniques, which are primarily focused on content analysis, the analysis of diagnostic data has received only limited research attention [1, 2]. A significant gap has been identified in terms of acquisition, analysis and the interpretation of the artefacts of android *dumpsys* analytical data.

Hence, the primary motivation for this study is to inspect the current state of Android *dumpsys* diagnostic data, identify artefacts which reflect specific driver activities, inspect their relevance and volatility, and demonstrate the applicability of the proposed method in a real-life investigation.

Besides the ability to avoid analysis of the user's personal data, the study explains how to extend the scope of prospective evidence providers and how to identify drivers' activities without the need to collect the data from ISPs. The study also demonstrates the possibility of determining those driver activities which are outside the analysis capabilities of currently available digital forensic solutions. The outcome of the study extends the perception of prospective digital forensic evidence, clarifying the circumstances leading to car accidents; and allow investigators to conduct more time- and cost-effective investigation.

The remainder of this paper is structured as follows: Sect. 2 reviews related work. Section 3 overviews the methodology and limitations of current work. Section 4 focuses on core Android *dumpsys* services, which are the most relevant to determine driver activities. Section 5 demonstrates the effectiveness of the proposed approach in a synthetic case study. The conclusions and future work are discussed in Sects. 6 and 7.

2 Related Work

The detection of driver distraction has received substantial attention in academia over the last decade. A significant portion of research has focused on how to detect driver distraction based on sensorial data, collected either from a smartphone or vehicle systems. The majority of the solutions propose to collect the data via custom applications or additional hardware installed in the vehicle. Mantouka et al. [3] attempted to identify driving styles (including distracted driving) based on data from gyroscope, accelerometer and GPS records. In addition to the previous, Papadimitriou et al. [4] added data from a magnetometer. The data collected is temporarily stored within the device itself and eventually uploaded to the cloud-based back-end and analysed. Concerning privacy, Mansor et al. [5] proposed a mechanism for secure vehicular data storage and cloud synchronization using a custom protocol, which complies with forensically sound evidence collection requirements.

Another perspective leverages a vehicle's built-in system. Khandakar et al. [6] demonstrated a portable solution to collect vehicular data from a 3-DOF accelerometer and ECU over the OBD-II port. This data is then sent to a mobile device for further analyses and to conduct autonomous decisions such as reducing speed. Khan et. al [7] presented the effect of smartphone activities on driving performance recorded in a vehicular lifelog, which could help to detect distracted driving.

A substantial amount of research has been dedicated to solutions that can differentiate between use of a phone by a driver or a passenger. Park et al. [8] studied typical driver activities, e.g. opening vehicle doors; Torres et al. [9] focused on reading text messages; Yang et al. [10] proposed advantages that could be gained from using a vehicle's speakers; Hald et al. [11], Liu et al. [12] and Manini and Sabatini [13] made strides in terms of differentiating between driver and passenger activities based on sensorial data from wearables. Lu et al. [14] analysed sensorial data to detect current driving activity and vehicle type (car, motorbike, bicycle or travelling on foot). These, and other detection techniques, were implemented in mobile applications which should discourage drivers from dangerous interactions with mobile phones [15].

Mobile phone diagnostic data has been used relatively little in research into driver distraction. Horsman and Conniss [1] analysed two major mobile operating systems, showing the most promising sources of digital evidence that could help investigators to indicate driver distraction. The study focused on artefacts that can reveal human interaction with a mobile device acquired from two primary internal evidence providers: Android's circular buffer log and iPhone's *CurrentPowerlog.powerlogsystem* file. The study provides several options how to identify the most probable activities such as interacting with social media, texting and calling, either directly from the mobile device or using hands-free equipment. Researchers described possible challenges to acquiring and analysing the *logcat* dump. Apart from the now obsolete operating system versions (AOS 4.3 (JellyBean) and 4.4 (KitKat)), the main drawback of the proposed solution was the extremely high volatility of the evidence. If the first responders did not react within a few minutes of the accident, the content of the buffer log might be overwritten and the evidence permanently lost. Similarly, the vast majority of the circular buffer log content would become unavailable after the device was rebooted. In addition, authors did not consider the *dumpsys* diagnostic data, which may indicate human interaction the best.

The *dumpsys* output data is not completely unknown to researchers either. However, recent research has been oriented mostly towards malware detection and malware classification techniques. Ferrante et al. [16] proposed a malware detection method, which, among other aspects, processes CPU and memory usage data acquired via *dumpsys* to identify which sub-parts of the executed application are malicious. Memory consumption data, application permissions, battery usage and network statistics collected via *dumpsys* were proposed by Lashkari et al. [17] as an additional type of feature to develop more comprehensive Android malware detection framework. Trivedi et al. [18] found that *dumpsys package* data helps with the correct application of a UID to application name resolution in a technique that identifies applications accessing malicious URLs.

Despite the fact that *dumpsys* offers powerful analytical options, it has not been utilised as a feature by many known malware datasets [19]. *Dumpsys* diagnostic data has also been found to be useful in other areas. Shoaib et al. [20] used *dumpsys* data to analyse how the recognition of human activity impacts resource consumption in smart devices. Dumpsys CPU statistics were included into the examination datasets to identify UI performance regressions in Android applications [21] and to identify the impact of logger-augmented mobile banking application on power consumption [22]. However, these implementations have only limited forensic value in terms of indicating driver distraction.

3   Analysis Background and Methodology

3.1   Introduction to Android *Dumpsys*

The primary purpose of the *dumpsys* tool is to allow developers to inspect diagnostic data generated by system services[1] such as process statistics, CPU consumption, network usage and battery behaviour. As with any other operating system, much of the analytical data generated by system services, installed applications or telemetry functions is not designed for digital forensic purposes. The same applies for Android devices and their system services. The primary drawback is that only a limited number of subject-relevant system events are time-stamped. Moreover, system services do not necessarily generate diagnostic events with a unified timestamp format. The time value might be expressed in epoch time, it may follow system time, or it may be expressed as a differential value, e.g. the number of seconds since the application was pushed to the *back-stack* until the *dumpsys* tool was executed. The time resolution of each set of events may also vary from milliseconds to minutes. Even if some diagnostic data does survive a system reboot, particular content was shown to be eventually overwritten, either due to user interaction or just after regular system runtime. The lifetime of the

---

[1] Authors in [23] use the term 'service' as a *dumpsys* option to specify the output from particular *dumpsys* plugins.

events kept by particular system services may also vary from seconds to months, regardless of whether or not the device is rebooted.

One of the main advantages of *dumpsys* data acquisition is that the command can operate under user level privileges. Meaning, the acquisition process does not require elevation to the root-level access, but rather the standard ADB shell. If the minimal set of requirements[2] is met, full diagnostic output can be acquired by the ADB *shell dumpsys* command without setting any additional arguments. Diagnostic information will be extracted from all supported services. The scope of the supported system services and the format of diagnostic data differ based on the installed platform. For instance, the primary tested model *Samsung Galaxy S9, SM-G960F/DSA* running on Android 8.0 supports 225 different services, while *Samsung Galaxy S3 (AOS 7.0)* supports 189 services and *Samsung Galaxy S5 (AOS 5.0)* altogether 196 services. Dumping all services may, however, produce quite verbose output in which not all events are valuable for forensic purposes.

3.2 Evidence Identification

The diagnostic data from a single service may contain either data from a related service or the aggregated data from multiple services. Since the output is highly verbose, the initial objective is to limit the scope of targeted services and exclude irrelevant diagnostic content. As the *dumpsys* services do not generate diagnostic data in a unified structure, the examination requires separate per-service data acquisition. Each *dumpsys* service is triggered and the output is manually examined. Since the intention is to construct a timeline dataset, the first filtering criterion requires the presence of time information. Should the service generate information (an event) without a timestamp, the service (the artefact) is excluded from further observation (see Fig. 1).

The next criterion inspects subject-relevant content which would reflect the driver's intentional interaction. The diagnostic data is categorised based on relevance to the investigation subject. As case-relevant data is essentially an event which reflects direct or indirect driver interaction; for instance, waking up the screen, unlocking the device, charging, changing settings, opening an application and switching between applications. Irrelevant content can be considered the portion of the diagnostic data which is not generated as a response to the driver's intentional interaction or that does not correspond to driver activity; for instance, an event which reports the volume of currently consumed memory or CPU is irrelevant.

Lastly, events which are not certainly irrelevant nor definitely attributed to the driver's intentional activity are examined and correlated in the context of all other events; for example, a diagnostic output from *WiFiController* could be irrelevant, but it tracks and logs activities such as screen on/off or user login, and so might be relevant.

The next stage requires empirical examination to identify under what conditions each individual event is or is not generated. To exclude a portion of uncertainty, the observation also considers whether the event can be generated without any user interaction. The scope of the tests is customised for each artefact being explored. For

---

[2] Steps to enable the ADB shell varies depending on the installed AOS [41].

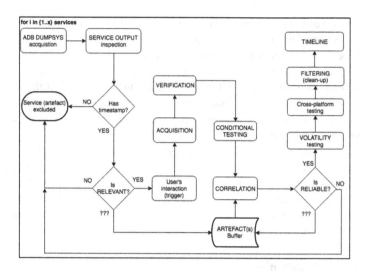

Fig. 1. Analyses process

instance, telephony activities are examined separately for a phone call which is conducted through the built-in earpiece, through the Bluetooth-connected car speaker or through a wired external handset. The behaviour is then observed for situations when the phone call is accepted, rejected or ignored. The full set of the conducted tests is outside the scope of this paper.

The output of this stage results in a set of triggers which can be responsible for generating each individual event. Following the principle of evidence reliability, each event is repeatedly invoked by the set of discovered triggers. Should the event be generated after a defined set of triggers is executed, the event is considered to be reliable. Any deviation from the expected output marks the event as unreliable and the event is excluded from the final timeline dataset.

Another examination criterion is the volatility of the event. The primary volatility test shows whether the event survives system reboot. If it does, the next stage is to determine the condition under which the event persists. The events might be erased after a particular buffer has been reached or if the user triggers a certain activity (e.g. the application is closed). The buffer might be defined by the maximum size of the log, by the number of events being stored within one log, or by the expiration time.

A preliminary examination returned a list of services in which the diagnostic data can be sufficient to indicate the driver's interaction with the mobile device. The list consists of 8 out of 225 supported services: *activity, bluetooth_manager, mount, statusbar, telecom, customfrequencymanagerservice, wifi,* and *usagestat*. A brief summary from the examination of each individual service is described in Sect. 4.

3.3   Post-acquisition Stage

The post-acquisition stage filters unnecessary content and unifies the event structure to build the timeline. First, the timestamp format across all accepted events is converted to the unified format. However, if multiple same-source events are generated within the same minute (which often is the case), all of them will have the same times-tamp. Consequently, the analyst may unintentionally break the relationship between individual events which might result in misinterpretation of the user's activities. To maintain the integrity of the timeline, the order of the generated events has to be preserved. For the purpose of this analysis, events which are not timestamped with at least one-second resolution were tagged by an *ORDER* number which maintains the order of events in which they initially were generated.

All extracted events are delimited into three fields: *DATE*; *TIME* and *MESSAGE* body. To enhance the usability and simplify further filtering, each individual event is enriched with additional fields: *SOURCE, CLASS, EVENT_TYPE* and *DESCRIPTION*. The *SOURCE* tag equates to the origin; that is to say, the name of the service which generates the event, e.g. *wifi* or *telecom*. The *CLASS* defines the specific application's class. For instance, the *wifi* service generates diagnostic output from but not limited to the following classes: *WifiStateMachine, AutoWifiController, WifiController* and *WifiConnectivityMonitor*. *EVENT_TYPE* and *DESCRIPTION* tags were constructed based on observation, researched theory and the contextual meaning. *EVENT_TYPE* refers to the group of same type events, regardless of which service or class generates a particular event. A good example is a login activity event type which refers to the user's login and logout events. The login activity event type aggregates the events from *wifi, mount* and *statusbar* services (see Table 1).

Table 1. Event types produced from individual *dumpsys* services

EVENT_TYPE	SOURCE (dumpsys service)
App activity	usagestats, CustomFreqencyManagerService
BT activity	bluetooth_manager, CustomFreqencyManagerService
Call activity	telecom, statusbar, CustomFreqencyManagerService
Charging activity	CustomFreqencyManagerService
Login activity	wifi, mount, statusbar
Screen activity	wifi, CustomFreqencyManagerService
Task activity	activity
Wifi activity	CustomFreqencyManagerService

The 'DESCRIPTION' field clarifies the meaning of the message body and the activity type with greater granularity. For instance, the screen activity distinguishes *screen on* and *screen off* events, and the call activity recognises *call started/ended*. Events for which their meaning is unclear were tagged as unknown (-) (see Table 2).

Table 2. Event type descriptions

Event type	Description
App activity	App launched; app moved to background; app moved to foreground; lastTime executed; (-)
BT activity	BT AUDIO connected; BT device connected; BT device disconnected; BT entered AUDIO; BT entered NORMAL; BT paired device; call answered; audio route; (-)
Call activity	Call ended; call started; (-)
Charging activity	Charging OFF, charging ON
Login activity	UI locked; UI unlocked; login detected; pwtype requested; pwtype confirmed; unlock requested; unlock confirmed;
Screen activity	Screen OFF; screen ON
Task activity	App exited
Wifi activity	WiFi OFF; WiFi ON

Consequently, each case-relevant event extracted from *dumpsys* diagnostic output appears in the timeline in a unified structure (see Fig. 2).

```
DATE:           04/27/19;
TIME:           13:17:11.253
ORDER:          (-);
SOURCE:         wifi;
CLASS:          WiFiConnectivityMonitor;
EVENT_TYPE:     screen activity;
DESCRIPTION:    screen OFF;
MESSAGE:        processed=DefaultState org=NotConnectedState
                dest=<null> what=135177(0x21009) (75938.065)
                EVENT_SCREEN_OFF 0 0
```

Fig. 2. An example of event with unified structure

3.4 Limitations

The primary limitation is the rapid development of the Android operating system and the application packages, which might invalidate certain results over the period of analysis. Significant changes have already been introduced in AOS 9 and 10. A considerable limitation is the scope of explored devices and installed operating systems. The research results might be limited to device-specific hardware and installed versions of the OS. Lastly, neither official resources [23, 24] nor Android project source code [25] revealed sufficient documentation to support the research results. The research outcomes are therefore highly depended on empirical examination supported by limited documentation.

4   Core Dumpsys Services to Indicate Driver Distraction

4.1   Application Activities

Activity manager is the Android built-in class available from API level 1 which interacts and provides the diagnostic data about running processes, services and their activities. The *Activity* command supports extended operation switches to limit the observation to a specific package, service or broadcast delivery.

For the purpose of this research, the analysis of the *Activity manager* output was limited to the *Recent Tasks* section. The data in the *Recent Tasks* dump provides granular information about tasks that the user has most recently started or visited [26]. Authors in [27] define a task as *'a collection of activities that users interact with when performing a certain job'*. All activities are arranged into a stack. If the user opens a new activity within the application, older activities are sent to the *back-stack*. Once the user exits the activity, the activity from the top of the *back-stack* will be retained with the configuration it contained before being sent to the *back-stack*. Task configuration holds details such as finger touch position, scroll position or even bar colours. Each record in the stack holds the time when the task had been last active (*lastActiveTime*).[3]

Tasks are accompanied by *Intent* [28, 29]. By default, *Intent's* structure consists of primary attributes as *Action* and *Data*. *Action* and *Data* are paired to define a specific action, e.g. *'ACTION_VIEW content://contacts/people/1'*. The secondary attributes such as *category*, *component* and *type* define expected action more specifically. For instance, the *category.Launcher (cat)* orders the application to start on top of all currently running applications. *Component (cmp)* defines an explicit name of the component to be executed, e.g. to start user login interface in *Revolut app* would be defined as *com.revolut.revolut/com.revolut.ui.login.pin.LoginActivity*. Further explanation of these attributes is beyond the scope of this paper.

Once the task is resumed, the combination of individual definitions (*act, cat, cmp*) and others orders the system to resume the exact configuration as the application had before it was pushed to the background. Meaning, retained tasks give the investigator the ability to recover identical situations which the user had faced in the past.

The activities within the *Recent Task* dump are listed from the most recent at the top of the list. The number of tasks running in the background relies on hardware configuration. If the user runs many background tasks at the same time, the system might start destroying them in order to recover memory. Even though the *Recent tasks* memory is reboot-resilient, the evidence can be irreversibly destroyed if the user (or the investigator) closes all running applications. The *back-stack* will be freed without the ability to recover any past activities. While examining the test device, it was possible to recover 32 tasks from last 22 h of user activities.

---

[3] The *Recent task* dump also allows to attribute past activities to a specific user (*EffectiveUiD*).

4.2   Application Usage Statistics

Application use statistics can be acquired from *dumpsys UsageStats* service, available for developers from API level 21. The statistics are collected for a package for a specific time range [30]. Data is stored separately for packages which are in the foreground or background of UI, or for packages which are idle for a specific time interval. The output can be divided into the following three categories:

1. *In-memory* statistics;
2. *Event type collector* statistics; and
3. *Package idle* statistics.

The *In-memory* statistics (stats) are aggregated into certain periods – day, week, month and year. However, regardless of the length of the aggregation period, the aggregated output of *in-memory* stats does not have to contain statistics through the whole aggregation interval. In fact, the data is collected within a system-defined time range (*timeRange*). For instance, *In-memory daily* stats may be limited to application use statistics over the last several hours, *'weekly stats'* to last several days, etc. While the start time of *timeRange* is system-defined, the end time equals the time of *dumpsys* acquisition.

Each aggregation period contains usage statistics for each individual package which was executed on the system over the defined *timeRange*. The *totalTime* is measured over the same period of time. The investigator may conclude that during the time interval (*timeRange*), the user had been using a particular application (*package*) for a specific amount of time (*totalTime*). The *lastTime* refers to the time of the last user interaction (see Fig. 3).

```
user=0
    In-memory daily stats
            timeRange="4/26/2019, 20:36 – 4/27/2019, 14:07"
            packages
            package=com.whatsapp totalTime="00:30" lastTime="4/26/2019, 20:59"
            package=com.waze totalTime="04:59" lastTime="4/27/2019, 13:23"
    <<output omitted>>
```

Fig. 3. Usagestats – An example of *In-memory daily stats* output

Furthermore, each time the application is called, the *Event type collector* denotes that the activity moved to the foreground or to the background and the time, application name and associated activity type are recorded. If the user pushes the application to the background, *UsageEvents.Event* object will generate a *MOVE_TO_BACKGROUND* event. If the user calls the application to the foreground, the *UsageEvents.Event* object will generate *MOVE_TO_FOREGROUND* event.[4] If the application consists of multiple activities, a separate event will be generated for each individual activity [31] (see Fig. 4).

```
<<output omitted>>
  time="4/27/2019, 22:58"    type=MOVE_TO_BACKGROUND package=com.google.android.gm
                             class=com.google.android.gm.ui.MailActivityGmail
  time="4/27/2019, 22:59"    type=MOVE_TO_FOREGROUND  package=com.google.android.gm
                             class=com.google.android.gm.ComposeActivityGmail
<<output omitted>>
```

Fig. 4. Usagestats – An example of *Event type collector* statistics

UsageEvents.Event object also reports the *class* which refers to a specific activity within the application. For instance, if a driver attempts to compose a new email, a new set of events with updated class definition will be generated (+*ComposeActivityGmail*) (see Fig. 4).

Although *In-memory* statistics and *Event type collector* events are logged only with a 1-min resolution[5], the investigator may still define the last execution time more precisely. An additional indication about the driver's interaction with the mobile device can be derived from *Package idle stats* which count the time since the application was last used. In comparison to the previous *Usagestats* categories, *Package idle stats* do not keep the history of the application usage, but only the most recent record per application. If the application or its internal activity is either executed or pushed to the background or to the foreground of the UI, the *lastUsedElapsed* counter will be restarted. While the *lastUsedElapsed* counter counts the time since the application was last used, the *lastUsedScreenOn* counter counts the time during which the screen is on (see Fig. 5).

```
<<output omitted>>
  package=com.facebook.orca lastUsedElapsed=+1h10m45s946ms lastUsedScreenOn=+7m0s774ms idle=n
  package=com.whatsapp lastUsedElapsed=+4m2s943ms lastUsedScreenOn=+1m0s491ms idle=n
<<output omitted>>
```

Fig. 5. Usagestats – An example of *Package idle* statistics

---

[4] As of API level Q (29), the 'MOVE_TO_' event types were deprecated and replaced by constants ACTIVITY_PAUSED and ACTIVITY_RESUMED [31].

[5] As of API level 28, events are generated with 1 s resolution.

4.3   WiFi Analytics and Screen Activities

ADB *dumpsys* offers several options to inspect WiFi behaviour, connectivity, configuration and statistics. The tested device supported five *dumpsys* services: *wifi*, *wifip2p*, *wifi_policy*, *wificond* and *wifiscanner*. Due to extensive output, further explanation will be limited to *wifi* service, which may best clarify the driver's activities.

Firstly, one may wonder why there is a need to inspect WiFi behaviour if the driver is most likely not connected to any WiFi network while driving the car. It is because selected classes keep tracking system activities and therefore the driver's behaviour.[6] For instance, any time a driver switches the screen on or off, the screen state change is reported. Screen state changes can be observed through multiple classes, primarily: *WifiController*, *WifiStateMachine*, *WifiConnectivityMonitor* and *AutoWifiController*. The change of screen state can be recognised in the body of the message instantly (as *'screen on'* or *'EVENT_SCREEN_ON'*) or it may require further decoding, as is the case for the *WifiController* class.

Individual classes report system changes the *WiFiManager*, which acts as a primary API for managing all aspects of WiFi connectivity [32]. Reported events contain so-called *msg.what codes* which serve primary API to identify the type of received message. Messages are constructed as a sum of the *Message.what* BASE message address and the class's specific state address. *Message.what* BASE message address is declared as a public static final integer [33], e.g. *WifiController's* BASE message address is 0x00026000 (155648). The class's specific state addresses are defined in each individual class's source code. For instance, *WifiController* declares the *screen on* state as BASE+2 and *screen off* as BASE+3 [34] thus reporting the change of the screen state as *msg.what=155650* for *screen on* and 155651 for *screen off* (see Fig. 6). The same principle is applied for all supported classes which use *'msg.what'* codes.

```
<<output omitted>>
  rec[2]: time=04-27 13:23:11.811 processed=DefaultState org=DeviceActiveState dest=<null>
          what=155651(0x26003)
  rec[3]: time=04-27 13:23:15.650 processed=DefaultState org=DeviceActiveState dest=<null>
          what=155650(0x26002)
<<output omitted>>
```

Fig. 6. Wifi - *WifiController* screen activity

The primary drawback, however, is that the vast majority of *dumpsys wifi* service diagnostic content does not survive system reboot. The lifespan of each individual class also varies. While testing, the *WifiController* and *WifiStateMachine* classes held diagnostic data from the last 2 h, *AutoWifiController* for approximately 10 h, and *WifiConnectivityMonitor* and *WifiConnectivityManager* for up to 36 h.

---

[6] The statement does not apply if the device is set to airplane mode.

4.4 Login Activities

The user's login activities can be perceived as the artefact which would indicate the driver's activity the best, but retrieving it is a considerable challenge. Android *dumpsys* output holds only fragmented and, in most cases, indirect evidence of user login activities, if anything. While logout activity can be indirectly attributed to *screen off* events, this is not necessarily true of login activity. Given that the screen may be woken up without any user interaction, *screen on* events by themselves are insufficient to indicate that the driver logged in. Nevertheless, the investigation revealed several options for how to detect login activities indirectly.

A driver's login activity can be determined from *WiFiManager* statistics, the *WifiController* class specifically. Applying the decoding approach described in the previous section, the investigator may identify login activities tagged as *what=155660 (0x2600c)* messages. The value is constructed as a sum of *WifiController's* base message address '*0x00026000 (155648)*' and *USER_PRESENT* state address *(12)*. Regardless of whether the WiFi module is enabled or not, and regardless of what authentication method is used, *WifiController* reliably reported all user logins (see Fig. 7).

```
<<output omitted>>
  rec[173]: time=05-04 20:42:27.884 processed=DefaultState org=StaDisabledWithScanState
            dest=<null> what=155660(0x2600c)
  rec[176]: time=05-04 20:43:46.186 processed=DefaultState org=StaDisabledWithScanState
            dest=<null> what=155651(0x26003
<<output omitted>>
```

Fig. 7. Wifi - User's login activity

Another indirect source of the prospective login artefacts is the Android disk encryption subroutine. Each time the user changes or provides credentials to unlock the UI, the *cryptfs connector* is initiated which is accordingly reflected in system events. *Cryptfs connector* activities (if FDE is present) can be obtained from *dumpsys mount* service. The main benefit is that behaviour is reliable and the log may trace login events over several hours. The tested device held logins from the last 7 h. However, if the user uses fingerprint or face recognition, the log is not generated. Lastly, *cryptfs* events are not reboot resilient.

A partial solution to this problem can be retrieved from *statusbar manager* service logs. Android processes can call a routine in another process using a binder to identify the method to invoke and pass the arguments between processes [35, 37]. The same mechanism is used to maintain binder tokens which are shared between *Notification* and *StatusBar* managers. Depending on the installed version of the OS, Android processes may communicate with others via native binder object – the *IBinder* – or via proxy – *the BinderProxy.java* [38].

Token activities can be acquired by the *adb shell dumpsys statusbar* command. Among other triggers, each time the user logs into the device, *statusbar manager* generates the *what=CLEAR* event. If the user or the system itself locks the user interface out, a secondary event *what=HOME RECENT* is generated. The events are ordered by time, with the most recent at the bottom of the list. The list holds up to 100 events. The primary drawback of this artefact is that the associated timestamps do not hold the date, just the time with millisecond resolution. The second downside is that the artefact is not reboot resilient. Regardless of what security measure is applied (PIN, pattern, fingerprint or face recognition), the events are reliably recorded.

4.5   Telephony Activities

Android *dumpsys telecom* service generates a list of recently conducted phone calls. Each call log contains call direction, the *startTime* and the *endTime* of the phone call. For each direction, the *callTerminationReason* is defined by *DisconnectCause* attributes, the *Code* and the *Reason*. These attributes show whether the phone call was missed, rejected, or ended by a caller or by the counterpart. Depending on used technology, *telecom* shows individual audio states. 'Each state is a combination of one of the four audio routes (earpiece, wired headset, Bluetooth, and speakerphone) and audio focus status (active or quiescent)' [39]. Whenever the driver conducts a phone call via the external handsfree kit and switches back to the earpiece or phone speaker, *the telecom audio_route* is switched and logged (see Fig. 8).

```
<<output omitted>>
  20:27:12.723 - SET_RINGING (successful incoming call) :(...
  20:27:12.924 - START_RINGER:( ...
  20:27:12.926 - SKIP_VIBRATION (hasVibrator=true, ...
  20:27:13.003 - AUDIO_ROUTE (Leaving state QuiescentBluetoothRoute) :(...
  20:27:13.003 - AUDIO_ROUTE (Entering state RingingBluetoothRoute) :(...
  20:27:16.623 - UNMUTE: BPSI.aC->CARSM.pM_MUTE_OFF@m8I
  20:27:16.649 - STOP_RINGER: BPSI.aC@m8I
  20:27:16.674 - REQUEST_ACCEPT: BPSI.aC@m8I
  20:27:16.958 - AUDIO_ROUTE (Leaving state RingingBluetoothRoute): ...
  20:27:16.959 - AUDIO_ROUTE (Entering state ActiveBluetoothRoute): ...
  20:27:16.993 - SET_ACTIVE (active set explicitly):CSW.sA@m8Q
  20:27:17.048 - CAPABILITY_CHANGE ...
  20:27:32.378 - SET_DISCONNECTED (disconnected set explicitly> DisconnectCause
  20:27:32.509 - DESTROYED:CSW.rC@m+E
<<output omitted>>
```

Fig. 8. Telecom - Switching audio routes

Yet another benefit is that *telecom* service preserves the phone log entries even if the user deletes the log from her user interface. The downside it that *telecom* log is not reboot resilient.

4.6   Bluetooth

Bluetooth manager has been available in Android source code since API 18. The most valuable artefacts reside in the base64-encoded *BTSnoop* file format log summary. *BTSnoop* log resembles the snoop format of *Host Controller Interface* (HCI) packets[7] [40]. Depending on the installed platform, *BTSnoop* log summary may contain an extended clear text log. If a driver conducts a phone call via a Bluetooth paired device, either incoming or outgoing, a unique event *HFSM-enter AUDIO* is generated. The event itself does not signal an answered call, but rather entering the ringing state. With incoming calls, if the call is answered, the service will generate *'HSFM-processAnswerCall'* event. If the call is outgoing, the BT manager generates the *HFSM-processDialCall* record. When the call is finished, the mobile device quits the *AUDIO* states which is signalled by *HFSM-enter Connected message* (see Fig. 9).

```
<<output omitted>>
   05-04 20:27:12.808--HFSM-setAudioParams(prev) - 0,1
   05-04 20:27:12.811--btif_hf.cc -- connect_audio([0] e0:ae:5e:f6:7c:XX)
   05-04 20:27:13.003--HFSM-msg 6, but mVoiceRecognitionDevice is null
   05-04 20:27:13.468--HFSM-setAudioParams - 0,1
   05-04 20:27:13.471--HFAM-clear pathChangeTone (false, false)
   05-04 20:27:13.507--HFSM-enter AUDIO (1/1) : F6:7
   05-04 20:27:16.575--HFSM-processAnswerCall : F6:7
   05-04 20:27:32.495--btm_sco.cc -- Send SCO Disc Req to 6
   05-04 20:27:32.522--btm_sco.cc -- Recv SCO Disc Comp 22 on 5 from 6
   05-04 20:27:32.530--HFSM-enter Connected (1/1)
<<output omitted>>
```

Fig. 9. Bluetooth manager - received phone call

If the call is conducted over cross-platform VoIP applications such as WhatsApp, the service records the events accordingly. The log integrity is not affected by system reboot, and log lifetime exceeds several months; the tested device held the log from the last 5 months.

4.7   SSRM Service (CustomFrequencyManagerService)

Android *dumpsys CustomFrequencyManagerService* (*SSRM service*) is the last of the documented services which may clarify the circumstances of the accident.[8] SSRM service has been identified only on Samsung devices. Despite this, if the investigated model is a Samsung, the investigator should include the output from the SSRM service in the range of observed artefacts.

---

[7] https://tools.ietf.org/html/rfc1761.

[8] As of API level 28, the data previously available under *CustomFrequencyManagerService* service are available under *sdhms* service. *CustomFrequencyManagerService* remains present but without any forensic value.

The content of the SSRM service can be acquired by *adb shell dumpsys CustomFrequencyManagerService*. The output can be divided into two main sections:

1. Application (process) statistics and *Recent Battery Level Changes*; and
2. SSRM memory dump.

Both sections hold battery statistics data, mainly about total operational time, the period of the time over which the device was charged, and the amount of data transferred while connected to WiFi or GSM networks. Device battery statistics are recorded separately for applications in the foreground and background when the state of the screen is on and off, while the phone is connected to a paired Bluetooth device, and while using different power modes.

Apart from the per-app statistics, the *Recent Battery Level Changes* section keeps an overall battery statistic which is summarised for both states separately when the screen is on and off. Each time the state of the screen changes, the *Start Time* and the *End Time* of a new state is recorded, and *Duration* of the state is calculated. Whenever the device's battery is charged, the *OnBatteryTime* value equals 0 ms. The primary drawback resides in the reliability of the artefact. In testing, the *Recent Battery Level Changes* did not contain *screen on/off* events each time as they were triggered. However, should the event be already present in the log, it can be considered as reliable information.

The content of the *SSRM memory dump* is dumped as a base64-encoded data stream delimited by *SSRM MEMORY DUMP** header and trailer. Decoded data stream resolves in a gzip-compressed data structure. The decompressed event log consists of fixed header and the SSRM service log body. Each event is tagged by a timestamp, followed by an event type tag and the log message. The decompressed SSRM service log body holds a fixed number of 8,002 events. Since the detailed description of the SSRM service log is beyond the scope of this paper, further explanation will be limited to a brief description of two of the twelve recognised event types, [SET] and [PKG]. An example of the SSRM service log limited to [SET] and [PKG] events is in Fig. 10.

```
<<output omitted>>
  2019-02-08 23:08:44 [SET]   [NDX0XRXXXOXXOX] [LCD] OFF
  2019-02-08 23:10:24 [SET]   [NDX0XRXXXOOXOX / BT: Volvo] [BT] CONNECTED
  2019-02-08 23:10:51 [PKG]  com.samsung.android.incallui
  2019-02-08 23:10:51 [SET]   [NDX0ORXXXOOXOX / BT: Volvo] [LCD] ON
  2019-02-08 23:11:04 [PKG]  com.facebook.katana
  2019-02-08 23:11:10 [SET]   [NDX0XRXXXOOXOX / BT: Volvo] [LCD] OFF
  2019-02-08 23:14:33 [PKG]  com.samsung.android.incallui
  2019-02-08 23:14:33 [SET]   [NDX0ORXXXOOXOX / BT: Volvo] [LCD] ON
  2019-02-08 23:14:34 [SET]   [NDX0OROXXOOXOX / BT: Volvo] > [Call] CallStateOffHook : true
  2019-02-08 23:15:05 [SET]   [NDX0XROXXOOXOX / BT: Volvo] [LCD] OFF
<<output omitted>>
```

Fig. 10. An example of SSRM service log

A [PKG] event types refer to application execution or activity. The body of the message refers to the name of the package which was executed. In comparison to the *UsageStats* artefacts, [PKG] events do not allow us to differentiate between activities within the same application. In addition, [PKG] messages may appear in the log even if the driver does not interact with the application. For instance, when a driver ignores an incoming phone call, once the ringing state is over the SSRM service will generate a [PKG] event which refers to the application on the top of the UI. Should the Facebook app be the last used application, the service will generate [PKG] *com.facebook.katana* event which can be misinterpreted as driver interaction. These and other discrepancies can be clarified.

A [SET] event type primarily reports power management changes. The SSRM service distinguishes two power-related functions, the power mode and the battery status. Depending on the version of AOS, the investigator may recognize *Normal Mode* [N], *Power Saving Mode* [P]; *Ultra Power Saving Mode* [U] and the *Emergency Mode* [E].[9] It also distinguishes battery status – charged or discharged. If the device is charged, the service tracks the charging methods standard *AC charging* [Ac], *USB charging* [Usb], *Wireless charging method* [W] or *Fast Charging* [F]. The information is combined in the first two bits at the beginning of the [SET] event bit string.[10] While the 1st bit represents the power mode – [SET] [Nxxxxx...] – the 2nd reports battery status – [SET] [xAxxxxx...]. For instance, a device which is set to *Power Saving Mode* [P] and charged by standard charger [Ac] will generate [SET] [PAxxxxx...] events.

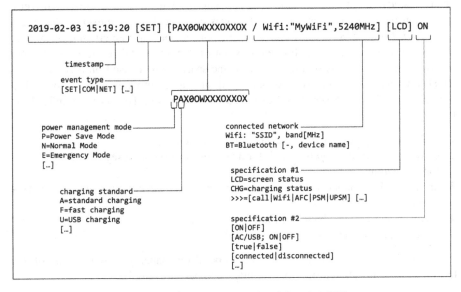

Fig. 11. SSRM [SET] - An example of decoded SET event

---

[9] A slightly different terminology can be identified in devices running AOS 7.0 +.

[10] The official terminology or definitions may differ.

Similarly, a device which is set to *Normal Mode* and discharged [D], generates the [NDxxxxx...] events (see an example in Fig. 11).

Each time the power mode is changed, a single or a combination of SET events is generated. Similarly, each time the device is connected or disconnected from the power source; the charging status change is logged.

A similar approach is applied for screen changes. Each time the screen is changed to on or off, the SET [LCD] ON, respectively SET [LCD] OFF event is generated. Consequently the 4th bit of the SET event bit string is switched to value 0 if the screen is on, or switched back to value X if the screen is off. The [LCD] ON|OFF events are reliably generated regardless of the trigger, be it user interaction, a received phone call or notification of a fully charged battery.

SSRM memory dump [SET] event content is not limited to power mode and charging status. It tracks any network-related changes such as connectivity to Bluetooth devices or WiFi networks. It tracks details such as SSIDs, Bluetooth friendly names, connection status, whether Bluetooth is enabled or if the device is also connected to an external device. A summary of decoded attributes is presented in Fig. 11.

The log lifetime depends on device activity, the primary tested device held the events from the last 5 days. Neither intentional reboot, nor several hours long power outage affected the integrity of the log.

5 Synthetic Case Study and Results

The case study demonstrated a simulated car accident which occurred after the driver's interaction with a mobile device. The test was conducted on a *Samsung Galaxy S9, SM-G960F/DSA*, AOS 8, connected by Bluetooth to the car's entertainment system. The evidence acquisition was limited to 8 out of 225 supported services which were described in the previous section. The timeline search was focused on a 20-min time window when the accident was reported. All simulated activities were conducted in accordance with testing script and executed by a co-driver. The script contained the following activities:

1. mobile device connected to the car's stereo system;
2. driver uses *Chrome app* to search for a new destination and uses *Google maps app* for navigation;
3. driver receives phone call, responds via handsfree kit and switches to device's earpiece;
4. driver is texting via Messenger; and
5. driver is taking pictures.

Since, the full analysis results exceed the scope of this paper, the applicability of this technique is demonstrated only on a limited number of examples.

5.1   Results

The analysis can be approached from multiple angles. The first option can be to focus on the driver's login and screen activities to identify whether a driver even attempted to log in. In the current case, multiple login activities were reported by *WifiController* (wifi), *BinderProxy* (statusbar) and *Crypt Connector* (mount) classes. Each login activity was followed by *Screen On* activity, which copies natural behaviour while logging into the device. Screen activities were proven reliably reported by all examined *wifi* classes (see Fig. 12).

Time	CLASS	DESCRIPTION	MESSAGE
13:45:47.285	WifiController	screen ON	processed=DefaultState org=DeviceActiveState dest=<null> what=155650(
13:45:47.286	AutoWifiControll	screen ON	processed=DefaultState org=InitialState dest=<null> what=12(0xc) CMD_
13:45:50.236	BinderProxy	UI locked	pkg=com.android.systemui userId=0 what=HOME RECENT token=android.os.B
13:45:53.420	CryptConnector	unlock requested	SND -> {168 cryptfs setpw_for_ext [scrubbed]}
13:45:53.421	CryptConnector	unlock confirmed	RCV <- {200 168 0}
13:45:53.862	BinderProxy	UI unlocked	pkg=com.android.systemui userId=0 what=CLEAR token=android.os.BinderP
13:45:53.918	WifiController	login detected	processed=DeviceActiveState org=DeviceActiveState dest=<null> what=15
13:48:47.623	AutoWifiControll	screen OFF	processed=DefaultState org=InitialState dest=<null> what=12(0xc) CMD_

Fig. 12. Driver's login activity

The second option is to observe *UsageStats – Event type collector* events which cannot be generated without user interaction. Within an observed timeframe, it was possible to detect all driver activity defined in a test script, including:

- home button touch, (*com.android.launcher*);
- run *Galaxy Finder* to search for an application;
- run *Waze* app and set up the navigation;
- USB connectivity (car's charger);
- switching between executed applications *Chrome* app, *Google maps*, *Messenger*, *Waze* and *Contacts*;
- browsing contacts, dialling, conducting a phone call;
- switch to PiP mode; and
- taking a camera picture.

An example of driver activities extracted from *Usage* statistics is in the figure below (Fig. 13).

Time	ORDER	SOURCE	MESSAGE
13:29:00.000	2053	usagestats	type=MOVE_TO_FOREGROUND package=com.samsung.android.app.galax
13:29:00.000	2054	usagestats	type=MOVE_TO_BACKGROUND package=com.samsung.android.app.galax
13:29:00.000	2055	usagestats	type=MOVE_TO_FOREGROUND package=com.sec.android.app.launcher
13:30:00.000	2056	usagestats	type=MOVE_TO_BACKGROUND package=com.sec.android.app.launcher
13:30:00.000	2057	usagestats	type=MOVE_TO_FOREGROUND package=com.android.chrome class=org.
13:30:00.000	2058	usagestats	type=MOVE_TO_BACKGROUND package=com.android.chrome class=org.
13:30:00.000	2059	usagestats	type=MOVE_TO_FOREGROUND package=com.google.android.apps.maps

Fig. 13. An example of *Usagestats* diagnostic output

Even the output from *UsageStats* could be sufficient to conclude that the driver did interact with the mobile device. When the driver conducted a phone call, the mobile device was already connected to the car's entertainment system. Therefore, the ring tone was routed through the car's audio system, which was signalled by both *bluetooth_manager* (at 13:22:37.839) and *telecom* services (at 13:22:38.012) (follow Fig. 14).

Time	CLASS	DESCRIPTION	MESSAGE
13:22:36.000	phone log	call started	"CallTC@15 [Apr 277
13:22:37.839	BT logs	BT entered AUDIO	---HFSM-enter AUDIO (1/1) : F6:7
13:22:38.011	phone log	audio route	AUDIO_ROUTE (Leaving state QuiescentBluetoothRoute)
13:22:38.012	phone log	audio route	AUDIO_ROUTE (Entering state RingingBluetoothRoute)
13:22:39.470	AutoWifiControll	screen ON	processed=DefaultState org=InitialState dest=<null>
13:22:40.667	BT logs	Call answered	---HFSM-processAnswerCall : F6:7
13:22:40.928	phone log	audio route	AUDIO_ROUTE (Leaving state RingingBluetoothRoute):E
13:22:40.928	phone log	audio route	AUDIO_ROUTE (Entering state ActiveBluetoothRoute):E
13:22:41.207	BT logs	BT AUDIO disconnected	---HFSM-enter Connected (1/1)

Fig. 14. A phone call conducted via BT handsfree device

Then the driver accepted an incoming call which was again signalled by both services, by *bluetooth_manager* at 13:22:40.667 and by *telecom* at 13:22:40.928. At 13:22:41.207 *bluetooth_manager* reported the change of state to *HFSM-enter Connected (1/1)* which signals a return to the 'normal' state without interactive connection to the Bluetooth-connected device (see Fig. 15). The device stayed connected to the car's entertainment system, but the call was not streamed via the audio system. Also, *telecom* service reported another change of state from *BluetoothRoute* to *EarpieceRoute* at 13:22:41:211 From this moment, the rest of the call was conducted via the phone's

Time ^	CLASS	DESCRIPTION	MESSAGE
13:22:41.207	BT logs	BT AUDIO disconnected	--HFSM—enter Connected (1/1)
13:22:41.211	phone log	audio route	AUDIO_ROUTE (Leaving state ActiveBluetoothRoute):BRM.oR->BRM
13:22:41.211	phone log	audio route	AUDIO_ROUTE (Entering state ActiveEarpieceRoute):BRM.oR->BRM
13:23:11.811	AutoWifiControll	screen OFF	processed=DefaultState org=InitialState dest=<null> what=12
13:23:15.576	phone log	call ended	DESTROYED:CSW.rC@DjA
13:23:15.649	AutoWifiControll	screen ON	processed=DefaultState org=InitialState dest=<null> what=12
13:23:19.270	BinderProxy	UI locked	pkg=com.android.systemui userId=0 what=HOME RECENT token=and
13:23:23.149	AutoWifiControll	screen OFF	processed=DefaultState org=InitialState dest=<null> what=12

Fig. 15. A phone call conducted via BT handsfree device

earpiece. Once the phone call was finished, the display switched on (13:23:15.649) and the UI was locked.

Similar results can also be retrieved from the SSRM service. The analyst can determine Bluetooth connectivity to car's audio system and the call, which is accompanied by screen activities. Analysts may also detect that the phone was set to *Power saving mode*, charged through the USB and connected to Volvo Car's entertainment system (see Fig. 16).

Time ^	CLASS	DESCRIPTION	MESSAGE
13:22:38.000	SSRM	app launched	[PKG] com.samsung.android.incallui
13:22:39.000	SSRM	screen ON	[SET] [PUX00RXXX00X0X / BT:My Volvo Car] [LCD] ON
13:22:41.000	SSRM	-	[SET] [PUX00R0XX00X0X / BT:My Volvo Car] >>> [Call]
13:23:11.000	SSRM	screen OFF	[SET] [PUX0XR0XX00X0X / BT:My Volvo Car] [LCD] OFF
13:23:15.000	SSRM	-	[SET] [PUX0XRXXX00X0X / BT:My Volvo Car] >>> [Call]
13:23:15.000	SSRM	screen ON	[SET] [PUX00RXXX00X0X / BT:My Volvo Car] [LCD] ON
13:23:19.000	SSRM	app launched	[PKG] com.waze
13:23:23.000	SSRM	screen OFF	[SET] [PUX0XRXXX00X0X / BT:My Volvo Car] [LCD] OFF

Fig. 16. A phone call conducted via BT handsfree device

In addition to the driver's behavioural activities, the investigator can determine other circumstances which might be relevant. For instance, analysts may detect the time when the mobile phone was connected or disconnected from the wireless network (*wifi*, *SSRM*), the time when the driver entered the car and started engine (*SSRM*, *Bluetooth_manager*) or even the approximate driving path (*wifi*). They may also detect whether the mobile device was charged (*UsageStats*, *SSRM*) or whether the system was rebooted (*Bluetooth_manager*, *SSRM*). *Recent Tasks* may also hold information about

Time	MESSAGE
13:48:47.038	* Recent #5: TaskRecord{daac8a3d0 #432 A=com.samsung.android.incallui U=0 StackId=-1 sz=0} mFullscreen=true mLastNonFullscreenBounds=null mLastDeXBounds=null intent={act=android.in tent.action.MAIN flg=0x10840000 cmp=com.samsung.android.incallui/com.android.incallui.InCall Activity} hasBeenVisible=true mResizeMode=RESIZE_MODE_RESIZEABLE_VIA_SDK_VERSION mSuppor tsPictureInPicture=false isResizeable=true firstActiveTime=1556362127038 lastActiveTime=1556 362127038 lastActiveElapsedTime=393605219 (inactive for 1091s)
14:04:11.385	* Recent #4: TaskRecord{e1e2ff0d0 #424 A=com.google.android.apps.maps U=0 StackId=1 sz=1} mFullscreen=true mLastNonFullscreenBounds=null mLastDeXBounds=null intent={act=android.in tent.action.VIEW cat=[android.intent.category.BROWSABLE] dat=https://maps.google.com/maps?q= stroomi+beach+address&client=ms-android-samsung-gs-rev1&um=1&ie=UTF-8&sa=X&ved=2ahUKEwj5n5vR iPDhAhVvsosKHa_XAsIQ_AUoAXoECAsQAQ flg=0x14000000 cmp=com.google.android.apps.maps/com.googl

Fig. 17. Restored Recent Task Intent

user activity (*Intent*). If the observed task is still in the stack, the investigator may obtain its content. Since in the current case the applications had not been closed but rather pushed to the background of UI, the content of the tasks could be restored (see Fig. 17).

6 Conclusion

The goal of the study was to analyse the scope of the prospective digital evidence which resides in diagnostic data acquired from the *adb dumpsys* tool. As was demonstrated, *dumpsys* analysis does not require anything other than standard user-level access with the developer's options enabled, and it allows the investigator access to system-level data. The results from the analysis and synthetic case study proved the applicability of this technique in a real-life car accident investigation. The analysts have several options to determine user interaction with a mobile device, including their logins, texting, calling, interaction with social media or browsing offline content. Analysts can also identify telephony activities and distinguish their operating modes, such as conducting the phone call via the phone's earpiece or external handsfree appliance. *Dumpsys* diagnostic data allows the recovery of deleted phone call entries or attempts to delete other artefacts, which could lead to conviction. Since evidence acquisition does not rely on specialised digital forensics equipment, it may be conducted outside digital forensics laboratories.

Like any other operating system, the range and structure of the events described may be invalidated by newly implemented upgrades. The logic of the described services is such that the structure of the events can be re-designed, re-placed or may be completely removed. Despite these facts, the core services, such as, *activity, Bluetooth_manager, usagestats* and *wifi* have been identified across a selection of different mobile device brands, types and operating system versions, from AOS 5 to AOS 10. Even if a portion of the events may still become unavailable, the results and the method described in this work can serve as a valid starting point to conduct further research and customized development on a wider selection of brands and operating systems.

The outcome of the study can assist digital forensic practitioners to reveal additional evidence while investigating any type of crime or supporting the intelligence operations. Discovered artefacts may clarify the scope of used applications, services, paired accounts, paired devices, connected networks, visited locations, etc. It enables differentiation between whether a certain activity was initiated by a system or a user. The demonstrated method can assist investigators to verify a suspect's alibi, build communication networks or even verify whether a device's security has been breached. It can also provide a vital framework for targeted preparation, automated evidence collection and further evidence visualisation.

7 Future Work

One of the biggest challenges identified in the study is to determine login activities. A significantly more believable artefact of the user's login activity can be extracted from the Android buffer log through *logcat*. However, the main drawback of a buffer log is its volatility, and future research should be focused either on less volatile evidence or methods to extend the artefact's lifetime.

As the scope of the analysed artefacts retrieved from Android *dumpsys* has not as yet been exhausted, further analyses should be extended to a number of additional topics. Activity manager has been found to be one of the most verbose plugins, responsible for almost 25% of *dumpsys* output. However, this analysis covered only 1 of 14 sections holding the information about user- and system-initiated activities. Correlation between *Recent Tasks*, *Broadcast Activities* and *Pending Items* activities might extend understanding of past user behaviour. The same applies to other services, mainly *wifi* and *bluetooth_manager*, which have not been explored in depth. Knowing how *msg.what* messages are constructed, additional research may deliver further evidence providers, which reflect human activities.

Since the structure of particular events from core services, such as *activity*, *bluetooth_manager*, *usagestats* and *wifi* has been changed with new AOS, demonstrated artefacts will require systematic verification. A significant challenge will be to keep track of newly implemented services. While the tested device (Samsung S9, AOS 8) offered 225 services, the same device upgraded to AOS 10 provides access to 303 services. Finally, automating post-acquisition analysis to build a structured timeline, be it JSON, CSV or other formats, would allow both effective examination and the correlation of results with external evidence providers across multiple cases.

Acknowledgments. I would like to thank Matthew Sorells for fruitful discussions and highly valuable feedback.

References

1. Lynne, C., Graeme, G.: Investigating evidence of mobile phone usage by drivers in road traffic accidents. Digit. Invest. **12**, S30–S37 (2015)
2. Tamma, R., Skulkin, O., Mahalik, H., Bommisetty, S.: Practical Mobile Forensics: A Hands-on Guide to Mastering Mobile Forensics for the iOS, Android, and the Windows Phone Platform, 3rd edn. Pack Publishing Ltd., Birmingham (2018)

3. Mantouka, E.G., Barmpounakis, E.N., Vlahogianni, E.I.: Identifying driving safety profiles from smartphone data using unsupervised learning. Saf. Sci. **119**, 84–90 (2019)
4. Papadimitriou, E., Argyropoulou, A., Tselentis, D.I., Yannis, G.: Analysis of driver behaviour through smartphone data: the case of mobile phone use while driving. Saf. Sci. **119**, 91–97 (2019)
5. Mansor, H., Markantonakis, K., Akram, R.N., Mayes, K., Gurulian, I.: Log your car: the non-invasive vehicle forensics. In: 2016 IEEE Trustcom/BigDataSE/ISPA, pp. 974–982. IEEE, Tianjin (2016)
6. Khandakar, A., et al.: Portable system for monitoring and controlling driver behavior and the use of a mobile phone while driving. Sensors **19**(7), 1563 (2019)
7. Khan, I., Khusro, S., Alam, I.: Smartphone distractions and its effect on driving performance using vehicular lifelog dataset. In: 2019 International Conference on Electrical, Communication, and Computer Engineering (ICECCE), pp. 1–6. IEEE, Swat (2019)
8. Park, H., Ahn, D., Park, T., Shin, K.G.: Automatic identification of driver's smartphone exploiting common vehicle-riding actions. IEEE Trans. Mob. Comput. **17**(2), 265–278 (2018)
9. Torres, R., Ohashi, O., Pessin, G.: A machine-learning approach to distinguish passengers and drivers reading while driving. Sensors **19**(14), 3174 (2019)
10. Yang, J., et al.: Detecting driver phone use leveraging car speakers. IEEE Trans. Mob. Comput. **11**(9), 1426–1440 (2012)
11. Cano, T.A., Junker, D.H., Mårtensson, M., Skov, M.B., Raptis, D.: Using smartwatch inertial sensors to recognize and distinguish between car drivers and passengers. In: 10th International Conference on Automotive User Interfaces and Interactive Vehicular Applications, AutomotiveUI 2018, pp. 74–84 (2018)
12. Liu, L., et al.: Toward detection of unsafe driving with wearables. In: Proceedings of the 2015 Workshop on Wearable Systems and Applications, WearSys 2015, pp. 27–32 (2015)
13. Mannini, A., Sabatini, A.M.: Machine learning methods for classifying human physical activity from on-body accelerometers. Sensors **10**(2), 1154–1175 (2010)
14. Lu, D.-N., Nguyen, D.-N., Nguyen, T.-H., Nguyen, H.-N.: Vehicle mode and driving activity detection based on analyzing sensor data of smartphones. Sensors **18**(4), 1036 (2018)
15. Oviedo-Trespalacios, O., King, M., Vaezipour, A., Truelove, V.: Can our phones keep us safe? A content analysis of smartphone applications to prevent mobile phone distracted driving. Transp. Res. Part F: Traffic Psychol. Behav. **60**, 657–668 (2019)
16. Ferrante, A., Medvet, E., Mercaldo, F., Milosevic, J., Visaggio, C.A.: Spotting the malicious moment: characterizing malware behavior using dynamic features. In: 11th International Conference on Availability, Reliability and Security (ARES), pp. 372–381. IEEE, Salzburg (2016)
17. Lashkari, A.H., Kadir, A.F.A., Taheri, L., Ghorbani, A.A.: Toward developing a systematic approach to generate benchmark android malware datasets and classification. In: 2018 International Carnahan Conference on Security Technology (ICCST), pp. 1–7. IEEE, Montreal (2018)
18. Trivedi N., Das M.L.: MalDetec: a non-root approach for dynamic malware detection in Android. In: Shyamasundar, R., Singh, V., Vaidya, J. (eds.) ICISS 2017. LNCS, vol. 10717, pp. 231–240. Springer, Cham (2017). https://doi.org/10.1007/978-3-319-72598-7_14
19. Taheri, L., Kadir, A.F.A., Lashkari, A.H.: Extensible android malware detection and family classification using network-flows and API-calls. In: 2019 International Carnahan Conference on Security Technology (ICCST), pp. 1–8. IEEE, Chennai (2019)
20. Shoaib, M., Incel, O.D., Scolten, H., Havinga, P.: Resource consumption analysis of online activity recognition on mobile phones and smartwatches. In: 2017 IEEE 36th International Performance Computing and Communications Conference (IPCCC), pp. 1–6. IEEE, San Diego (2017)

21. Gómez, M., Rouvoy, R., Adams, B., Seinturier, L.: Mining test repositories for automatic detection of ui performance regressions in android apps. In: 2016 IEEE/ACM 13th Working Conference on Mining Software Repositories (MSR), pp. 13–24. IEEE, Austin (2016)
22. Basara, O.E., Alptekina, G., Volakaa, H.C., Isbilenb, M., Incela, O.D.: Resource usage analysis of a mobile banking application using sensor-and-touchscreen-based continuous authentication. Proc. Comput. Sci. **155**, 185–192 (2019)
23. Dumpsys. https://developer.android.com/studio/command-line/dumpsys. Accessed 25 Jan 2019
24. Logcat command-line tool. https://developer.android.com/studio/command-line/logcat#alter nativeBuffers. Accessed 30 Dec 2018
25. Google Git Google repositories on Android. https://android.googlesource.com/. Accessed 24 Jan 2019
26. RecentTasksInfo. https://developer.android.com/reference/kotlin/android/app/ActivityManager. RecentTaskInfo.html. Accessed 15 Apr 2020
27. Understand Tasks and Back Stack. https://developer.android.com/guide/components/ activities/tasks-and-back-stack. Accessed 15 Apr 2020
28. Intent. https://developer.android.com/reference/android/content/Intent.html. Accessed 10 Apr 2020
29. Intents and Intent Filter. https://developer.android.com/guide/components/intents-filters. Accessed 10 Apr 2020
30. UsageStats. https://developer.android.com/reference/android/app/usage/UsageStats. Accessed 17 Mar 2020
31. UsageEvents.Event. https://developer.android.com/reference/android/app/usage/UsageEvents. Event.html. Accessed 17 Mar 2020
32. WiFiManager. https://developer.android.com/reference/android/net/wifi/WifiManager. Accessed 02 Mar 2020
33. Google Git, Protocol.java. https://android.googlesource.com/platform/frameworks/base.git/ +/master/core/java/com/android/internal/util/Protocol.java. Accessed 01 Mar 2020
34. Google Git, WifiController.java. https://android.googlesource.com/platform/frameworks/ base/+/02ba86f/services/java/com/android/server/wifi/WifiController.java. Accessed 07 Mar 2020
35. Binder. https://developer.android.com/reference/android/os/Binder.html. Accessed 25 Jan 2020
36. IBinder. https://developer.android.com/reference/android/os/IBinder.html. Accessed 25 Jan 2020
37. Android_Binder. https://elinux.org/Android_Binder. Accessed 04 May 2019
38. Google Git, BinderProxy.java. https://android.googlesource.com/platform/frameworks/base/ +/master/core/java/android/os/BinderProxy.java. Accessed 25 July 2019
39. Google Git, CallAudioRouteStateMachine.java. https://android.googlesource.com/platform/ packages/services/Telecomm/+/android-7.0.0_r7/src/com/android/server/telecom/CallAudio RouteStateMachine.java. Accessed 29 Apr 2019
40. Android source, Bluetooth and NFC. https://source.android.com/devices/bluetooth/verify ing_debugging. Accessed 02 May 2019
41. Configure on-device developer options. https://developer.android.com/studio/debug/dev-options. Accessed 23 Jan 2019

Adapting to Local Conditions: Similarities and Differences in Anonymous Online Market Between Chinese and English Speaking Communities

Gengqian Zhou[1] and Jianwei Zhuge[1,2(✉)]

[1] Institute for Network Sciences and Cyberspace,
Tsinghua University, Beijing, China
zhougq17@tsinghua.org.cn, zhugejw@tsinghua.edu.cn
[2] Beijing National Research Center for Information Science and Technology
(BNRist), Beijing, China

Abstract. In this paper, we have conducted a comparative analysis of anonymous online market between Chinese and English speaking communities. First, we collect public data of multiple Chinese and English anonymous online markets. Then, we conduct a comparative analysis of the Chinese and English anonymous online markets from three aspects: market operation mechanism, market security mechanism, and goods sales situation. We find that Chinese and English anonymous online markets are both affected by factors such as market demand and relevant laws and regulations, and there are differences in the goods sales situation. In contrast, English anonymous online markets are relatively mature in market operation mechanism and market security mechanism, while Chinese anonymous online markets are still on their developing stage. We finally discuss the impact of law enforcement agencies' crackdown on Chinese and English anonymous online markets, as well as the focus and methods of Chinese and English anonymous online market governance.

Keywords: Anonymous online market · Comparative analysis · Market governance

1 Introduction

Anonymous online markets are online shopping platforms that run in a special network environment such as Tor [14], and they allow both buyers and vendors to hide their identities, making it difficult for others to identify their real identities or trace them. As a result, many illegal goods, such as drugs, leaked information data, and hacking services, have become the popular goods in anonymous online markets.

S. Goel et al. (Eds.): ICDF2C 2020, LNICST 351, pp. 164–181, 2021.
https://doi.org/10.1007/978-3-030-68734-2_9

Since the emergence of "Silk Road", the first large-scale anonymous online market in 2011 [4], the scale and the number of anonymous online markets worldwide have increased. Like other Internet applications, the anonymous online market is developing in multiple languages, with different participants and different goods sold. Those differences usually depend on the specific needs of market audiences, which may help researchers understand the development trends and relevance of cybercrime in different language communities. In recent years, with the increasing influence of the anonymous online market in Chinese speaking community, the number of Chinese anonymous online markets is also increasing, and a market system that can meet the needs of Chinese users has been formed. In this paper, we first collect public data of multiple anonymous online markets, then conduct a research on the anonymous online market in Chinese. We combine with previous work on anonymous online markets in English, extract the similarities and differences between anonymous online markets in Chinese and English speaking communities. In short, we make the following contributions:

1. We have collected public data on multiple anonymous online markets in Chinese and English, and combine with previous research on the English anonymous online market. We have analyzed and summarized the characteristic of Chinese and English anonymous online markets.
2. We have studied into Chinese and English anonymous online markets from three aspects: market operation mechanism, market security mechanism and goods sales situation. We have revealed the similarities and differences between Chinese and English anonymous online markets.
3. We have analyzed and explained the reasons for the similarities and differences between the Chinese and English anonymous online markets.

The rest of the paper is organized as follows. We give an anonymous online market overview and describe the methods for collecting public data in Sect. 2. Then we compare and analyze Chinese and English anonymous online markets from the three aspects as market operation mechanism, market security mechanism and goods sales situation in Sect. 3, and point out the similarities and differences between these two. We discuss our research results in Sect. 4, including ethical considerations, the crackdowns of law enforcement in Chinese and English speaking communities against the anonymous online market, and the focus and methods of law enforcement in these two communities. We outline related work in Sect. 5 and we give our conclusion and future research directions in Sect. 6.

2 Anonymous Online Market Overview and Data Collection

In this section, we will first give a overview of anonymous online market. Then we introduce our methods of collecting anonymous online market public data.

2.1 Anonymous Online Market Overview

As the name implies, anonymous online market is an online market that operates in an anonymous network. Anonymous online market is built by combining onion service and web server software together. Common web server software is used to build anonymous online market, such as Apache, Nginx and Windows IIS Server. In fact, the anonymous online market itself does not sell goods. Its role is to provide a risk manageable platform for participants in transaction, such as vendors and buyers. In general, anonymous online markets usually have the following characteristics:

1. The anonymous network market operates in an anonymous network, which makes the communication between participants(buyers and vendors) highly anonymously, so that participants can be protected from the interference by law enforcement to some extent.
2. The anonymous online market provides better security mechanism in protecting users' accounts. Users need to enter account password and CAPTCHA when logging in to the account, or log in to the account through two-factor authentication(2FA) based on PGP [1].
3. Anonymous online markets build their payment system with cryptocurrencies (such as Bitcoin [19]), which can effectively avoid the trace ability of assets that exist when using traditional electronic payment system (such as wire transfers or credit card payments).
4. Anonymous online markets usually use advanced settlement methods such as escrow to reduce transaction risks. When the buyer have purchased goods in the market, the payment will not be directly transferred to the vendor's account, but be managed by the market first. After the buyer confirms the receipt of the goods, the market will transfer the payment to vendor. Similar settlement methods are commonly used in anonymous online markets such as finalized early (FE) and multisig.

2.2 Data Collection

We have collected the public data of multiple anonymous online markets. Table 1 lists the markets we crawled, the time the measurements spanned, and the number of snapshots that were taken.

Table 1. Anonymous online markets crawled. (* denote the English market, and ⁻ denote the Chinese market.)

Market	Measurement dates	# snap.
Chinese trading market⁻	07/02/2019–10/27/2019	115
Tea-Horse Road⁻	10/15/2019–11/11/2019	28
Darknet China⁻	12/16/2019–03/14/2020	79
Empire Market*	01/15/2020–03/12/2020	46

We design and use the Python crawler framework based on Selenium [3] and Requests-HTML [2] library to collect the public data in Chinese anonymous online market. The crawler framework uses the Selenium library to and corresponding Firefox drivers to simulate real user's behavior of logging in to the market, so that the crawler framework can run normally in a complex login environment. After logging in to the market, the crawler framework obtains cookies from the browser and updates the cookies to the HTMLSession object of the Requests-HTML library. In order to improve the efficiency of the crawler framework, the data collection after login will be continued by the HTMLSession object in Requests-HTML.

Kanich et al. [16] emphasized that the measurement should not be detected by the targets in measurement, otherwise they could change their behaviors, which would taint the measurements. So, hiding trace is important during crawling. In order to enhance the hidden effect, for each page request, the crawler replaces the circuit once. We implement this functionality by using stem [5]. We start our crawling thread at random time every day. For example, in the adjacent two days, we start to crawl at 5am and 2pm respectively.

3   Comparative Analysis of Anonymous Online Market in Chinese and English

In this section, we analyze and compare the Chinese and English anonymous online markets from three aspects: market operation mechanism, market security mechanism and goods sales situation. Then we extract the similarities and differences between the Chinese and English anonymous online markets.

3.1   Market Operation Mechanism

Similar to the online market running on the surface network, anonymous online markets are also built on common web server software, including Apache, Nginx and Windows IIS Server. Among them, most anonymous online markets prefer to use Nginx. We have tested 8 Chinese and English anonymous online markets and found 6 of them are built using Nginx. Only 1 anonymous online market is built by Apache and the other 1 by Windows IIS Server. We show the result in Table 2. Compared with the English anonymous online market, Chinese anonymous online market are more likely to use the Nginx server. For example, the 3 Chinese anonymous online markets we collect in Table 2 are all built on Nginx.

For the anonymous online market with a large number of users, Nginx server has shown great advantages in reverse proxy, anti-concurrency and anti-DDoS attacks. Those advantages can help the owner of anonymous online market to operate stably when accessed by multiple users. On the other hand, it also enables the anonymous online market to better respond to DDoS threats.

Anonymous online markets use crypto-currencies for transactions. Common crypto-currencies in anonymous online markets include Bitcoin (BTC), Litecoin

Table 2. Web server software used by anonymous online market.

Market	Web server software
Chinese Trading Market	Nginx
Tea-Horse Road	Nginx
Darknet China	Nginx
Empire Market	Apache
Square Market	Windows IIS Server
Yellow Brick	Nginx
Bitbaz Market	Nginx
Pax Romana	Nginx

(LTC) and Monero (XMR). Since the price of crypto-currencies fluctuates frequently, the anonymous online market usually displays the real-time price of crypto-currencies against conventional currencies in the homepage. As shown in Fig. 1, users can evaluate the prices of goods in the market more intuitively.

Fig. 1. Anonymous online market crypto-currency to real currency price display.

English anonymous online markets usually support multiple crypto-currencies, and the crypto-currencies supported in different markets are also different. As shown in Fig. 1, this market supports Bitcoin, Bitcoin Cash(BCH), Ethereum, Monero, Litecoin and Dash at the same time. For comparison, "Empire Market" supports three crypto-currencies, Bitcoin, Litecoin and Monero while "Dream Market" only supports Bitcoin and Bitcoin Cash [28]. Although different markets support different types of crypto-currencies, all markets support Bitcoin. Unlike English anonymous online markets, Chinese anonymous online markets usually only support Bitcoin. For example, the three Chinese anonymous online markets listed in Table 1 are all only support Bitcoin. It can be found that in terms of support for crypto-currency, the Chinese anonymous online market is relatively simple.

Escrow is currently the most popular transaction settlement method used in the anonymous online market, and is also the transaction settlement method commonly used in the Chinese anonymous online market. In addition to escrow, many English anonymous online markets also support FE and multisig. FE allows the transaction to be settled immediately after the buyer pays for the goods, without waiting for the buyer to confirm the receipt. But this method has a fraud risk and only a few vendors can use it with the permission of the market administrator. Multisig is a new type of transaction settlement method, which allows transaction settlement under the approval of two-thirds of the transaction parties (any two parties in the market, buyers and vendors). Figure 2 shows a commodity that supports multisig. Multisig can effectively prevent the loss of transaction money when the market is suddenly offline or closed.

Fig. 2. A commodity that support multisig. ("[MS]" tag is in the front of the commodity title.)

3.2 Market Security Mechanism

Account Security. When the user registers an account in the market, the username and login password need to be set. In addition, English anonymous online markets usually require users to set a 6-digit personal identification number(PIN) when registering an account. The PIN can improve the security of the user's account, and is usually used when the user trades with others or resets account, which can better protect the account from the threeat of password leak. Similar to the PIN, the Chinese anonymous online market usually supports payment password. As shown in Fig. 3, payment password is used to protect the user's property and is usually used when the user pays for the goods. In addition to the above mechanisms for the security of user's accounts, anonymous online market users also need to enter a CAPTCHA when logging into their accounts. Before the end of 2019, the most of Chinese anonymous online markets have not set up CAPTCHA in their login pages and registration pages. From the end of 2019 to the beginning of 2020, many Chinese anonymous online markets have improved the platform, and set up CAPTCHA on their login pages and registration pages.

In order to improve the security of user accounts, English anonymous online markets recommend that users should set up PGP public key after registering accounts. The account that sets the PGP public key can login through 2FA. As shown in Fig. 4, 2FA requires users to use the corresponding PGP private key to decrypt the message displayed in the login page, and enter the content (such as security code) required on the page. Therefore, only the user with the correct

今年400W身份信息，身份证，手机，地址等；超划算价！

Fig. 3. Payment password in Chinese anonymous online market transactions.

PGP private key can login through 2FA. The PGP can also be used for communication between buyer and vendor, thereby protecting the communication between the two parties from the impact of middleman attacks.

The Chinese anonymous online markets have not yet deployed the PGP to ensure the security of user accounts and transactions. However, Chinese anonymous online markets pay more attention on the privacy of vendors. Many Chinese anonymous online markets have specially processed personal information such as vendor ID. For example, in "Chinese Trading Market", only the vendor number is used to distinguish vendors; "Darknet China" hides the middle part of the vendor ID and only shows the first and last characters (for example "A***e"). Although the above two methods can protect the vendor's information to a certain extent, making it more difficult for law enforcement to identify the vendor, it also increases the difficulty of identifying the buyer. In the anonymous online market, reputation is the most critical factor in determining the success of a vendor. Usually, buyers identify their trusted vendors by vendor ID. For "Chinese Trading Market", buyers can use the vendor number to distinguish vendors. But for "Darknet China", because the buyer can only observe the first and last characters of the vendor ID, the scammers in the market can use the vendor ID with the same first and last characters as the high-reputation vendor ID to sell the goods to defraud the buyer's money, which is often difficult for buyers to discern.

Website Security. In recent years, with the increasing number of anonymous online markets, there have been more and more attacks on anonymous online market. For example, "Dream Market" had suffered serious cyber-attack from unidentified attackers. Regarding the source of this attack, there are conjectures in the relevant forums of the anonymous network showing that the attack

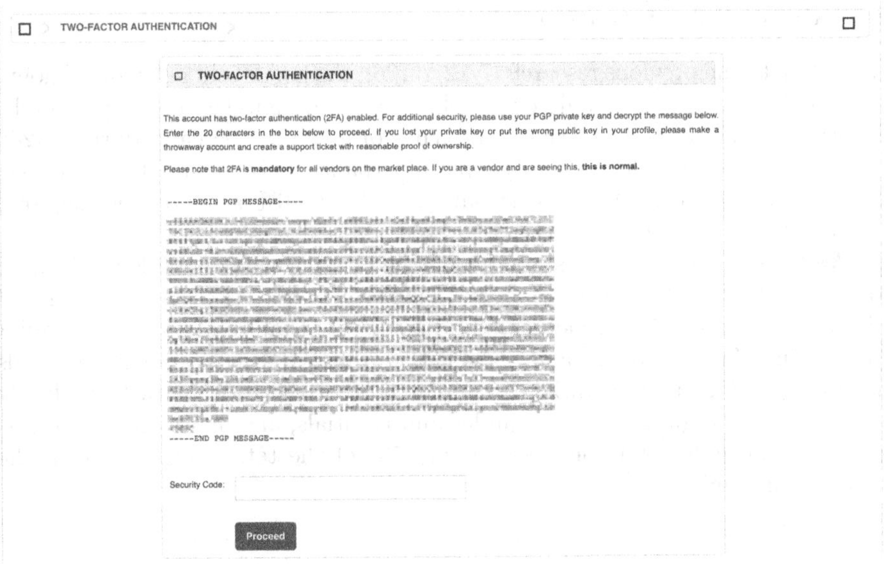

Fig. 4. Anonymous online market with 2FA login.

is coming from competitors of "Dream Market", and there are other conjectures saying that the attack is coming from the law enforcement [28]. Similar to "Dream Market", "Chinese Trading Market" and "Tea-Horse Road" also suffered cyber-attacks from unidentified attackers during 2019. In response to this, "Chinese Trading Market" published a message on its web homepage showing that the attack came from the law enforcement. On the other hand, "Tea-Horse Road" administrator made an announcement in its market forum stated that the cyber attack suffered by "Tea-Horse Road" came from a competitor, and pointed out that this competitor had recruited hackers publicly through Telegram. From these attacks we can be seen that the anonymous online markets are constantly facing cyber threats from law enforcement and competitors with similar businesses.

Many anonymous online markets have adopted relevant security measures to deal with cyber-attacks. The most typical countermeasure is the multi-domain strategy, which uses multiple domain names for mapping to the same market. Because ".onion" domain is generated by the Tor software running on the onion server, the anonymous online market administrator can generate multiple ".onion" domains for his market. The list of domains is called mirrors list. When a certain domain name of the market cannot be accessed, users can access through other domain names in the mirror list. Currently, most English anonymous online markets and some Chinese anonymous online markets use this strategy. However, with the increment in the number of domain names in the same market, and the difficulty for ".onion" domains to remember, many malicious users take advantage of it for phishing.

3.3 Goods Sales Situation

According to the previous research [7, 12, 23, 26], the goods sold in English anonymous online market are mainly drugs, chemicals and digital goods. For example, the left side of Fig. 5 shows the main types of goods in "Dream Market" [28], including drugs, digital goods, drugs paraphernalia, services and others. Among them, drugs and digital goods account for about 50% and 40% of the total "Dream Market" goods, respectively.

We have also carried out statistics on the classification of goods in "Empire Market". The classification of goods in "Empire Market" is shown on the right of Fig. 5. During our measurement, we find goods in "Empire Market" are similar to "Dream Market": drugs and chemicals are also the most important goods in "Empire Market', accounting for about 68% of the total market goods. At the same time, digital products, guides and tutorials, and digital goods such as software and malware account for about 25% of the total merchandise in the "Empire Market".

Fig. 5. "Dream Market" (left) and "Empire Market" (right) main categories.

For Chinese anonymous online market, each market in Chinese anonymous online markets has its own classification criteria. Therefore, we have developed a classification standard and trained a classifier to reclassify all products in the market.

To build and confirm the classifier, we select 4,331 pieces of goods information of the determined classification to form a data set, divide them into training set, test set and verification set, and use the "goods title" and "goods description" fields in the goods information as the classification characteristics. The input of the classifier is processed by the Convolutional Neural Network (CNN) algorithm with high accuracy. Then we feed to the model to train the classifier. The accuracy of the final classifier on the test set can reach 80%.

The goods in all markets are finally divided into seven categories: "Information Data", "Physical Goods", "Pornography", "Services", "Digital Products", "CVV" and "Private Auction". Figure 6 shows the goods classification of the Chinese anonymous online markets after reclassification, in which information data, digital products and pornography are the most important goods in the

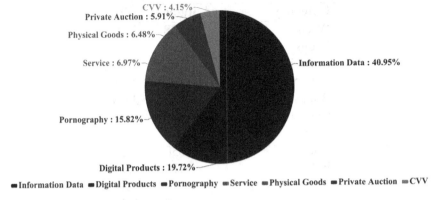

CVV : 4.15%
Private Auction : 5.91%
Physical Goods : 6.48%
Service : 6.97%
Information Data : 40.95%
Pornography : 15.82%
Digital Products : 19.72%

■Information Data ■Digital Products ■Pornography ■Service ■Physical Goods ■Private Auction ■CVV

Fig. 6. Main categories of Chinese anonymous online markets.

Chinese anonymous online markets, accounting for almost 40%, 20% and 16% respectively.

The goods sold in English anonymous online markets are usually dominated by drugs, chemicals and digital goods. Goods in Chinese anonymous online market are mainly information data and other digital goods, and information data dominate the market. Therefore, there are certain differences between the English anonymous online markets and the Chinese anonymous online markets.

Next, we will analyze the reasons for the differences in the anonymous online markets between Chinese and English, and make a comparative analysis of the most important online goods in Chinese and English anonymous online markets, including information data, pornographic films and hacking technologies.

Important Goods in English Anonymous Online Market. As we known, the drug trade has high profits. The most important goods in the "Silk Road", the first large-scale integrated anonymous online market, was drugs. As shown in Fig. 7, Christin listed the 20 types of goods with the largest number of goods in "Silk Road" [12]. Among them, 16 types are related to drugs. At the same time, the number of soft drugs such as weed, cannabis and hash in "Silk Road" is greater than hard drugs such as opiates. And we also observed similar phenomena in "Empire Market".

The sale of goods in the "Silk Road" reflects the huge demand for soft drugs. Since the rise of the anonymous online market, this demand has never changed. British journalist Wensley Clarkson mentioned in his book "Hash: The Secret and Chilling Story Behind the Drug's Deadly Underworld" [13] says: "As a lucrative cash crop, the global gross output value of cannabis exceeds the sum of corn and wheat. Hash is a concentrated product of hemp, and is a recreational drug considered to be the most acceptable to society. It is estimated that the largest source of economic income for organized criminal groups worldwide is Hash." Meanwhile, Cannabis such as Hash are not included in the scope of control or have a low degree of control in some countries and regions. Therefore,

Category	#. items	Pct.
Weed	3338	13.7%
Drugs	2194	9.0%
Prescription	1784	7.3%
Benzos	1193	4.9%
Books	955	3.9%
Cannabis	877	3.6%
Hash	820	3.4%
Cocaine	630	2.6%
Pills	473	1.9%
Blotter (LSD)	440	1.8%
Money	405	1.7%
MDMA (ecstasy)	393	1.6%
Erotica	385	1.6%
Steroids, PEDs	376	1.5%
Seeds	374	1.5%
Heroin	370	1.5%
DMT	343	1.4%
Opioids	342	1.4%
Stimulants	291	1.2%
Digital goods	260	1.1%

Fig. 7. Top 20 product categories by number of "Silk Road".

cannabis have lower trade risks than other drugs. Additionally, the anonymous online market has provided a safer sale method for vendors of this high-profit industry, allowing both parties in the transaction to hide their identity, Cross-border transactions can be conducted without contacting the other party.

Important Goods in Chinese Anonymous Online Market. With the continuous advancement of China's online real-name system process, users' online virtual identities are matched with real identity information. More and more personal information is used in various web applications, which provides convenience for the management of Internet governors in China. However, due to the lack of data security management in many Internet applications, lack of legal awareness for network administrators and lack of relevant regulations, there is a great information leakage risk of personal information data stored in these Internet applications, even causing large-scale leakage of personal information data. Personal information data can be used by fraud gangs to implement precise fraud. According to relevant reports, Chinese police have cracked 200,000 online telecommunications fraud cases and captured 163,000 suspects in 2019, up 52.7% and 123.3% year-on-year respectively. This shows that China's fraud cases are on the rise, and precise fraud can greatly increase the success rate, thereby bringing greater benefits to criminals. The popularity of the Chinese anonymous online market provides a safer trading platform for black industry practitioners and precise fraud groups engaged in the sale of personal information data. Driven by profits and criminal needs, information data have gradually become the most important goods in Chinese anonymous online markets.

Information Data. The information data sold in Chinese and English anonymous online markets are very similar. The information data in the Chinese anonymous online market mainly include personal real-name, asset, network accounts, bank accounts and passwords in many industries such as finance, e-commerce platforms, transportation and education. Information data in English anonymous online markets mainly include Social Security Number (SSN), birthday, bank card account and password, and "Fullz"[1].

Although the information data sold in Chinese and English anonymous online markets have certain similarities, due to the difference in social environment, buyers of information data may be used for different purposes. Data buyers in Chinese anonymous online market will usually use these data for precise marketing and precise fraud; while data buyers in English anonymous online market usually use information data for identity theft or tax fraud. For example, a purchaser of information data in the United States can use the SSN of the minor he purchased to carry out tax fraud [6], that is, use the child tax credit when submitting a tax return. Due to that parents usually pay little attention to the credit status of their children, purchasers of information data can also use a synthetic identity with a minor social security code to apply for a credit card, which will cause the victim a double loss of credit and money.

The proportion of information data in English anonymous online markets is relatively small. For example, the volume of information data in "Empire Market" only accounts for 4.9% of the total market goods, which is far lower than 40.95% in Chinese anonymous online markets. Although the proportion of information data in "Empire Market" is relatively small, the actual number of information data in the two markets is not different, since the total number of market goods in "Empire Market" is about 7 times that of "Chinese Trading Market", and the number of information data in "Chinese Trading Market" is slightly higher than "Empire Market". On the other hand, we have studied the cumulative trading of information data in "Empire Market" and "Chinese Trading Market" from February 2018 to mid-March 2020. During this period, the average cumulative information data of "Empire Market" goods transactions were approximately 69,725; the average cumulative information data transactions of "Chinese Trading Market" were approximately 56,146. This shows that the overall situation of the information data in "Empire Market" and "Chinese Trading Market" is similar. In terms of goods number, "Chinese Trading Mar-

---

[1] Fullz is a slang term used by credit card hackers and data resellers which means full packages of individuals' identity information. "Fullz" usually contains an individual's name, Social Security number, birth date, account numbers and other data.

ket" is slightly higher than "Empire Market"; but in terms of actual trading, "Empire Market" is slightly higher than "Chinese Trading Market".

Pornography. Another important online goods in anonymous online markets is pornography. Among them, pornography in Chinese anonymous online market accounts for about 15.82% of the total market goods; while in English anonymous online market, pornography accounts for about 4%. But on the other hand, users in Chinese anonymous online market usually do not show a strong willingness to pay for pornography. We use the buyer's purchase probability to measure the buyer's willingness to purchase a certain type of goods. The buyer's purchase probability is defined as in Eq. 1. Let the total sales of a certain category of goods be S and the total number of user's browsing of goods be V, the purchase probability P of the buyer of the goods is:

$$P = \frac{S}{V} \tag{1}$$

In this subsection, the pornography purchase probability in "Chinese Trading Market" and "Empire Market" are calculated respectively. The pornography purchase probability in "Empire Market" reached 5.96%, which is about 46 times that of the "Chinese Trading Market". It can be seen from the above that for pornography, although the Chinese anonymous online market has a larger market share, English anonymous online market users have shown a stronger purchase intention than Chinese anonymous online market users.

Hacking Technology. In recent years, the rapid development of the anonymous online market not only provides a safer and more convenient trading platform for leaked information data and pornography, but also enables hacker technology transactions to be conducted in a more covert way. Hacking technology in the anonymous online market can usually be divided into two types: actual hacking resources and teaching resources. The actual combat resources mainly include malware, exploit kit, hacking tools, and cyber-attack services. The teaching resources usually include text and video, which are mainly used to provide technical guidance for technical enthusiasts.

We further divide hacking technology products into 4 categories: malware, tools, tutorials, and services. Table 3 shows the basic situation of the 4 categories of hacking technology goods in Chinese and English anonymous online markets. The hacking technology goods sold in Chinese and English anonymous online markets are very similar, but there are certain differences due to different audiences.

It can be seen from Table 3 that, in addition to some common hacking tools and malicious programs, malware and tools in Chinese anonymous online market are more focused on private information theft; while similar goods in English anonymous online markets are more focused on phishing, social network account theft and property theft. In terms of tutorial, English anonymous online market is still more focused on phishing, account theft and property theft, but Chinese anonymous online market is more focused on low-cost sales of Kali Linux, penetration testing and well-known online security training platforms for fee-based teaching videos. In terms of service, most vendors in Chinese anonymous online markets have limited the scope of their services. They usually only target illegal or overseas websites involving black and gray products, and usually do not accept the target of attacks on websites of sensitive businesses such as government and education. However, there are a few vendors in Chinese anonymous online markets that have not restricted their service scope. In the English anonymous online market, most vendors that provide service do not restrict the scope of service demand.

Table 3. Hacking technology goods in anonymous online markets

Category	Chinese anonymous online market	English anonymous online market
Malware	Include monitoring software, CVE vulnerability exploit kits, various viruses and Trojan	Include 0-day exploit, ransomware and Trojan
Tools	Include website penetration, Wifi attack, password cracking, Android remote control, camera attack, and SQL injection	Include phishing site deployment, SQL injection, Wifi attack, Android remote control, Bitcoin theft, and social network account theft
Tutorials	Involves Kali Linux, penetration test, DDoS attacks, paid tutorials on security training platforms, and hacking technology books	Involves basic hacking tutorials, phishing site construction, social network account theft, and payment service theft
Services	Involves DDoS attacks, website penetration, Domain Name System (DNS) hijacking, and SMS bombing	Involves DDoS attacks, botnets, website attacks, SMS bombing and email bombing

4 Discussion

In this section, we give our discussions on Chinese and English anonymous online markets. First, we discuss ethical considerations. Then we discuss the impact of external attacks on anonymous online market and the focus and methods of Chinese and English anonymous online market governance.

4.1 Ethical Considerations

For ethical considerations, first of all, the data we collected is public. Anyone can observe these data by browsing the market pages, so there is no risk of exposing the users' privacy. In addition, we adopt a relatively conservative data crawling method, and limits the frequency of crawler to a certain extent, so as not to cause cyber-attack on any market.

4.2   Law Enforcement Intervention and Anonymous Online Market Governance

At present, many researchers such as [11,23] have shown that English anonymous online markets usually have a certain "resilient" for the crackdown by law enforcement agencies. The crackdown by law enforcement agencies cannot completely prevent the trading behavior of market users, but only force them to move to other markets. For example, the closure of "AlphaBay" and "Hansa" in 2017 caused a large number of anonymous online market users to move to "Dream Market" [27]. The Chinese anonymous online market usually does not completely disappear after being subjected to a malicious network attack, but will continue to operate after a short repair. It can be seen that Chinese anonymous online market has shown a certain degree of stability.

Therefore, regardless of English anonymous online market or the Chinese anonymous online market, the strategy of forcibly closing the market or attacking the market through cyber-attacks cannot deter anonymous online markets. Since the anonymous online market is dominated by profits and demand, reducing people's demand for illegal goods will play a decisive role in the governance of the anonymous online markets. However, the reduction in demand will be a protracted process, and the illegal transactions in anonymous online market threaten the security of cyberspace is imminent. Law enforcement agencies need to formulate more targeted market interventions. For example, for the transactions of physical goods, law enforcement agencies can strengthen the control of logistics, thereby blocking the illegal transactions at the transport phase.

However, the main goods sold in Chinese anonymous online market are information data, and logistics control has no effect on these virtual goods. Therefore, when governing the anonymous online market, Chinese government should strengthen its network supervision and the protection of various information and data, together with network security companies. At the same time, increase the level of attention to precise marketing and crack down on precise fraud, increasing the criminal costs of criminals.

4.3   Market Demand and Vendor Behavior

Considering the differences between Chinese and English anonymous online market goods, we found that the types of goods sold in the market mainly depend on the specific needs of members of the language community to which the market belongs. At the same time, the language community to which the market belongs may not be directly related to the language community to which the vendor belongs. For example, a study by Scourfield et al. [22] shows that many vendors from China sell goods in English markets, and the goods they sell occupy a larger market share. Vendors usually decide in which (language community) market they will sell their goods based on the potential consumers of their goods.

Therefore, researchers can focus more on the consumption habits of consumers in the language communities where the market belongs, and then discover potential cybercriminal goods and behaviors, take measures before they appear in the anonymous online market.

5 Related Work

In most anonymous online markets, drugs are the most important goods, which has made the research in recent years mostly focus on drug market transactions such as [8,10,17,18,21], transaction participants [24,25] and the geographical characteristics of transaction trafficking in [9,15,20]. In this work, besides drugs, we also pay attention on other types of goods such as digital goods.

In 2015, Christin et al. [23] measured and analyzed the anonymous online market ecosystem, and similar studies include [12,26,28]. However, their research target is the anonymous online market in English, which usually does not include anonymous online markets in other languages. And we have conducted a research on the Chinese anonymous online market and the first (to our knowledge) comparative analysis of the Chinese and English anonymous online markets.

6 Conclusion

In this work, we first collect the public data about Chinese and English anonymous online markets. Then we combine with previous research results and conduct a study on the characteristics of Chinese and English anonymous online markets.

We finish a comparative analysis of Chinese and English anonymous online markets from three aspects: market operation mechanism, market security mechanism and goods sales situation. The analysis results that the English anonymous online market is relatively mature in terms of market operation mechanism and market security mechanism, while the Chinese anonymous online markets are still on their developing stage. In addition, due to the influence of market demand and relevant laws and regulations, there are certain differences in the goods sales situation between anonymous online markets in Chinese and English. Finally, we discuss the impact of law enforcement crackdowns on Chinese and English anonymous online markets, as well as the focus and methods of Chinese and English anonymous online market governance.

The same vendor may sell goods in the markets of different language communities, so they may be a true international vendors proficient in multiple languages. Although our paper does not discuss this type of vendor, we can use our research as a basis and combine with more types of data for in-depth research in the future.

Acknowledgement. We thank the anonymous reviewers for their constructive feedback. This work is supported by the NSFC fund (Grant No. U1936121) and BNRist Network and Software Security Research Program (Grant No. BNR2019TD01004).

References

1. Pretty Good Privacy. https://en.wikipedia.org/wiki/Pretty_Good_Privacy. Accessed 29 Apr 2020
2. Requests-HTML: HTML Parsing for Humans (writing Python 3)! http://requests-html.kennethreitz.org/. Accessed 29 Apr 2020
3. SeleniumHQ Browser Automation. https://www.selenium.dev/. Accessed 29 Apr 2020
4. Silk Road (marketplace). https://en.wikipedia.org/wiki/SilkRoad(marketplace). Accessed 29 Apr 2020
5. Welcome to Stem! Stem 1.8.0 Documentation. https://stem.torproject.org/. Accessed 29 Apr 2020
6. Why does my 3-year-old son have a bad credit history? Dark web world surge. http://tech.sina.com.cn/csj/2019-02-27/doc-ihrfqzka9518025.shtml. Accessed 11 Apr 2020
7. Aldridge, J., Décary-Hétu, D.: Not an 'Ebay for Drugs': the cryptomarket 'Silk Road' as a paradigm shifting criminal innovation. Available at SSRN 2436643 (2014)
8. Bancroft, A., Reid, P.S.: Concepts of illicit drug quality among darknet market users: purity, embodied experience, craft and chemical knowledge. Int. J. Drug Policy **35**, 42–49 (2016)
9. Broséus, J., Rhumorbarbe, D., Morelato, M., Staehli, L., Rossy, Q.: A geographical analysis of trafficking on a popular darknet market. Forensic Sci. Int. **277**, 88–102 (2017)
10. Buxton, J., Bingham, T.: The rise and challenge of dark net drug markets. Policy Brief **7**, 1–24 (2015)
11. Calis, T.: Multi-homing sellers and loyal buyers on darknet markets (2018)
12. Christin, N.: Traveling the silk road: a measurement analysis of a large anonymous online marketplace. In: Proceedings of the 22nd International Conference on World Wide Web, pp. 213–224 (2013)
13. Clarkson, W.: Hash: The Secret and Chilling Story Behind the Drug's Deadly Underworld. Not Avail (2013)
14. Dingledine, R., Mathewson, N., Syverson, P.: Tor: the second-generation onion router. Technical report, Naval Research Lab Washington DC (2004)
15. Dittus, M., Wright, J., Graham, M.: Platform criminalism: the 'last-mile' geography of the darknet market supply chain. In: Proceedings of the 2018 World Wide Web Conference, pp. 277–286 (2018)
16. Enright, C.K.K.L.B., Savage, G.M.V.S.: The Heisenbot uncertainty problem: challenges in separating bots from chaff (2008)
17. Leontiadis, N., Moore, T., Christin, N.: Measuring and analyzing search-redirection attacks in the illicit online prescription drug trade. In: USENIX Security Symposium, vol. 11 (2011)
18. Martin, J.: Drugs on the Dark Net: How Cryptomarkets are Transforming the Global Trade in Illicit Drugs. Springer, London (2014). https://doi.org/10.1057/9781137399052

19. Nakamoto, S.: Bitcoin: a peer-to-peer electronic cash system. Technical report, Manubot (2019)
20. Norbutas, L.: Offline constraints in online drug marketplaces: an exploratory analysis of a cryptomarket trade network. Int. J. Drug Policy **56**, 92–100 (2018)
21. Rhumorbarbe, D., Staehli, L., Broséus, J., Rossy, Q., Esseiva, P.: Buying drugs on a darknet market: a better deal? Studying the online illicit drug market through the analysis of digital, physical and chemical data. Forensic Sci. Int. **267**, 173–182 (2016)
22. Scourfield, A., et al.: Synthetic cannabinoid availability on darknet drug markets-changes during 2016–2017. Toxicol. Commun. **3**(1), 7–15 (2019)
23. Soska, K., Christin, N.: Measuring the longitudinal evolution of the online anonymous marketplace ecosystem. In: 24th {USENIX} Security Symposium, {USENIX} Security 2015, pp. 33–48 (2015)
24. Van Hout, M.C., Bingham, T.: 'Surfing the silk road': a study of users' experiences. Int. J. Drug Policy **24**(6), 524–529 (2013)
25. Van Hout, M.C., Bingham, T.: Responsible vendors, intelligent consumers: silk road, the online revolution in drug trading. Int. J. Drug Policy **25**(2), 183–189 (2014)
26. Van Wegberg, R., et al.: Plug and prey? Measuring the commoditization of cybercrime via online anonymous markets. In: 27th {USENIX} Security Symposium, {USENIX} Security 2018, pp. 1009–1026 (2018)
27. van Wegberg, R., Verburgh, T.: Lost in the dream? Measuring the effects of operation Bayonet on vendors migrating to dream market. In: Proceedings of the Evolution of the Darknet Workshop, pp. 1–5 (2018)
28. Zhou, G., Zhuge, J., Fan, Y., Du, K., Lu, S.: A market in dream: the rapid development of anonymous cybercrime. Mobile Netw. Appl. **25**(1), 259–270 (2020). https://doi.org/10.1007/s11036-019-01440-2

Remote Air-Gap Live Forensics

Tom Van der Mussele[(⊠)] [iD], Babak Habibnia[iD],
and Pavel Gladyshev[iD]

DFIRe Lab, School of Computer Science, University College Dublin,
Dublin, Ireland
tom.van-der-mussele@ucdconnect.ie,
tomvandermussele@gmail.com
{babak.habibnia,pavel.gladyshev}@ucd.ie

Abstract. This paper describes a solution to build a scalable means to perform remote live forensics, which introduces minimal and traceable changes to the air-gap systems. The solution can respect the air-gap and not introduce network connectivity to the air-gap systems. It provided a central management system with the solution; this allows the solution to be used in an incident across multiple systems. Full traceable actions, built in the solution, allow the investigator to respect the second ACPO rule during the live forensics. The solution introduces low impact changes to aim for maximum stability and preservation of evidence during the investigation of the air-gap system. The solution needs to be operational with minimal interaction behind the keyboard. In this paper, it will compare and benchmark other industry solutions with proposed solution in this research.

Keywords: Digital forensics · Live forensics · Air-gap · Remote forensics · Forensic dongle

1 Introduction

Today, malicious software for air-gap systems is becoming more common. To investigate the active threat as part of the incident response, it is well accepted to perform live forensics. Due to the isolation of these air-gap systems from the normal network connected systems, it is not always straightforward to perform live forensics. Any remote live forensics is difficult to perform without introducing large changes to the infrastructure.

In the case of a confirmed incident, speed of analysis is a contributing factor for success. With air-gap systems, it can be a challenge to bring the skills behind the keyboard when there is no network connectivity. Making systems "air-gapped" is a well-known defence against attackers for high-value target or critical systems such as SCADA (Supervisory Control and Data Acquisition), ICS (Industrial Control Systems) and HMI (Human Machine Interface) of PLC (Programmable Logic Controller). The attacks on air-gap systems are becoming more common, often driven by strategic interest such as cyber warfare. Attacks on air-gapped systems such as Stuxnet [1] and

© ICST Institute for Computer Sciences, Social Informatics and Telecommunications Engineering 2021
Published by Springer Nature Switzerland AG 2021. All Rights Reserved
S. Goel et al. (Eds.): ICDF2C 2020, LNICST 351, pp. 182–203, 2021.
https://doi.org/10.1007/978-3-030-68734-2_10

Flame demonstrate the need for forensic capabilities in the incident response phase of an attack [2].

The main fundamental forensic investigation and incident response principles apply for "air-gapped" controllers as much as "non air-gapped" or connected controllers. However, as air-gapped systems are not connected to the enterprise network or common networks such as the internet, a remote and instant incident response is a challenge. This research will try to solve this by introducing a combination of hardware and software that simulates low impact devices which can be used as a bridge to an 802.11 network. The solution needs to be able to communicate remotely with the system, have a small footprint on the system, be scalable and able to perform live forensics and not expose the system to a network.

2 Scenario

2.1 Problem

In 2010, Stuxnet was found to be distributed and infecting air-gapped systems of a nuclear plant to target the PLCs operating the power plant and potentially damage the plant. Since the system was air-gapped, the infection took place using a USB thumb drive. Described in the analysis by Farwell and Rohozinski (2011) [3], the PLCs were operated by engineers onsite using Siemens software, this Siemens Human Interface or HMI was installed on a standard Windows CC operating system. The engineers, operating the HMI, are not experts in live forensics and only use the Siemens software to provide instructions to the PLCs, not the operating system. In case of an incident, providing field engineers with instructions on how to investigate the system live is a risk. In a typical incident scenario, the forensic investigator needs to travel physically to the site to have the option to investigate the air-gap system. Travel time is a big disadvantage in incident response, the state of the system might change a lot, or an attacker might disappear during that travel time. Often air-gap systems are used in hard to reach places such as oil rigs, nuclear plants, military equipment, kiosks, ... and therefore travel time can be long and travel costs can be expensive. This only works against the success rate of the incident response.

2.2 Importance of Remote Live Air-Gap Forensics

Often SCADA use historian servers for storing data and have Human Management Interface (HMI) to display data and controllers to interact with the control systems. Many of these are built on traditional operating systems with special control software to interact with the PCLs [4]. Van der Knijf, in 2014 [5], classified engineering stations (controllers), databases and historians with a priority 3 in value of possible sources of forensic artifacts. The priority was derived by applying the algorithm priority = (2*Likely value) − (effort) + (4*volatility). This makes it a moderate source of value within the investigation strategy [5].

3 Approach

3.1 Common Approach and Its Risks

One might think, simply connecting the air-gap system to a network and use a remote session to perform the forensics real-time is a straightforward approach. This could allow the investigator to connect, authenticate and start the investigation of the HMI. The HMI operating systems often have a longer lifespan and operate critical processes [4, 6]. The introduction of a new network adapter or connection can be risky; a high impact driver change might destabilize the system. Additionally, a network connection might tip off the attacker and even allow for further infection beyond the air-gap system.

To perform live forensic acquisitions on systems, there are two options available. The first one requires the pre-installation of an agent, capable of performing tasks that can extract the data over the network [2]. This is an option frequently used in enterprise networks but can be a challenge in air-gap systems due to the missing connectivity. These agents, usually part of an Endpoint Detection and Response solution are installed on the systems and will connect back to a central server deployed in the cloud or on-premise. The post-installation of an agent on the system can heavily increase the footprint on the air-gap system and requires additional items, such as network connectivity to an on-premise controller or cloud controller. Malware might be monitoring for the installation of agents, after its successful infection, and alter its behavior to avoid detection. A second method is using a modified agent or a tool which are commonly used in incident response to extract or find specific signs of malicious activity. These can be native built-in commands or 3rd party tools such as Mandiant Redline [7].

3.2 Proposed Approach

The goal of this research is to avoid or reduce the risks described in the common approach section. Meanwhile, it wants to respect the air-gap and not introduce any typical network connectivity, by for example connecting an IEEE 802.11 adapter directly to the air-gap system. Instead, it would use a combination of cheap, readily available hardware and custom software which make up a "dongle". To "operate" the air-gap system it would suggest that on one end, the investigator is connected to an IEEE 802.11 network and communicates over TCP/IP with the dongle.

The other end of the dongle is connected via USB to the air-gap system and simulates a keyboard, COM port and two removable drives. This allows a small footprint on the system, connect the air-gap system to the investigator over unlimited distance and should not destabilize the system. The aim is to send keystrokes via a simulated keyboard to the system which would be a substitute of the typing of an investigator behind the keyboard and use a low impact COM port for communicating with a custom written component running on the air-gap system (Fig. 1).

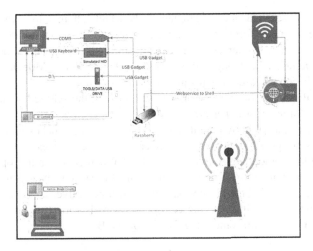

Fig. 1. Overview

The solution needs to be scalable so that multiple systems can be investigated at the same time. This would require some form of the central management system to communicate and interact with the dongles connected to each separate air-gap system. Live forensics does, in contrast with offline forensics, change the state of the system. To respect ACPO rule 2 [8], investigators must demonstrate what and for what reasons changes have been made to the system. The device is simulated on the air-gap system, it allows for setting unique identifiers (i.e.: USB Vendor ID, Device ID) and differentiating itself from other manufacture devices.

Using audit trails and timestamping of the commands issued, the aim is to provide the investigator with enough means to prove the changes and that he/she can demonstrate the impact on the system. The solution will be able to link every executed action on the air-gap system with the original command issued by the investigator. An independent review should be able to prove what commands were executed by the investigator, in light of the investigation. The proposal is to use unique tracking IDs for every executed command, synchronization of time sources using Network Time Protocol (NTP) and sufficient logging.

The final goal for this study is to come up with a solution (named *Forensic Dongle*) that,

- can perform live forensics on air-gap systems
- has a small footprint on the systems
- is scalable
- can respect ACPO rule 2
- is cheap

The research selected and researched tools which attempt to address the same problem of remote live forensics (on air-gap systems). It was the intention to select tools which fall in a similar cost range. The solutions that match closest with the "*Forensic Dongle*", are "Google Rapid Response" (GRR)[1], "Mozilla Investigator" (MIG)[2] and "Facebook osquery" (osquery)[3].

For each of goals, a benchmark or comparison with the selected solutions capable of remote live forensics was performed.

"Facebook osquery" is by default a local solution which makes remote live (real-time) forensics not possible. "Facebook osquery", however, comes with plugins which allow logging to a remote log source (i.e.: syslog). When choosing this option, the tool will query the system using a schedule and send the system data to the remote log source. This makes it, that the last option is not real-time or live. To separately compare these configurations, it will name the configuration with a local logging "osquery A" and the configuration with remote logging "osquery B".

3.3   Overview

The solution exists of 3 major logic components (Fig. 2).

The physical dongle ("*Forensic Dongle*"), which is connected to the air-gap system by a field engineer. The dongles can be used on a regular connected machine as well. The dongle will be able to execute tasks/scripts/commands on the connected host. To operate the dongles in a scalable way, they need to communicate with the "*Forensic Dongle Console*". This VB.NET[4] program serves as a master polling console which allows to task the dongles with different commands in real-time. This central management system also allows adding/remove or edit dongle configurations of expected dongles.

The "*Forensic Dongle Console*" keeps track of the deployed dongles and allows the investigator to submit tasks on multiple hosts involved in the incident in real-time. The third component is the "*Air Controller*", this component is the execution piece on the air-gap system. The program captures the commands from the simulated devices and is responsible for decoding & executing the commands and returning the output over the simulated devices. The program is written in Visual Basic 6.0[5] for maximum compatibility with legacy systems and systems lacking the latest updates and features.

---

[1] https://storage.googleapis.com/releases.grr-response.com/grr-server_3.3.0-4_amd64.deb.

[2] https://github.com/mozilla/mig/archive/20170308-0.e7a93ea.dev.zip.

[3] https://github.com/osquery/osquery/releases/.

[4] https://docs.microsoft.com/en-us/dotnet/visual-basic/.

[5] https://en.wikipedia.org/wiki/Visual_Basic.

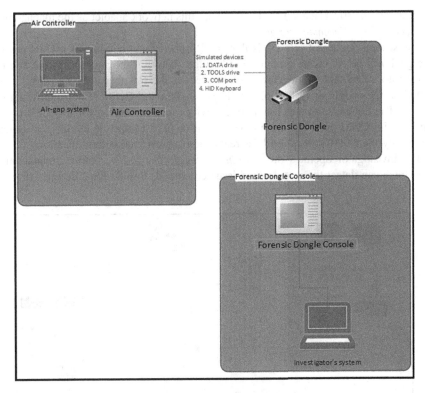

Fig. 2. Major components

4 Goals

4.1 Can it perform remote live forensics on an air-gap system?

There are 3 main aspects to this goal:

- Remote; an investigator must have the ability to be in a different physical location and operate the technology.
- Live forensics; the process of performing analysis and preserving evidence on a running system. This is performed real-time.
- Air-gap; the system has no direct network connection to the investigator or other systems.

Remote. The Raspberry Pi Zero[6] W is a low-cost piece of hardware with limited resources and capable of booting Raspbian OS[7], a Linux variant. There are included two features that will apply of them. One, the Raspberry Pi Zero W comes with an

---

[6] https://www.raspberrypi.org/products/raspberry-pi-zero-w/.

[7] https://www.raspberrypi.org/downloads/raspberry-pi-desktop/.

integrated IEEE 802.11n adapter. That will use this network adapter as the management interface of the *"Forensic Dongle"*.

The second feature of interest is that the Raspberry can be used as a USB device. The goal will be, to create a controlled "bridge" between the air-gap system and the investigator. The 802.11 interfaces, embedded in the Raspberry Pi Zero W, is not hosted on the operating system of the air-gap system and therefore not interfering the air-gap. The dongle simulates low impact devices such as USB keyboard, USB thumb drives and a COM port. All these devices will be used to operate the air-gap system, while only the COM port is used for real-time bi-directional communication.

The investigator operates the *"Forensic Dongle Console"*, a central management tool which can detect the dongles and issue commands to individual dongles (Fig. 3).

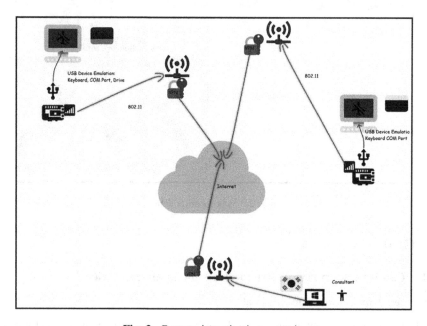

Fig. 3. Remote investigation scenario

For the investigator to address each dongle individually, each dongle needs to be unique. The hostname as a unique identifier for a dongle was chosen. An investigator can change the hostname using the *"Forensic Dongle Console"* or via quick editing a plain-text configuration file. The *"Forensic Dongle Console"* can, by using mDNS, detect all the dongles in the field and does not need to know any IP addresses assigned to the dongle, as they might be assigned by a DHCP server of for example the Wi-Fi access point. The solution deliberately uses mDNS. A field engineer, who is no expert, can just plug in a guest Access Point and connect the dongle. The investigator does not need to send a pre-configured image with fixed IPs in it and this allows him/her the maximum flexibility and speed. Once the *"Forensic Dongle Console"* can "see" the dongle, the investigator can issue an encoded command to the Flask Web service of the dongle. The Web service will pass the command over to the air-gap system via the simulated hardware. A simulation of 4 devices will happen on the air-gap system.

1. A read-only USB Drive containing all the investigator's tools. (i.e.: Microsoft Sysinternals) (TOOLS drive)
2. A writable USB Drive which will be used by the *"Air Controller"* to preserve all captured evidence. (DATA drive)
3. A HID keyboard which will be used to send keystrokes to the system. (i.e.: simulating the investigator behind the keyboard)
4. A COM port which will be used for receiving commands and sending the output back to the investigator.

The commands will be passed through the COM port or the keyboard to the air-gap system. The *"Air Controller"* captures the encoded command and decodes the exact payload. The *"Air Controller"* is then responsible for the execution of the command, capturing of evidence and returning data through the COM port (Fig. 4).

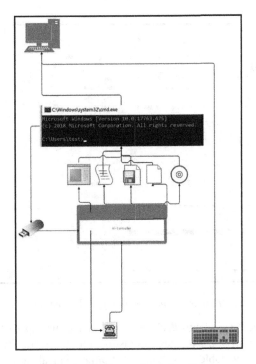

Fig. 4. Hardware simulation flow

When the *"Air Controller"* sends back data, a service running on the dongle called *"Forwarder"* hosts a TCP listener where the *"Forensic Dongle Console"* can retrieve that data from. When comparing the provided solution in this research with the other solutions, it was observed that all, except "osquery A", require a central management system or remote logging server (i.e.: syslog). The IP connections towards these central management solutions must originate from the air-gap system. This will defeat the air gap. The overview can be found in Table 1.

Live Forensics. Live forensics is the capturing and preserving of evidence on systems while they are running. In contrast with dead box or offline forensics, the data which is of interest could be volatile. This means that the data is only available while the system is running, turning off the system might render the evidence useless. The magnitude and type of incident might favour for live forensics, it can be too labor-intensive to perform dead box forensics over multiple systems. As shown in Fig. 1, the "*Forensic Dongle Console*" communicates in real-time with the Flask Web service of each dongle. By using the "*Forensic Dongle Console*" (Fig. 5), the investigator can send commands in real-time to the dongles. The command gets encoded and packaged with a UUID and the "*Forensic Dongle Console*" will send it to the Web service of that specific dongle.

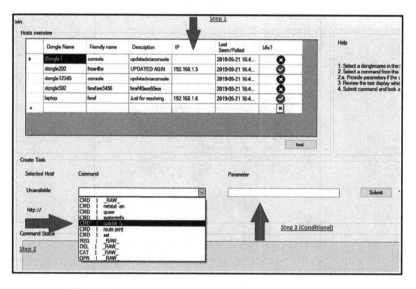

Fig. 5. "*Forensic Dongle Console*" – Issuing a command

In real-time, the "*Air Controller*", running on the air-gap system, intercepts the input of the COM port and executes the instructions received. Two methods of capturing evidence are available. The "*Air Controller*" will always write the details or pieces of evidence on the simulated DATA drive. For each execution, two files will be written, the job details and the job output (evidence). This makes that all details will be easily available for the investigator to analyze. The second method of capturing data is the "*Air Controller*" sending real-time output through the simulated COM port.

A service, called "*Forwarder*", that runs on the dongle, hosts a TCP listener. All data received by the COM port will be streamed to the TCP listener. The output is displayed to the investigator (Fig. 6) through the "*Forensic Dongle Console*", the same tool which is used to issue the commands. This output can only be text, binary captures will not be displayed and only written to the DATA drive for later investigation.

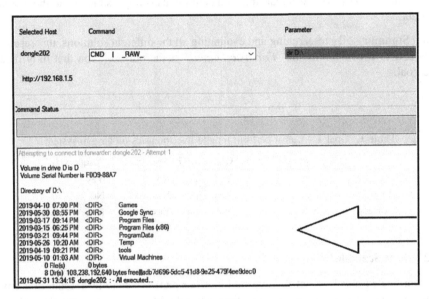

Fig. 6. "*Forensic Dongle Console*" – Real-time output

Air-gap. Air-gap systems are deliberately physically separate and have no connectivity (i.e.: TCP/IP, IPX, ...) to other systems or the internet. Since this approach has been chosen for a security reason, it is important to respect this. To maintain the air-gap aspect of the system and yet being able to operate, choosing for simulating low-impact devices on the air-gap system. The simulated hardware, which is not capable of working as a network controller, is operated in a controlled environment by the investigator.

The air-gap system does not receive any network capability but instead for any two-way communication; a COM port is simulated. By putting this COM port in a controlled environment, from the "*Air Controller*" to the "*Forwarder*", this respects the air-gap. The simulation would probably not tip off an attacker and further infection of other systems remains impossible.

GRR and MIG require a TCP/IP connectivity from the air-gap system to the central controller and is thus not air-gap. Osquery A is a local solution and needs to be operated locally, so the air-gap is maintained, however, the investigator needs to be physically behind the system and there does not meet the first goal as mentioned above. Osquery B requires an IP connection to use alternative logging tested using syslog, and therefore is not air-gapped. Additionally, osquery B requires scheduling of sending the data to the syslog server, as a real-time and continuous is impossible due to the amount of data.

Goal Summary. By researching and evaluating all the different solutions, this research was able to conclude that the *"Forensic Dongle"* is the only solution that fully meets the goal.

Table 1. Goal 1 – Can it perform remote live forensics on air-gap systems?

	Forensic Dongle	GRR	MIG	"osquery A"	"osquery B"
Remote	Yes	Yes	Yes	No	Yes
Live forensics	Yes	Yes	Yes	Yes	No
Air-gap	Yes	No	No	Yes	No

4.2   Is It Scalable?

A coordinated attack might involve multiple (air-gap) systems. In a connected environment, an attacker might be infecting multiple hosts and pivoting through the environment. An attack on multiple air-gap systems would be advanced and requires a good bit of planning but is feasible. In the case of cyber warfare, attacking multiple power plants at the same time would be of significant advantage for the country that is attacking. The enemy's defence will be weakened significantly due to the lack of regular power sources. The goal is to build a flexible solution that allowed an investigator to analyze multiple systems, in real-time and with minimal configuration effort. Every dongle deployed in the field should be similar for the investigator.

When using multiple dongles, it needs to make sure that every dongle is unique, so it is possible to task each dongle with individual commands. The aim for a very simple setup is using the hostname as a unique identifier. When adding a dongle to the *"Forensic Dongle Console"*, 3 parameters are needed (Fig. 7).

- A unique hostname – a unique name which could have no meaning to the investigator (i.e.: dongle + incremental number) (Fig. 7).
- A friendly description – A meaningful name for the investigator to provide transparency over the dongles (Fig. 7).
- A comment or note – A comment to enhance the context of the dongle (Fig. 7).

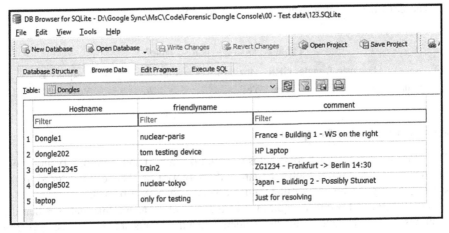

Fig. 7. *"Forensic Dongle Console"* – Dongle list.

Using the hostname and the friendly name, the investigator can create a context of which dongle is placed where. By using the hostname as a unique identifier, the investigator could use mDNS to "discover" the dongles, the investigator does not need to know the IP address assigned to the dongle. This allows the field engineer to just "plug in" the dongle with nothing to configure. The goal here was to make it as easy as possible for the field engineer, all he/she must do, tell what system he/she connects it to. The field engineer should have no ability to configure an address for the dongle or any access to the operating system of the dongle.

The solution also chooses an easy configuration for the investigator. The investigator can prepare dongle (images) upfront by either using the *"Forensic Console Dongle"* or editing a single plain-text configuration file. The image can easily be hosted and has no IP address and only a generic name. The dongle is now ready to be deployed. Once the dongle is plugged in, the *"Forensic Dongle Console"* can discover the dongle and perform a mapping from generic name to friendly name and IP address. This gives maximum flexibility for the investigator.

GRR packages binaries for deployment. The package can be installed on multiple hosts, once the hosts are reporting back to the GRR server, the investigator can use "hunts" to perform investigations on multiple systems, that can be concluded that GRR is scalable.

Mozilla Investigator can be installed on multiple hosts and offers the possibility to prepare tasks, these tasks are distributed to the different agents in batch fashion. It is concluded that MIG is scalable.

Facebook osquery B, using a remote logging mechanism, is scalable and sends data from multiple hosts to the log server. On a scheduled basis, data is collected and sent to a remote logging mechanism. The results of the remote logging can be analyzed using a log analysis tool. It is concluded it is scalable. In contrast with osquery A, where the data is kept locally, and queries must be performed behind the keyboard.

The conclusion is that osquery A is not scalable.

Table 2. Goal 2 – Is it scalable?

	Forensic Dongle	GRR	Mozilla Investigator	"osquery A"	"osquery B"
Scalable	Yes	Yes	Yes	No	Yes

4.3   Has It a Small Footprint?

The goal for having a small footprint is to minimize impact and therefore try and avoid system instability. Additionally, the larger the footprint or changes introduced to the system, the bigger the chance that valuable volatile data will be lost.

GRR, MIG and osquery require the installation of an agent, this makes it that the solutions are less suitable during the incident when the agents are not pre-installed. The *"Forensic Dongle"* is the sole solution which does not require a pre-installed agent and thus can easily be used in an unprepared or uncontrolled environment.

To measure the footprint change, the research focused on areas which are typically affected when changes are introduced due to insertion of hardware, persistence keeping, or file system changes.

- Driver installation
  The *"Forensic Dongle"* solution simulates hardware to achieve the first goal (Remote-Live Forensic on air-gap systems). On a Windows 7 system, an extra driver needs to be installed for the COM port and mass storage simulation to work simultaneously.
- Simulated hardware
  The *"Forensic Dongle"* solution simulates hardware. This area will measure the number of simulated hardware devices that are initialized by Windows.
- Windows Services
  Windows Services is a mechanism to have Windows automatically start programs and DLLs. This mechanism is often used to achieve persistence. These services are started by the Service Control Manager and can be run under a different user context, including high privileged ones, such as SYSTEM.
- Registry Changes
  The number of unique changes is introduced, changed or deleted. These changes can be made for persistence, configuration settings, hardware functionality. The requirement for the change count was that it was directly linked to the technology, not inherited effects of the Operating System. i.e.: MRU...
- Persistent file changes/ additions (Windows, AppData, Program Files, ProgamData, Program Files (x86))
  Persistent file changes which are needed for the functionality of the solution, this could be installation files, DLLs, configuration files, ... Inherited file changes, such as prefetch items are not included in this count.

Table 3. Goal 3 – Has it a small footprint?

	Forensic Dongle		Google Rapid Response		Mozilla Investigator		"osquery"	
	Win7	Win10	Win7	Win10	Win7	Win10	Win7	Win10
Driver installation	1	0	0	0	0	0	0	0
Simulated hardware	4	4	0	0	0	0	0	0
Windows Services	0	0	1	1	1	1	1	1
Registry Changes	46	46	17	17	10	10	0	0
File Changes	1	0	75	75	9	9	20	20

Comparing the impact of the solutions, it shows that GRR, MIG and osquery change the filesystem heavily and are persistent. Even though the *"Forensic Dongle"* generates the most Registry entries, many of them are volatile. And many of them are traceable as shown in 4.4.

The devices simulated to the air-gap system are of low impact, most operating systems have built-in drivers and modules to support these devices.

4.4   Is It Able to Respect ACPO Rule 2?

"In circumstances where a person finds it necessary to access original data, that person must be competent to do so and be able to give evidence explaining the relevance and the implications of their actions" [8].

An investigator needs to be able to demonstrate that actions performed are necessary for the investigation. One necessity is that the investigator can demonstrate the changes he/she made from the normal operational computer activity and/or attacker activity. Therefore, any activity needs to be documented, have an audit trial and timestamps to correlate it back with changes on the filesystem. Within the *"Forensic Dongle"* solution, in this research, it was able to create 3 features that allow an investigator to respect ACPO rule 2 [8]. That incorporated "Unique identification of issued commands", "Timestamps on issued commands" and log capacity on both Central Management side as client-side.

Unique Identification of Issued Commands. To have a full trace of an investigator preparing a command and have it executed on the air-gap system.

The investigator must be able to correlate the output with the original command, so it requires a unique identifier with sufficient randomness. That used Microsoft's implementation of RFC 4122[8] (Fig. 8).

---

[8] https://tools.ietf.org/html/rfc4122.

```
Public Function GenerateID() As String
    GenerateID = System.Guid.NewGuid.ToString()
End Function
```

Fig. 8. "Forensics Dongle Console" – GenerateID().

When issuing a command to a dongle using the "*Forensic Dongle Console*", a UUID (Universally unique identifier) gets generate using GenerateID(). Then prepare command and encode the UUID in the command (Fig. 9).

```
tempUUID = GenerateID()
tempType = Trim(stuk(0))
tempPayload = Trim(stuk(1))

payload = tempUUID & "|" & tempType & "|" & tempPayload
encodedpayload = ConvertBase64(payload)
Log2File(timestamp() & " - " & tempIP & ":3000/payload?ID=" & encodedpayload & " - " & payload, LogFile)
```

Fig. 9. "*Forensic Dongle Console*" – Encoding UUID in command.

The encoded command is passed onto the Flask Web service and without change sent to the COM port. The "*Air Controller*" will then capture this and decode the instructions, containing the UUID (Fig. 10).

```
Function RawSplit(ByVal RAW As String, ByRef refUUID As String, ByRef refCommand As String, ByRef refpayload As String) As Boolean
Dim argNo As Integer
Dim midden As String
argNo = 1
For I = 1 To Len(RAW)
    midden = Mid(RAW, I, 1)
    If midden <> "|" Then
        If argNo = 1 Then
            'UUID
            refUUID = refUUID & midden

        ElseIf argNo = 2 Then
            'COMMAND
            refCommand = refCommand & midden
        Else
            'payload
            refpayload = refpayload & midden
        End If
    Else
        argNo = argNo + 1
    End If
Next I
ID = refUUID
RawSplit = True
End Function
```

Fig. 10. "*Air Controller*" – Parsing UUID RawSplit().

After execution of the parsed instruction, the "*Air Controller*" encodes the output including the UUID and sends it to the investigator (Fig. 11).

```
'Dump Passwords'
If InStr(1, PA, "Dump Password") Then
    Call CMD(ID, toolsDrive & "lazagne.exe")
    DoEvents
    Sleep 1500
    inhoud = SimpleReadFromFile(DataDrive & ID & ".txt")
    SendToConsultant (inhoud)
End If
```

Fig. 11. "Air Controller" – SendToConsultant().

The output is received by the "*Forensic Dongle Console*" via the "Forwarder" service and before the data is presented to the investigator in the output window, the UUID gets parsed out (Fig. 12) and saved in the database (Fig. 13).

```
Dim tijdUUID As String
Dim encodedTempData As String
tijdUUID = GetUUIDfromSTring(tempData)
encodedTempData = ConvertBase64(GetOutputFromString(tempData))
RichTextBox1.SelectionColor = Color.Blue

    RichTextBox1.AppendText(Trim(tempData))
    RichTextBox1.SelectionColor = Color.Green
    RichTextBox1.AppendText(timestamp() & "   " & tempHost & "   :  - All executed..." & vbNewLine)
    RichTextBox1.SelectionStart = Len(RichTextBox1.Text)
RichTextBox1.ScrollToCaret()
Database.InsertOutputPayload(tijdUUID, encodedTempData)
```

Fig. 12. "Forensic Dongle Console" – GetUUIDfromString().

	UUID	timestamp	hostname	type	payload	response
	Filter	Filter	Filter	Filter	Filter	Filter
1	34cb68ed-73f7-4798-a872-29e975e7a7fe	2019-06-4 20:49:10	dongle202	CMD	dir c:\windows	DS8Wb2x1bWUgeW4gZHJpdmtIgQy8dVXMgbm8gbGFIZWvuDS8Wb2x1bWUgU...
2	5c975a12-560e-4cee-9b00-beae86a682e0	2019-06-4 20:49:30	dongle202	CMD	route print	DT09PT09PT09PT09PT09PT09PT09PT09PT09PT09PT09PT09PT09PT09P...
3	a742cc67-9eaa-45d0-b451-e8beb5e973a7	2019-06-4 20:50:08	dongle202	CMD	route print	DT09PT09PT09PT09PT09PT09PT09PT09PT09PT09PT09PT09PT09PT09P...
4	02e7cfd5-45af-47c7-bafc-23645226359a	2019-06-4 20:50:39	dongle202	REG	QUERY HKLM\Software\Micro...	DQ1IS9ViZX0xPQ0FMX0L8Q0hJTkVcU29mdHdhcmvcTWfjcm9zb2Z0XFdpbmRv...
5	211be251-6339-4614-8352-f06d2281475f	2019-06-4 20:50:55	dongle202	EXE	Autorun list	DVbyb2Nic3Ivci8wZXJmb3JtYW9jZS8vYmplY3Qgbm90lSZvdW5sXi9j9uIEx8UFRP...
6	986f0ff9-4d77-42f2-9b74-e2d65e3ae063	2019-06-4 20:51:46	dongle202	CAT	C:\windows\ODBC.ini	DVtFR6J0IDMyISlpdC8EYiXRh3FHvdxJjDXHdDVZpc3VhbC8Gb3hQcm8gVGFbGV...

Fig. 13. "Database" – commands table

Connecting a USB device to a system will generate artifacts in the operating system's registry. Because devices that the "*Forensic Dongle*" simulates are USB based, Windows will generate entries for each of the devices in:

- HKLM\HARDWARE\DEVICEMAP\KeyboardClass\\Device\KeyboardClass2: "\REGISTRY\MACHINE\SYSTEM\ControlSet001\services\kbdclass"
- HKLM\HARDWARE\DEVICEMAP\SERIALCOMM\\Device\USBSER000: "COM4"
- HKLM\SYSTEM\CurrentControlSet\services\Disk\Enum\2: "USBSTOR\Disk&Ven_Linux&Prod_File-Stor_Gadget&Rev_0414\7&d267530& 0&0102030405060708&0"

- HKLM\SYSTEM\CurrentControlSet\services\Disk\Enum\3:
  "USBSTOR\Disk&Ven_Linux&Prod_File-Stor_Gadget&Rev_0414\7&609a70e&
  0&0102030405060708&0"

This allows Windows to make a distinction between the devices. Windows includes SerialID and VendorID in the entries created in the registry (Fig. 14). Therefore, that made it possible to tweak the dongle with custom VendorID and SerialID. These parameters are contained in a text file and can easily be edited manually or by using the "*Forensic Dongle Console*".

```
HKLM\SYSTEM\CurrentControlSet\Enum\USBSTOR\Disk&Ven_Linux&Prod_File-
Stor_Gadget&Rev_0414\7&609a70e&0&0102030405060708&0\Control

HKLM\SYSTEM\CurrentControlSet\Enum\USBSTOR\Disk&Ven_Linux&Prod_File-
Stor_Gadget&Rev_0414\7&d267530&0&0102030405060708&0\Control
```

Fig. 14. Registry – USBSTOR.

Timestamps. The solution exists of several components, capable of generating a timestamp.

- "*Forensic Dongle Console*" – uses the clock of the investigator's workstation
- "*Forensic Dongle*" – uses the clock of the Raspberry Pi
- "*Air Controller*" – uses the clock of the air-gap system

Not all of these are components are in the same time zone and not guaranteed that they are correctly set. To ensure that the timestamps are as reliable as possible, it has opted for NTP. The "*Forensic Dongle Console*" can be synchronized using NTP or Windows time, the time zone is known to the investigator. The "*Forensic Dongle Console*" has the option to set all its timestamps in the local time or UTC. The "*Forensic Dongle*" is by default synchronized using NTP (2.debian.pool.ntp.org) and set to Irish Time.

Since these 2 devices are in control of the investigator the timestamps of these devices can be trusted to be accurate. The investigator can always poll the time of the "*Forensic Dongle*" by using the Flask Web service (http://donglename:3000/time). The "*Air Controller*", however, relies on the time of the air-gap system, this time can be off, purposely set to the wrong time or in the incorrect or different time zone. To counter this, the "*Air Controller*" will capture the time settings and local time of the computer before beginning the investigation (Fig. 15).

```
Public Function TimeSettings() As String
Dim zoneinfo As TIME_ZONE_INFORMATION
Dim bias As Long
Dim tmp As String
tmp = "Timezoneinformation: "
Select Case GetTimeZoneInformation(zoneinfo)
        Case 0:  test = "Cannot determine current time zone"
        Case 1:  test = zoneinfo.StandardName
        Case 2:  test = zoneinfo.DaylightName
    End Select
    tmp = tmp & StripT(CStr(test)) & " -- "

    Select Case GetTimeZoneInformation(zoneinfo)
    Case TIME_ZONE_ID_DAYLIGHT
        dwBias = zoneinfo.bias + zoneinfo.DaylightBias
    Case Else
        dwBias = zoneinfo.bias + zoneinfo.StandardBias
    End Select

    gmt = DateAdd("n", bias, Now)
    test = Trim(Format$(gmt, "yyyy mm dd hh:mm:ss"))
    tmp = tmp & "CurrentGMTTime " & test & " -- "
TimeSettings = tmp
End Function
```

Fig. 15. "Air Controller" – TimeSettings()

As described above, every command executed receives its unique UUID. The UUID gets a timestamp in the *"Forensic Dongle Console"* (Fig. 13).When the *"Air Controller"* captures and saves the evidence on the DATA drive, it will have a local timestamp from the air-gap system. The *"Air Controller"* saves every piece of evidence using the UUID, so the investigator can calculate the time difference between the air-gap system and the time recorded in the *"Forensic Dongle Console"*. The time to generate the evidence and the speed of writing the evidence might influence this calculation. During the research, some of the Sysinternals[9] commands took more than a few seconds. All the job details are also saved in a separate file on the drive, this is written prior execution of the instructions and will have a more accurate representation of the time difference (Fig. 16).

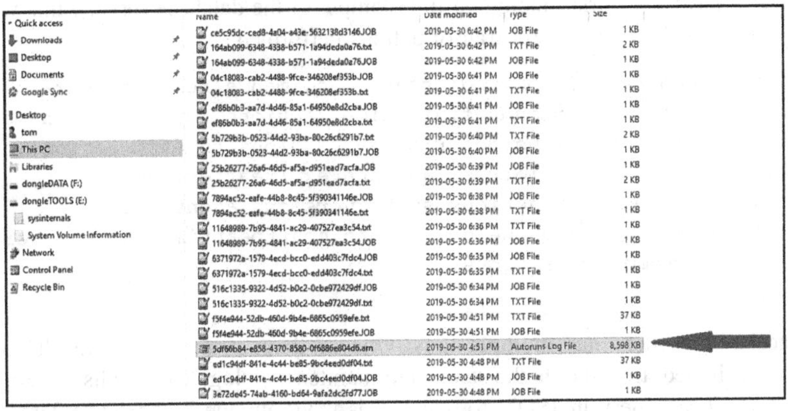

Fig. 16. "Air Controller" – DATA drive timestamps

[9] https://docs.microsoft.com/en-us/sysinternals/.

Logging. Logging takes place in several places of the solution.

- *"Forensic Dongle Console"*
- *"Forensic Dongle"*
- DATA drive (via the *"Air Controller"*)

The *"Forensic Dongle Console"* will have 3 places where logging is made available. The GUI screen will display the status of the console, status of the dongles, command input, command output and error messages, these messages are non-persistent. Within the *"Forensic Dongle Console"*, the solution was created with the option to log most events to a plain-text file. This logging will contain full command input, error messages with timestamps from the investigator's workstation. The most important logging takes place in the database. It will record the UUID, Timestamp, Command Type, Command payload and output in the database.

The *"Forensic Dongle"* will contain logging such as operating system messages and flask Web service messages, all these are NTP synchronized. The *"Air Controller"* will log all job details, received from the dongle on the DATA drive.

These job details will contain the UUID, full payload and type of command. When correlating these 3 log types, the investigator can present a good level of audit that supports his/her actions within the investigation.

Goal Summary. When creating Google Rapid Response "hunts", a batch of tasks is prepared for each client within the criteria set by the investigator. Each of these hunts receives a unique identifier. Every client is assigned a unique identifier and can query the local time. An investigator can combine the timestamp, localtimestamp, huntID and ClientID, to uniquely identify which command was run and when this was running.

The flow of a MIG investigation is that an "investigator" creates an "action" which executes a "command" on an "agent". These elements would allow the unique identification of commands issued. Each of these elements is stored in a separate table in the database and receives a unique ID. When drafting a SQL statement as following, it is possible to have a full trial, including timestamps (of the database server), this will be enough to provide a good audit trial of actions performed.

```
SELECT commands.id, commands.status, commands.results, com-
mands.starttime, commands.finishtime, actions.id, actions.name,
actions.target, actions.description, actions.threat, actions.op-
erations, actions.validfrom, actions.expireafter, ac-
tions.pgpsignatures, actions.syntaxversion, agents.id,
agents.name, agents.queueloc, agents.heartbeattime, agents.ver-
sion FROM commands, actions, agents;
```

Facebook osquery has multiple logs. One of them is the output results of the commands issued, the other is the status and maintenance log. The results log contains the output of the query in JSON format and is made unique by "calendarTime" and "hostIdentifier". Because the "calendarTime" is based on the time of the air-gap system there is no reliability.

Table 4. Goal 4 – Is it able to respect ACPO rule 2?

	Forensic Dongle	Google Rapid Response	Mozilla Investigator	osquery
Unique identification of issued commands	Yes	Yes	Yes	No
Sufficient timestamping	Yes	Yes	Yes	Yes, but unreliable time source
Audit trial	Yes	Yes	Yes	Yes

4.5   Is It Cheap?

The *"Forensic Dongle"* consists of two hardware pieces, a Raspberry Pi Zero W and in this case a Samsung MicroSD 64 GB. During the study, it was able to purchase the Raspberry at 24,90 euro and the Samsung MicroSD at 14,40 euro.

GRR, and Facebook osquery are licensed under the Apache License 2.0 and therefore free for private and commercial use. Mozilla Investigator is free for private and commercial use under the Mozilla License 2.0.

The *"Forensic Dongle"* is the more expensive solution, however, when it benchmarks to one of the original goals, saving on travel costs (+ time), it seems a cheap solution.

A simple example:

- Investigator lived in Munich at the time of writing
- For this example, the *"Forensic Dongle"* costs 39.3€ and a random airport is chosen (KBP – Kyiv Boryspil - Ukraine)
- Using Skyscanner[10] a single flight was chosen from MUC to KBP (Fig. 17)
- A direct price comparison (*"Forensic Dongle"* vs Airline price) comes out at least 5 times cheaper, for the use of 1 dongle. (this excludes the cost of 9h15 travel time of the investigator)

Fig. 17. "Skyscanner" – MUC to KBP

---

[10] https://www.skyscanner.ie.

5 Conclusion

"*Forensic Dongle*" provides functionalities and options that meet in intended goals in this research. The dongle can cover a bridge from the investigator's workstation to the air-gap system without introducing network connectivity on the air-gap system. The emulation of a COM port and keyboard allows the dongle to perform forensic actions whenever the investigator issues the commands, therefore real-time.

The devices, simulated on the air-gap system, are of low impact, most operating systems have built-in drivers and modules to support these. It does not require any pre-installed agent and therefore it does not need major file changes to the operating system. Additionally, it is very uncommon that malware would monitor for these simulated devices and assume that the system is under investigation, in contrast with a pre-installed agent.

With a cost of approximately 40€, the solution is cheap enough to expand it over multiple hosts. The other evaluated solutions are far more scalable and thus a better fit for a very large incident or threat hunting. For smaller incidents, the "*Forensic dongle*" becomes a cheap scalable solution. The biggest advantages of the solution are compared to the other technologies is the true remote air-gap forensics and the lack of the need for a pre-installed agent. With the idea of reducing travel costs, response time and performing forensics on difficult to reach places (i.e.: oilrig, train, medical equipment...), the "*Forensic dongle*" seems a viable solution for these situations.

6 Future Work

6.1 Capabilities

The "*Forensic Dongle*" is a proof of concept, developed within a limited timeframe. Comparing the solution with the other selected technologies, As described above it has been discovered opportunities to expand the capabilities of the "Air Controller". This would allow an investigator to gather forensic artifacts which are currently not possible to capture through the solution. The solution runs under the context of the logged-on user. SYSTEM level execution could be implemented using tools such as psexec and administrative access. The reading of files is currently impossible, which are not captured on the DATA drive first.

6.2 Security

Currently, the "*Forensic Dongle*" relies a lot on trust between the different components. There are currently no security features implemented to assure the integrity of the commands, the authenticity of the commands and the respective output. Many of the components used within the solution are built on default settings and services which are not advised for production use. Future work must be performed to explore options to ensure integrity, availability, and authenticity of the solution.

7 Stabilization and Limitation

During testing and evaluation, it encountered several shortcomings or limitations of the *"Forensic Dongle"*.

The COM port poses a limit on bandwidth; therefore, it is currently impossible to retrieve the large output of commands in real-time. The output will be saved on the simulated DATA drive but not displayed back to the investigator real-time.This could potentially be solved by introducing a timing mechanism and using the fragmentation of the output.

The delivery of the commands to the *"Air Controller"* and the output pass through several asynchronous components. The command passes the web service, the COM port and then the *"Air Controller"*. The output from the *"Air Controller"* goes through the COM port to the "forwarder" and gets picked up by the *"Forensic Dongle Console"*. This method is prone to timing failures and time-outs. Research for more reliable methods of delivery is something needs to explore.

Acknowledgements. This research has received funding from the European Union's Horizon 2020 research and innovation programme under grant agreement No 700381.

References

1. Langner, R.: Stuxnet: dissecting a cyberwarfare weapon. IEEE Secur. Priv. **9**(3), 49–51 (2011)
2. Ahmed, I., Obermeier, S., Naedele, M., et al.: SCADA systems: challenges for forensic investigators. Computer **45**(12), 44–51 (2012)
3. Farwell, J.P., Rohozinski, R.: Stuxnet and the future of cyber war. Survival **53**(1), 23–40 (2011)
4. Zhu, B., Joseph, A., Sastry, S.: A taxonomy of cyber attacks on SCADA systems. In: 2011 International Conference on Internet of Things and 4th International Conference on Cyber, Physical and Social Computing, pp. 380–388 (2011)
5. Van der Knijff, R.M.: Control systems/SCADA forensics, what's the difference? Digital Invest. **11**(3), 160–174 (2014)
6. Spyridopoulos, T., Tryfonas, T., May, J.: Incident analysis & digital forensics in SCADA and industrial control systems. In: 8th IET International System Safety Conference Incorporating the Cyber Security Conference 2013, vol. 2013, no. 620, p. 6a.1 (2013)
7. Wu, T., Jason, N.: Exploring the use of PLC debugging tools for digital forensic investigations on SCADA systems. J. Digital Forensics Secur. Law **10**(4), 79 (2015)
8. Association of Chief Police Officers: New ACPO guide for forensics. Comput. Fraud Secur. **2007**(7), 20 (2007)

A Digital Forensic Approach
for Optimizing the Investigation
of Hit-and-Run Accidents

Marian Waltereit[1]([✉]), Maximilian Uphoff[2], Peter Zdankin[1], Viktor Matkovic[1], and Torben Weis[1]

[1] University of Duisburg-Essen, Duisburg, Germany
{marian.waltereit,peter.zdankin,viktor.matkovic,torben.weis}@uni-due.de
[2] RheinByteSystems GmbH, Oberhausen, Germany
uphoff@rheinbyte.systems

Abstract. We present a novel digital forensic approach that facilitates the investigation of hit-and-run accidents. Based on wheel speeds gathered by forensic data loggers, our approach provides a priority ranking of the suspects in order to optimize further investigations. For this, we propose two investigation steps to get key information about a suspect's trip. First, we analyze the likely traveled routes of a suspect to determine whether the suspect could have been at the accident location. Second, we analyze the driving behavior of the suspect in terms of aggressiveness, since aggressive driving behavior is a major reason for traffic accidents. Our evaluation with real driving experiments shows that our approach is suitable for analyzing likely routes and driving behavior in order to prioritize suspects in an investigation.

Keywords: Digital forensic approach · Hit-and-run accidents · Route reconstruction · Driving behavior · Driving maneuvers

1 Introduction

Today's vehicles are equipped with a variety of inertial sensors to gather vehicle data, enabling the development of digital forensic approaches to investigate crimes involving vehicles. In this context, vehicle data is used to provide digital evidence as a complement to physical evidence [21]. In digital forensic investigations, vehicle data is usually obtained from event data recorders (EDR) integrated in the vehicle [16]. An EDR stores vehicle data covering the time period shortly around an accident. In contrast, forensic data loggers enable continuous gathering of vehicle data from the Controller Area Network (CAN bus) [15,18]. This is beneficial because the entire trip can be considered in the investigation. Forensic data loggers store vehicle data in a manner suitable for forensic investigations by ensuring integrity, authenticity, etc. In the era of connected vehicles, it is also possible to store vehicle data in the cloud [18,25].

S. Goel et al. (Eds.): ICDF2C 2020, LNICST 351, pp. 204–223, 2021.
https://doi.org/10.1007/978-3-030-68734-2_11

In this paper, we focus on the digital forensic investigation of hit-and-run accidents, as the number of hit-and-run accidents increases steadily [24]. Attention to this type of accident is important because a hit-and-run often proves to be fatal, either as a result of the collision or because of refusing first aid [3,24]. Hit-and-run accidents are typically investigated using third-party information such as surveillance cameras or eyewitnesses [8].

As our contribution, we propose a novel digital forensic approach to optimize the investigation of hit-and-run accidents based on in-vehicle data[1]. Our approach comprises two investigation steps. First, we reconstruct and analyze the likely routes of a suspect to determine whether the suspect could have been at the accident location. Then, we analyze the suspect's driving behavior in terms of aggressiveness. For example, we determine whether the suspect engaged in aggressive driving maneuvers near the accident location. This is of particular interest as aggressive driving behavior is a leading cause of traffic accidents [22]. The result of both steps is a priority ranking of suspects that enables law enforcement agencies to optimize subsequent investigations. In case of a hit-and-run, the perpetrator's vehicle often has physical evidence of the accident. By ranking suspects, law enforcement agencies can focus on the likely perpetrators when there are several suspects. This minimizes the risk of covering up physical evidence by the perpetrator.

We use wheel speeds gathered by a forensic data logger in our approach, as the use of wheel speeds is advantageous over other data sources such as GPS or inertial measurement units (IMU). Wheel speeds are available on the CAN bus of contemporary vehicles because of the mandatory anti-lock braking system (ABS) [23]. Thus, our approach is potentially applicable to a large number of today's vehicles. Whereas not every vehicle is equipped with an IMU and GPS is not always available, e.g. when driving in tunnels. Furthermore, wheel speeds are preferable from a data protection and privacy point of view, as our approach shows that wheel speeds are the minimal data set adequate and required for the investigation of hit-and-run accidents. As a result, our approach is in line with the principle of data minimization as defined in the EU General Data Protection Regulation (GDPR) [10]. In addition, wheel speeds are less privacy-invasive than, for example, surveillance cameras or GPS. Unlike surveillance cameras, wheel speeds are focused on the individual and do not monitor several people on suspicion. When GPS data is used, the actual traveled route and all places visited during the trip are revealed. This is particularly problematic if an unauthorized third party gains access to the GPS data. In contrast, wheel speeds can only be used to reveal this information if the area in which the trip took place is known [28,29]. As this information is known in a hit-and-run accident, wheel speeds are suitable for our approach. Although law enforcement agencies can gain insight into the places a suspect might have visited, they cannot clearly determine which of the likely routes the suspect actually took if more than one route is found. Thus, our approach helps law enforcement agencies to focus on

---

[1] A preliminary stage of this research was presented as an extended abstract at the PerCom PhD Forum 2019 [27].

suspects at an early stage, and yet innocent suspects in particular do not need to disclose where they actually traveled.

The rest of this paper is organized as follows. We discuss related work in Sect. 2 and introduce our digital forensic approach in Sect. 3. Then, we present details about both investigation steps in Sects. 4 and 5. In Sect. 6, we demonstrate that the presented approach is well suited for investigating hit-and-run accidents. Finally, we conclude the paper in Sect. 7.

2   Related Work

In our digital forensic approach, we investigate hit-and-run accidents by analyzing likely traveled routes. Existing algorithms for the reconstruction of a driver's likely routes differ in the requirements for the reconstruction and the sensors used. Some approaches require the start and/or the end positions of the trip [11,13], while other approaches require knowledge of the area in which the trip took place [17,20,28,29]. Typically, accelerometer, gyroscope and/or magnetometer readings are used as input data [17,20]. A further way is to use the vehicle's velocity or wheel speeds [11,13,28]. In this paper, the investigation of likely routes is based on an algorithm that we developed in prior work [29]. This algorithm uses distances and turns to determine a driver's likely routes in a given urban area. Distances and turns can be calculated from wheel speeds [28]. An advantage of this algorithm is its robustness against distance and turn errors. Furthermore, the algorithm does not require any additional information about the traveled route besides the area in which the trip took place, e.g. no start and/or end position. Since the perpetrator might lie about his start/end positions, algorithms that require any additional information do not work in forensic approaches. In case of a hit-and-run accident, we know the accident location and adapt the algorithm to leverage this information.

Furthermore, we analyze driving behavior in our digital forensic approach. Most existing algorithms for assessing driving behavior require data from different sources, e.g. accelerometer, magnetometer and GPS [5,7,12]. In our approach, we only use wheel speed sensors as data source, resulting in a minimal data set as explained in Sect. 1. In prior work [30], we introduced a scoring algorithm to measure driving behavior while driving in a driver feedback system. This algorithm calculates acceleration characteristics from the vehicle's wheel speeds and determines the closeness of the driving behavior to a physically unsafe driving situation based on a safety domain introduced by Eboli et al. [12]. Our digital forensic approach, however, focuses on the retrospective analysis of the driving behavior of a suspect in terms of aggressiveness. For this, we introduce severity levels to categorize driving maneuvers at any point of the suspect's trip based on the findings of our prior work [30]. In addition, we incorporate another physical quantity in our behavioral analysis, namely the vehicle's jerk.

In terms of digital forensic investigations, Cebe et al. [8] presented a blockchain-based system for collecting and managing vehicle data and environmental data to address digital forensics for connected vehicles in smart cities with smart infrastructure such as traffic lights. They briefly discuss how to resolve hit-and-run accidents using their system, but only in the sense of recognizing a hit-and-run by proving that a vehicle has fled the accident scene. Our aim is to prioritize suspects for subsequent investigations if a hit-and-run accident has occurred. Furthermore, the approach of Cebe et al. is only designed for connected vehicles in a smart city. In contrast, our approach can potentially be used in a large number of today's vehicles by retrofitting forensic data loggers. The work of Hoppe et al. [15] is most related to our work. They presented a forensic route reconstruction approach using vehicle data gathered by a forensic data logger in order to provide digital evidence in hit-and-run accidents. However, this approach provides only manual or semi-automated route reconstruction. For manual route reconstruction, the vehicle's velocity is used to estimate the traveled distance. If a position of the trip is known, e.g. the start or end position, the traveled route can be manually reconstructed in the street network by plausibility checks, such as verifying whether the estimated distance is correct. For semi-automated route reconstruction, a hardware-based navigation system is used to simulate a trip and generate possible routes based on the gathered vehicle data. However, the semi-automated approach requires a suspected start position and manual configuration as well as interaction steps. Instead, our approach allows for a fully-automated route reconstruction. Al-Kuwari et al. [4] proposed a probabilistic algorithm based on Bayesian inference to reconstruct the likely routes of a suspect when parts of the route are known, e.g. from surveillance cameras and GPS. In contrast to Hoppe et al. and Al-Kuwari et al., we do not require any additional information about the traveled route apart from the already known accident location. This is crucial, as it makes us independent of the possibly untrue statements of the suspects. Finally, in contrast to the other approaches, we consider driving behavior in the investigation and thus advance the state of the art.

3   Digital Forensic Approach

In this section, we provide an overview of our digital forensic approach to optimize the investigation of hit-and-run accidents. In our approach, we assume the following scenario [15,27]: *A law enforcement agency is investigating a traffic accident in which a driver caused bodily injury and fled the accident scene (hit-and-run accident). In addition to the accident location, the law enforcement agency knows the approximate accident time and the vehicle model from eyewitness reports. Based on this information, the number of suspects can be reduced. The suspects' vehicles are equipped with forensic data loggers that continuously store vehicle data such as wheel speeds locally or in the cloud. The law enforcement agency asks the suspects to voluntarily provide the wheel speeds of the trips in question for forensic analysis, comparable to a voluntary DNA profiling in other criminal investigations. The law enforcement agency uses the wheel speeds to find indications of the suspects' involvement in the accident by applying the*

digital forensic approach presented in this paper. This enables the law enforce-
ment agency to prioritize the suspects, e.g. to determine which suspects will be
interrogated first.

We follow the digital forensic process model of the German Federal Office for
Information Security (BSI) [1], which is divided into different phases describing
steps to be taken before, during and after a forensic investigation. This includes,
for example, the installation of forensic data loggers in vehicles to enable continuous gathering and storing of wheel speeds from the CAN bus. Hoppe et al. [15]
also applied this model to the investigation of automotive incidents. In this paper,
we focus on the phases during a forensic investigation, i.e. the inspection and
data analysis phases. The inspection phase involves calculating vehicle-related
data from wheel speeds as preprocessing for the data analysis phase. During
the data analysis phase, we investigate whether a suspect may have committed
the hit-and-run. For more details about the process model, refer to the digital
forensics guideline of the BSI [1]. In the following we describe the course of both
phases in our digital forensic approach.

3.1 Inspection Phase

In the inspection phase, we use the wheel speeds to calculate vehicle-related
data as preprocessing for the data analysis phase. We require a sampling rate
of at least 1 Hz. Furthermore, the wheel speeds must be timestamped by a synchronized clock, as the data is used for forensic purposes. Otherwise, we cannot
determine whether the vehicle of a suspect was driven during the time of the
accident. However, this is a reasonable assumption, since the forensic data logger
can be equipped with a radio clock or the time can be synchronized over the
network if the wheel speeds are stored in the cloud.

We define a wheel speed measurement $\mathcal{W}(t)$ at time t as a tuple of right
and left front wheel speeds $w_{\mathrm{rf}}(t)$ and $w_{\mathrm{lf}}(t)$ as well as right and left rear wheel
speeds $w_{\mathrm{rr}}(t)$ and $w_{\mathrm{lr}}(t)$ (each in ms^{-1}):

$$\mathcal{W}(t) = (w_{\mathrm{rf}}(t), w_{\mathrm{lf}}(t), w_{\mathrm{rr}}(t), w_{\mathrm{lr}}(t)) \tag{1}$$

The vehicle's velocity $v(t)$ (in ms^{-1}) at time t can be estimated as the mean of
the right and left rear wheel speeds $w_{\mathrm{rr}}(t)$ and $w_{\mathrm{lr}}(t)$ [6]:

$$v(t) = \frac{w_{\mathrm{rr}}(t) + w_{\mathrm{lr}}(t)}{2} \tag{2}$$

The first and second derivatives of the velocity $v(t)$ are the longitudinal acceler-
ation $a_{\mathrm{lon}}(t)$ and the longitudinal jerk $j_{\mathrm{lon}}(t)$ respectively. The yaw rate $r(t)$ of
a vehicle at time t can be estimated using the right and left rear wheel speeds
$w_{\mathrm{rr}}(t)$ and $w_{\mathrm{lr}}(t)$ as well as the vehicle's rear track width $\mathcal{T}$ (in m) [6]:

$$r(t) = \frac{w_{\mathrm{rr}}(t) - w_{\mathrm{lr}}(t)}{\mathcal{T}} \tag{3}$$

Neglecting the sideslip angle, the vehicle's heading $\psi(t)$ at time t can be estimated by integrating the yaw rate $r(t)$ [9]:

$$\psi(t) = \int_0^t r(t)\,dt \tag{4}$$

The vehicle's lateral acceleration $a_{\text{lat}}(t)$ can be estimated using the velocity $v(t)$ and the yaw rate $r(t)$, neglecting the sideslip angle [9]:

$$a_{\text{lat}}(t) = v(t) \cdot r(t) \tag{5}$$

The derivative of the lateral acceleration $a_{\text{lat}}(t)$ is the lateral jerk $j_{\text{lat}}(t)$. The vehicle's orientation-independent total acceleration $\|a(t)\|$ is the magnitude of the acceleration vector $(a_{\text{lon}}(t), a_{\text{lat}}(t))$:

$$\|a(t)\| = \sqrt{a_{\text{lon}}(t)^2 + a_{\text{lat}}(t)^2} \tag{6}$$

Accordingly, the vehicle's total jerk $\|j(t)\|$ is the magnitude of the jerk vector $(j_{\text{lon}}(t), j_{\text{lat}}(t))$:

$$\|j(t)\| = \sqrt{j_{\text{lon}}(t)^2 + j_{\text{lat}}(t)^2} \tag{7}$$

3.2 Data Analysis Phase

For the data analysis phase, we propose two investigation steps: (1) investigating the likely routes of a suspect and (2) investigating the driving behavior of a suspect. In the first investigation step, we analyze whether a suspect could have been at the accident location based on the gathered vehicle data. In the second investigation step, we analyze the driving behavior of the suspects and determine which suspects tended to drive aggressively. Furthermore, we investigate whether a suspect performed extreme driving maneuvers, e.g. sudden braking or strong acceleration, near the accident location. We describe both investigation step in detail in Sects. 4 and 5.

Each investigation step provides a ranking of suspects. The smaller the rank of a suspect, the more likely he or she was involved in the accident according to our analysis. We merge the rankings of both investigation steps into a single priority ranking. The smaller the rank of a suspect in each ranking of the investigation steps, the smaller his or her rank in the resulting priority ranking (where a small rank means a high priority). Due to the prioritization of suspects, we do not risk dropping the perpetrator as a suspect. We suggest to consider high-ranked suspects first in subsequent investigations.

4 Investigating Likely Routes

The aim of investigating the likely routes of the suspects is to determine which of the suspects could have been at the accident location and should thus be considered as possible perpetrators. In the following, we first present the reconstruction of likely routes. Then, we describe how to analyze the likely routes of a suspect in an investigation.

4.1   Reconstruction of Likely Routes

In order to reconstruct the likely routes of a suspect, we use an algorithm that determines the likely routes of a driver in a given urban area using the distances and turns caused by traveling the route [29]. Distances and turns as a representation of a route are used, for example, in turn-by-turn navigation to guide travelers to their destination. The basic idea of the route reconstruction algorithm is to map the distances and turns onto the street network of the trip area using a dynamic programming-based approach, resulting in a list of likely routes [29].

However, mapping distances and turns onto the street network is error prone due to measurement errors [29]. In case of a hit-and-run accident, the measured distances may not exactly match the distances in the street network, e.g. due wheel spin caused by an emergency braking followed by strong acceleration. In terms of turns, a *false positive* (*FP*) turn error can occur when a turn was measured although there was no junction in the street network. This type of error can be caused, for example, by an evasive maneuver in an accident. A *false negative* (*FN*) turn error can occur when a turn was not measured although there was a junction in the street network, e.g. due to a very slight turn. As stated in Sect. 2, the route reconstruction algorithm is robust against distance and turn errors and thus suitable for the investigation of hit-and-run accidents. The algorithm allows for an absolute distance deviation of up to ϵ_d percent. The number of tolerable *FP* and *FN* turn errors is denoted as ϵ_{FP} and ϵ_{FP} respectively. The algorithm ranks the reconstructed likely routes according to their distance and turn errors. The smaller the rank, the more likely a reconstructed route is to match the traveled route [29].

Below, we first show how to calculate distances and turns from the vehicle-related data introduced in Sect. 3.1. Then, we present how to determine the urban area in which the likely routes are reconstructed.

Distances and Turns. We use the vehicle-related data introduced in Sect. 3.1 to calculate the distances and turns as input for the route reconstruction algorithm. A turning maneuver is characterized by a significant change in the vehicle's heading $\psi(t)$. We consider an absolute change in heading of 20° between two times t_i and t_j with $i < j$ as significant. This allows for the recognition of turning maneuvers with interruptions, e.g. due to oncoming traffic. However, to minimize the chance of classifying a lane change or a slight curve as a turn, there must be an absolute change in heading of at least 10° within a single time step [20]. If the heading change is positive, the vehicle is turning *left*. A turn is also considered to be a *U-turn* if the positive heading change exceeds 160°. If the heading change is negative, the vehicle is turning *right*. We approximate the distance traveled between two consecutive turns by integrating the vehicle's velocity $v(t)$ over time.

Trip Area. The algorithm is capable of reconstructing likely routes in urban areas of about $1200\,\text{km}^2$, as we demonstrated in prior work [29]. A hit-and-run accident, however, provides information that can be used to significantly narrow down the area in which the perpetrator must have been driving (referred to as *trip area*). We use the accident location and the total distance d of a suspect's trip (in km) to approximate the trip area as a rectangle on the street network map with the accident location at the center. The street network is modeled as a graph. Streets and parts of streets are vertices (also referred to as *segments*) and turns between these streets are edges [29]. The trip area is bounded by the geographic coordinates (ϕ^-, λ^-) and (ϕ^+, λ^+), where ϕ denotes the latitude and λ the longitude (both in rad). Given the geographic coordinates of the accident location (ϕ_a, λ_a) in rad and the earth radius R in km, the bounding coordinates (ϕ^-, λ^-) and (ϕ^+, λ^+) are calculated as follows [19]:

$$\phi^- = \phi_a - \frac{d}{R}, \quad \phi^+ = \phi_a + \frac{d}{R} \tag{8}$$

$$\lambda^- = \lambda_a - \arcsin\left(\frac{\sin(\frac{d}{R})}{\cos(\phi_a)}\right), \quad \lambda^+ = \lambda_a + \arcsin\left(\frac{\sin(\frac{d}{R})}{\cos(\phi_a)}\right) \tag{9}$$

The trip area includes all locations within a distance d from the accident location [19]. Thus, the trip area includes all locations to which the perpetrator could have traveled from the accident location after committing the accident.

4.2 Analysis of Likely Routes

By analyzing the likely routes of a suspect, we address the question:

Did the suspect take a route that leads through the accident location?

In prior work [29], we found that the traveled route is among the 10 best ranked likely routes in 97% cases if no turn errors occurred. However, the probability does not increase significantly if more than 10 likely routes are considered. Thus, we suggest to consider the 10 best ranked likely routes in the analysis. However, it is not our goal to determine the exactly traveled route of a suspect. In our hit-and-run scenario, it is sufficient to show that a suspect could have been at the accident location.

To determine which suspects are likely to have driven along the accident location, we introduce a score s for the accident location. The higher the number of likely routes that include the accident location, the higher the score. In addition, the score is the higher, the better these likely routes are positioned among the 10 best ranked likely routes. A suspect is more likely to have driven along the accident location if the accident location has a comparatively high score. To calculate the score for a suspect, we first need the ranking position of each likely route among the 10 best ranked likely routes (denoted as p). The set P contains the ranking positions p of all likely routes that include the accident location. Using the ranking positions P, the score s of the accident location is calculated as follows:

$$s = \begin{cases} 0 & \text{if the accident location is not on a likely route} \\ \sum_{p \in P} \frac{1}{p} & \text{otherwise} \end{cases} \tag{10}$$

If there is a likely route among the 10 best ranked likely routes that includes the accident location, the score of the accident location is greater than 0, indicating that the suspect could have been at the accident location. Since we consider the 10 best ranked likely routes, the maximum score is about 2.93, meaning that the accident location is located on all of the 10 likely routes.

For the trip of each suspect, we determine the 10 best ranked likely routes and calculate the score of the accident location. We rank the suspects according to their scores in descending order. In the resulting ranking, the suspect at position 1 has most likely driven along the accident location. Accordingly, the higher the rank of a suspect, the less likely it is that the suspect drove along the accident location.

5   Investigating Driving Behavior

By investigating the driving behavior of the suspects, we aim to find out which of the suspects tended to drive aggressively during the trip in question and in particular near the accident location. In the following, we first introduce the assessment of the severity of driving maneuvers. Then, we describe how the driving behavior of suspects can be analyzed based on the severity of driving maneuvers.

5.1   Severity of Driving Maneuvers

We introduce the following severity levels with numerical values for assessing driving maneuvers (in ascending order): *not severe (1), low (2), medium (3), high (4),* and *extreme (5)*. Since the wheel speed measurements are a time series (see Sect. 3.1), we can assign one of the severity levels to each time t of the trip. The severity level of the driving maneuver performed at time t is determined using the vehicle's total acceleration and total jerk as introduced in Sect. 3.1. First, we calculate an individual severity level for each of the two aforementioned quantities, resulting in two possible severity levels for time t. Then, we assign the maximum of these two possible severity levels to the time t as the severity level of the driving maneuver performed at time t. As a result, we have a severity level for each time t of the trip in question.

Total Acceleration. We use the vehicle's total acceleration $\|a(t)\|$ (see (6)) to determine the severity of driving maneuvers. The advantage of using the total acceleration is that it is composed of longitudinal and lateral acceleration. Thus, the total acceleration covers three components (acceleration, braking and turning) that are sufficient to represent all types of driving maneuvers [26].

In order to determine the severity of driving maneuvers, we utilize a threshold $\theta_{v(t)}$ introduced by Eboli et al. [12]. This threshold is based on physical limitations of vehicle dynamics and depends on the velocity of the vehicle. The threshold $\theta_{v(t)}$ (in ms^{-2}) is calculated with the vehicle's velocity $v(t) \leq 150 \, km \, h^{-1}$ as

Table 1. Conditions for determining the severity of a driving maneuver based on the total acceleration $\|a(t)\|$ and the total jerk $\|j(t)\|$.

Conditions for $\|a(t)\|$	Conditions for $\|j(t)\|$	Severity of maneuver (numerical value)
$\|a(t)\| < 0.3 \cdot \theta_{v(t)}$	$\|j(t)\| < 2$	not severe (1)
$0.3 \cdot \theta_{v(t)} \leq \|a(t)\| < 0.53 \cdot \theta_{v(t)}$	$2 \quad \leq \|j(t)\| < 4.67$	low (2)
$0.53 \cdot \theta_{v(t)} \leq \|a(t)\| < 0.77 \cdot \theta_{v(t)}$	$4.67 \leq \|j(t)\| < 7.33$	medium (3)
$0.77 \cdot \theta_{v(t)} \leq \|a(t)\| < \quad \theta_{v(t)}$	$7.33 \leq \|j(t)\| < 10$	high (4)
$\theta_{v(t)} \leq \|a(t)\|$	$10 \quad \leq \|j(t)\|$	extreme (5)

follows:

$$\theta_{v(t)} = g \cdot \left[0.198 \cdot \left(\frac{v(t)}{100} \right)^2 - 0.592 \cdot \frac{v(t)}{100} + 0.569 \right], \tag{11}$$

where g is the gravitational acceleration on Earth [12]. However, the threshold is only defined for velocities up to $150\,\mathrm{km\,h^{-1}}$ [12]. Thus, we calculate the threshold with $v(t) = 150\,\mathrm{km\,h^{-1}}$ for velocities greater than $150\,\mathrm{km\,h^{-1}}$.

If the total acceleration $\|a(t)\|$ exceeds the threshold $\theta_{v(t)}$, the severity of the driving maneuver is *extreme* because it is physically unsafe to drive the vehicle under these conditions [12]. On the other hand, driving is safe if the total acceleration is below the threshold $\theta_{v(t)}$ [12]. To have a more fine-grained assessment of the severity, we introduce the conditions listed in Table 1 to determine the severity of a driving maneuver based on the total acceleration $\|a(t)\|$. Assuming that a hit-and-run accident leads to a total acceleration close to or above the threshold $\theta_{v(t)}$, we set the limit for *extreme* severity to 100% of the threshold $\theta_{v(t)}$ to reflect an unsafe driving condition. In prior work [30], we found a total acceleration of less than 30% of the threshold $\theta_{v(t)}$ to be a suitable indicator for non-aggressive driving behavior. Thus, we set the limit for *low* severity to 30%. The remaining limits are evenly distributed between these boundaries.

Total Jerk. We also use the vehicle's total jerk $\|j(t)\|$ to determine the severity of driving maneuvers. In terms of driving comfort, a total jerk of $1\,\mathrm{ms^{-3}}$ is considered comfortable and a total jerk of $2\,\mathrm{ms^{-3}}$ is still acceptable [31]. In extreme situations, however, the total jerk can exceed $10\,\mathrm{ms^{-3}}$ [31]. We introduce the conditions specified in Table 1 to determine the severity of a driving maneuver based on the total jerk $\|j(t)\|$. We set the limit for *low* severity to $2\,\mathrm{ms^{-3}}$, as this is still an acceptable value for the total jerk. Based on Wei et al. [31], we set the limit for *extreme* severity is set to $10\,\mathrm{ms^{-3}}$. The remaining limits are evenly distributed between these boundaries.

5.2 Analysis of Driving Behavior

In this section, we introduce the use of the severity levels to analyze the driving behavior of a suspect with respect to the following questions:

1. Did the suspect drive aggressively?
2. Did the suspect perform risky driving maneuvers near the accident location?

To answer the first question, the likely routes found in the first investigation step are not required. Thus, the investigation of this question is independent of the first investigation step and can be addressed even if no likely routes were found. For the second question, however, we use the likely routes. A suspect may have been involved in the hit-and-run accident if the driving behavior of the suspect was aggressive or the suspect performed risky driving maneuvers near the accident location.

Did the Suspect Drive Aggressively? As stated in Sect. 5.1, at any time t of the suspect's trip, we have the severity level of the driving maneuver performed at time t. Using this information, we can assess the aggressiveness of suspects by evaluating the expected severity level of each suspect's trip.

Let X represent the severity level $l \in \{not\ severe, low, medium, high, extreme\}$ of a driving maneuver performed a time t within a suspect's trip. The possible values of X are $1, 2, 3, 4, 5$ for the severity levels *not severe*, *low*, *medium*, *high* and *extreme* (see Sect. 5.1). Within the trip of a suspect, the severity levels l occur with the empirical probabilities f_l. We calculate the severity rating r of a suspect's trip as the expected value of X as follows:

$$r = E[X] = f_{not\ severe} + 2 \cdot f_{low} + 3 \cdot f_{medium} + 4 \cdot f_{high} + 5 \cdot f_{extreme} \quad (12)$$

The more the distribution of severity levels shifts towards the extreme level, the higher the rating. Therefore, a higher rating means a more aggressive driving behavior during the trip.

By sorting the suspects in descending order according to the severity ratings, we obtain a ranking that expresses the aggressiveness of the suspects relative to each other. The position in the ranking is related to the possible involvement in the hit-and-run accident, because aggressive driving increases the risk of accidents [2]. The smaller the rank of a suspect in the aggressiveness ranking (due to a high severity rating), the more aggressive the driving behavior was compared to the other suspects. However, the perpetrator may have a high rank if other suspects have driven more aggressively. For documentation purposes, we suggest to depict the severity ratings of all suspects in descending order to illustrate the aggressiveness ranking.

Did the Suspect Perform Risky Driving Maneuvers Near the Accident Location? Although the approximate accident time is known in our scenario (see Sect. 3), we refrain from using this information in answering the question whether a suspect performed risky driving maneuvers such as sudden braking or strong acceleration near the accident location. The time period in which the accident happened could be long and cover a large part of the trip. Consequently, the approximate accident time is not a suitable information to investigate the question addressed in this section. In contrast, the accident location is typically precise.

We use the likely routes found in the first investigation step to determine whether a suspect performed risky driving maneuvers near the accident location, i.e. maneuvers with high or extreme severity. Each of the likely routes that includes the accident location provides a point in the suspect's trip where the accident could have occurred. For each of these likely routes, we can determine the presence of risky driving maneuvers at the point where the accident could have occurred, as we are able to determine the severity level of a suspect's driving maneuver at any point of a trip (see Sect. 5.1). The presence of risky maneuvers near the accident location for any of the likely routes is an indication of an accident. We use this information to refine the aggressiveness ranking obtained in Sect. 5.2 by positioning all suspects with risky driving maneuvers near the accident location above those without risky driving maneuvers near the accident location.

For documentation purposes, the numerical values of the severity levels, i.e. $1, 2, 3, 4, 5$ for *not severe*, *low*, *medium*, *high* and *extreme*, can be plotted against distance traveled. Using this figure, risky driving maneuvers near the accident location can be easily identified.

6 Evaluation

In the following, we evaluate our digital forensic approach. First, we describe the data sets used in the evaluation. Then, we evaluate the investigation of likely routes and the investigation of driving behavior as presented in Sects. 4 and 5. Finally, we outline how to use our digital forensic approach in an investigation.

6.1 Data Sets

We collected two data sets to evaluate the investigation steps. Both data sets include wheel speeds gathered while driving a Ford C-Max. The wheel speeds were recorded at 100 Hz by a Raspberry Pi 2 connected to the vehicle's CAN bus. However, we sample the wheel speeds down to 1 Hz as this is sufficient for our approach. Below we briefly describe the characteristics of each data set.

Data Set 1. We performed a total of eight trips with different driving behavior in the urban area of Duisburg in Germany to create our first data set (referred to as data set D_1). Besides the wheel speeds, we also gathered GPS data as ground truth. We use this data set in the evaluation of both investigation steps.

First, we let the two drivers A and B drive the same route in a calm manner (referred to as *calm trips*). The route of these trips consists of 13 turns and has a total distance of about 3.5 km. For both drivers, we measured these 13 turns and thus have no turn errors. Then, both drivers drove the route again in a considerably more aggressive manner (referred to as *aggressive trips*). We measured 14 turns for driver A and 12 for driver B. Thus, we have one *FP* turn error for driver A and one *FN* turn error for driver B. A few weeks before, the two drivers drove a comparable route in a normal manner, i.e. without any instruction regarding the driving behavior (referred to as *normal trips*). The route of these two trips consists of 13 turns and has a total distance of about 4 km. For driver A, we measured 14 turns, i.e. we have one *FP* turn error. We measured 13 turns for driver B. Finally, the two drivers drove around the university building once each and performed an emergency braking followed by strong acceleration as typical maneuvers in hit-and-run accidents (referred to as *accident trips*). The route of these two trips consists of four turns and has a total distance of about 625 m. We measured four turns for both drivers A and B.

Data Set 2. To create our second data set (referred to as data set D_2), a driver performed three driving maneuvers that are common in accidents: emergency braking, evasive maneuver and change of direction [14]. We use this data set in the evaluation of the second investigation step. We instructed the driver to perform each maneuver three times with increasing aggressiveness, i.e. from *low* to *medium* to *high* aggressiveness.

6.2   Investigation of Likely Routes

In this section, we evaluate the first investigation step. This investigation step addresses the question *"Did the suspect take a route that leads through the accident location?"* and provides a ranking of suspects, expressing which suspects most likely drove along the accident location (see Sect. 4.2). We evaluate this investigation step using the trips from the data set D_1.

Throughout the evaluation, we consider two cases: 1) the suspect drove along the accident location and 2) the suspect did not drive along the accident location. The suspects of the first case are potential perpetrators and should be positioned at the top of the ranking, whereas the suspects of the second case are innocent should be positioned at the bottom of the ranking. We analyze the risk of considering potential perpetrators as innocent and innocent suspects as potential perpetrators. In addition, we analyze the risk that potential perpetrators will be at the bottom of the ranking and innocent suspects at the top.

In the following, we first provide the algorithm parameters used in our evaluation as well as information about the trip areas of data set D_1. Then, we present the results of the evaluation with regard to the two cases mentioned above.

Algorithm Parameters and Trip Area. For each trip of data set D_1, we determine the 10 best ranked likely routes as suggested in Sect. 4.2. We set the tolerable distance error ϵ_d to 15% [29]. We determine the number of tolerable *FN* and *FP* turn errors ϵ_{FN} and ϵ_{FP} depending on the number of measured turns, resulting in a turn error tolerance that is comparable to the distance error tolerance. If n turns were measured, we calculate ϵ_{FN} and ϵ_{FP} using the method of round half away from zero (denoted as $\lfloor \rceil$):

$$\epsilon_{FN} = \epsilon_{FP} = \lfloor 0.15\, n \rceil \tag{13}$$

Table 2. Parameters of the route reconstruction algorithm as well as information about the trip area for each trip in data set D_1. The road density is the ratio of the length of the area's road network (in km) to the area's size (in km^2).

Trip	Driver	ϵ_{FN}	ϵ_{FP}	Size of trip area	Road density
Calm	A	2	2	65.9 km^2	10.7
Calm	B	2	2	66.1 km^2	10.7
Normal	A	2	2	86.7 km^2	10.6
Normal	B	2	2	86.4 km^2	10.6
Aggressive	A	2	2	65.8 km^2	10.7
Aggressive	B	2	2	65.9 km^2	10.7
Accident	A	1	1	2.1 km^2	20.5
Accident	B	1	1	2.1 km^2	20.7

In an investigation, we would use the accident location to determine the trip area in which the perpetrator must have been driving (see Sect. 4.1). However, the trips of data set D_1 do not include real accidents. Thus, we use the central point of each trip to determine the respective trip area instead. For each segment in the trip area, we assume that an accident has happened on this segment, which leads to a complete analysis of the trip area. We calculate the central point of the trip as the coordinate (ϕ_c, λ_c) using the latitudes ϕ and longitudes λ of the trip:

$$(\phi_c, \lambda_c) = (\frac{\min(\phi) + \max(\phi)}{2}, \frac{\min(\lambda) + \max(\lambda)}{2}) \tag{14}$$

Using this central coordinate and the total distance of the respective trip, we determine the bounding coordinates of the trip area as described in Sect. 4.1. However, we increase trips's total distance by 15% to account for any distance errors. Table 2 provides the tolerable *FN* and *FP* turn errors ϵ_{FN} and ϵ_{FP} as well as information about the trip area for the trips from data set D_1.

Case: The Suspect Drove Along the Accident Location. We estimate the risk of considering a potential perpetrator as innocent to be low. For all trips from data set D_1, the traveled route is among the 10 best ranked likely routes with ranking positions between 1 and 6. As a result, we would have considered all drivers from data set D_1 as possible perpetrators if the accident had happened on the traveled routes.

Moreover, we estimate the risk of positioning potential perpetrators at the lower end of the ranking to be low. In contrast, potential perpetrators are likely to be put at the top of the ranking of the first investigation step. Among the likely routes, segments located on the traveled route have on average a higher score than segments that are not located on the traveled route (2.27 vs. 0.42). Thus, all drivers of data set D_1 would be positioned at the top of the ranking if the accident had happened on a segment located on their traveled routes.

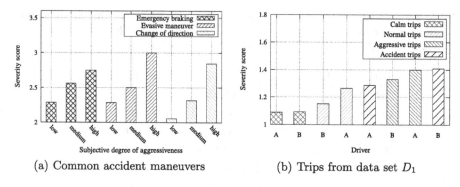

Fig. 1. (a) Shows the severity ratings of common accident maneuvers (emergency braking, evasive maneuver and change of direction) from data set D_2 performed with increasing aggressiveness (*low*, *medium*, *high*). The severity rating increases with increasing aggressiveness. (b) Shows the severity ratings of the trips from data set D_1. The severity ratings are sorted in ascending order. The severity ratings correctly represent the respective driving behavior.

Case: The Suspect Did Not Drive Along the Accident Location. Overall, we estimate the risk of considering an innocent suspect as a potential perpetrator to be low, since for the trips from data set D_1 on average only 0.4% of all segments in the trip area are located on a likely route, but not on the traveled route. However, for an innocent suspect to be considered a potential perpetrator, an accident must have happened on one of these segments.

We estimate the risk of considering an innocent suspect as a potential perpetrator to be highest if the suspect's traveled route is short and common in urban areas. The route of the accident trips is short and less unique in the trip area than the routes of other trips. For the accident trips, the proportion of segments that could lead to considering an innocent suspect as a potential perpetrator is higher than for the other trips, namely 6.8%, leading to an increased risk.

Finally, we estimate the risk of positioning innocent suspects at the top of the ranking to be low. Overall, most segments that are located on a likely route, but not on the traveled route, have a comparatively low score with a mean value of 0.42. Thus, all drivers of data set D_1 are likely to be positioned at the bottom of the ranking if an accident had occurred on one of these segments. In contrast, potential perpetrators are likely to be positioned above the innocent suspects as we found in Sect. 6.2.

6.3   Investigation of Driving Behavior

In the following, we evaluate the second investigation step. In this investigation step, we rank the suspects according to the aggressiveness of their driving behavior. Furthermore, we determine the presence of risky driving maneuvers near the accident location to refine the ranking.

Aggressiveness of Driving Behavior. In this section, we evaluate the severity rating introduced in Sect. 5.2. The severity rating is used to address the question *"Did the suspect drive aggressively?"* phrased in Sect. 5.2.

Severity of Driving Maneuvers. First, we evaluate whether the severity rating can be used to distinguish between different degrees of severity of driving maneuvers. This is the fundamental prerequisite for the analysis of the driving behavior of a suspect during his or her entire trip. We use the common accident maneuvers (emergency braking, evasive maneuver and change of direction) from data set D_2 that were performed with increasing aggressiveness (*low, medium, high*).

For each of the accident maneuvers, we calculate the severity rating as defined in (12). The results are illustrated in Fig. 1(a). For each accident maneuver, the severity rating is higher, the higher the aggressiveness with which the accident maneuver was performed. Thus, we conclude that the severity rating can be used to distinguish between different degrees of severity of driving maneuvers. For the emergency braking, the severity rating increases from 2.29 to 2.75 when increasing the subjective degree of aggressiveness from *low* to *high*. The severity ratings of the evasive maneuvers with a *low, medium* and *high* degree of aggressiveness are 2.29, 2.5 and 3 respectively. For the change of direction maneuver, the severity rating increases from 2.06 to 2.85 as the degree of aggressiveness is raised from *low* to *high*.

Assessment of Driving Behavior. Next, we evaluate whether the severity rating-based ranking expresses the aggressiveness of the suspects relative to each other. Here, we consider the entire trips of the suspects. We use the eight trips from data set D_1. These trips include calm, normal and aggressive driving behavior as well as accident maneuvers.

We calculate the severity rating for each trip and sort the trips according to their severity ratings, resulting in a ranking of the drivers. The results are shown in Fig. 1(b). Overall, the severity ratings are in line with the ground truth of our data set, as the severity ratings of the calm and normal trips are lower than the ratings of the aggressive and accident trips. Hence, the severity rating increases with increasing aggressiveness of the driver. We conclude that the severity rating is suitable for representing different kinds of driving behaviors. Furthermore, the ranking of the trips expresses the aggressiveness of the drivers relative to each other and can thus be used to rank the suspects in an investigation as described in Sect. 5.2.

Presence of Risky Driving Maneuvers. In the following, we evaluate whether our approach can be used to determine the presence of risky driving maneuvers such as sudden braking or strong acceleration within a trip. This information is used to address the question *"Did the suspect performed risky driving maneuvers near the accident location?"* phrased in Sect. 5.2.

We use the two accident trips from data set D_1, in which the drivers performed a common accident maneuver, i.e. emergency braking followed by strong

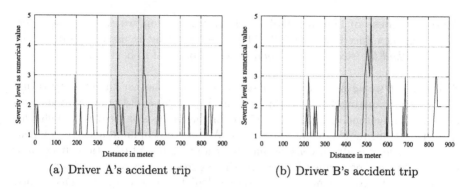

(a) Driver A's accident trip   (b) Driver B's accident trip

Fig. 2. Severity levels plotted as numerical values (1, 2, 3, 4, 5 for *not severe*, *low*, *medium*, *high* and *extreme*). For both trips, there are extreme driving maneuvers when the accident maneuver was performed (highlighted in red). (Color figure online)

acceleration, after the second turn (see Sect. 6.1). For each trip, we rate the driving maneuvers as described in Sect. 5.1, resulting in a severity level for each time step of the trip. Figure 2 shows the severity levels of the driving maneuvers plotted as numerical values against the distance traveled as suggested in Sect. 5.2. The distance ranges in which the accident maneuvers were performed are highlighted in red. For both drivers, there are risky driving maneuvers with high and/or extreme severity in the respective distance range. As a result, there are indications of potential accidents in both trips. This demonstrates that our approach is well suited to discover risky driving maneuvers at a certain position of the route, e.g. near the accident location.

6.4   Using the Digital Forensic Approach in an Investigation

Here, we briefly outline how our digital forensic approach can be used in an investigation. We use data set D_1 and assume that the trips from data set D_1 were performed by different suspects. Furthermore, we assume that the accident happened at the location where the accident maneuvers of the accident trips were performed (see Fig. 2). Thus, the perpetrator is among the drivers of the accident trips and we expect these drivers to be positioned at the top of the priority ranking.

First, we analyze the likely routes of the suspects, resulting in a first ranking of suspects. The score of the accident location for the drivers of the normal and the accident trips are higher than for the other drivers, as these trips include the accident location. However, the score for the normal trips is higher than the score for the accident trips. Thus, the drivers of the normal trips are positioned above the drivers of the accident trips. The other drivers are positioned behind the drivers of the normal and the accident trips.

Next, we analyze the driving behavior, resulting in a second ranking of suspects. Figure 1(b) shows the ranking of the suspects based on the severity rating of their trips. The drivers of the aggressive and the accident trips are ranked above the other drivers. As Fig. 2 shows, there are risky driving maneuvers with high and/or extreme severity near the accident location for both accident trips, whereas there are no such maneuvers for the other trips. Thus, we can refine the ranking shown in Fig. 1(b), resulting in drivers of the accident trips being ranked above the drivers of the other trips.

We combine both aforementioned rankings into a single priority ranking. In the first ranking, the drivers of the accident trips are ranked at positions 3 and 4 and in the second ranking at positions 1 and 2. Finally, these suspects are positioned at the top of the final priority ranking and are prioritized in subsequent investigations.

7   Conclusion

We presented a novel digital forensic approach for optimizing the investigating hit-and-run accidents. For data protection and privacy reasons our approach is solely based on wheel speeds. This data is easy to gather if the vehicles are equipped with forensic data loggers and is available even when GPS is not, e.g. in tunnels or between tall buildings. We analyze the wheel speeds to identify the following key information about a suspect and his or her trip:

1. The possibility that a suspect took a route that led him or her through the accident location.
2. An analysis of the driving behavior of a suspect in terms of aggressiveness compared to the other suspects.
3. A rating of the driving behavior near the accident location to determine whether the suspect engaged in aggressive and risky driving maneuvers.

Based on this information, law enforcement agencies can prioritize suspects for subsequent investigations. This allows to focus on suspects which have most likely traveled along the accident location and had a suspicious driving behavior. This could make investigations more efficient and minimize the risk of covering up physical evidence. In contrast to GPS analysis, our approach only generates a list of likely routes that the suspect could have taken. For innocent suspects this implies that their whereabouts cannot be exactly identified, but law enforcement agencies can assign a low priority to them nonetheless.

For future work, we suggest to extend our approach by determining whether a suspect was actually driving the vehicle during the trip in question or whether another person was driving the vehicle. Future work could also investigate whether the driving behavior of a suspect became aggressive at a certain point, e.g. by fleeing quickly from the accident location.

Acknowledgment. We thank the Chair of Mechatronics of the University of Duisburg-Essen and in particular Dieter Schramm for providing the Ford C-Max, which was used to evaluate our approach.

References

1. Leitfaden "IT-Forensik": Version 1.0.1 (März 2011). Bundesamt für Sicherheit in der Informationstechnik - BSI (2011)
2. Abojaradeh, M., Jrew, B., Ababsah, H.: The effect of driver behavior mistakes on traffic safety. J. Civ. Environ. Res. **6**, 39–54 (2014)
3. Aidoo, E.N., Amoh-Gyimah, R., Ackaah, W.: The effect of road and environmental characteristics on pedestrian hit-and-run accidents in Ghana. Accid. Anal. Prev. **53**, 23–27 (2013)
4. Al-Kuwari, S., Wolthusen, S.D.: Probabilistic vehicular trace reconstruction based on RF-visual data fusion. In: De Decker, B., Schaumüller-Bichl, I. (eds.) CMS 2010. LNCS, vol. 6109, pp. 16–27. Springer, Heidelberg (2010). https://doi.org/10.1007/978-3-642-13241-4_3
5. Carfora, M.F., et al.: A "Pay-how-you-drive" car insurance approach through cluster analysis. Soft Comput. **23**(9), 2863–2875 (2019)
6. Carlson, C.R., Gerdes, J.C., Powell, J.D.: Practical position and yaw rate estimation with GPS and differential wheelspeeds. In: Proceedings of AVEC 2002 (2002)
7. Castignani, G., Derrmann, T., Frank, R., Engel, T.: Driver behavior profiling using smartphones: a low-cost platform for driver monitoring. IEEE Intell. Transp. Syst. Mag. **7**(1), 91–102 (2015)
8. Cebe, M., Erdin, E., Akkaya, K., Aksu, H., Uluagac, S.: Block4Forensic: an integrated lightweight blockchain framework for forensics applications of connected vehicles. IEEE Commun. Mag. **56**(10), 50–57 (2018)
9. Chen, W., Xiao, H., Wang, Q., Zhao, L., Zhu, M.: Integrated Vehicle Dynamics and Control. Wiley, Singapore (2016)
10. Council of the European Union, European Parliament: Regulation (EU) 2016/679 of the European Parliament and of the Council of 27 April 2016 on the protection of natural persons with regard to the processing of personal data and on the free movement of such data, and repealing Directive 95/46/EC (General Data Protection Regulation). OJ L 119, pp. 1–88 (May 2016)
11. Dewri, R., Annadata, P., Eltarjaman, W., Thurimella, R.: Inferring trip destinations from driving habits data. In: Proceedings of the 12th ACM Workshop on Workshop on Privacy in the Electronic Society, WPES 2013, pp. 267–272. ACM, New York (2013)
12. Eboli, L., Mazzulla, G., Pungillo, G.: Combining speed and acceleration to define car users' safe or unsafe driving behaviour. Transp. Res. Part C: Emerg. Technol. **68**, 113–125 (2016)
13. Gao, X., Firner, B., Sugrim, S., Kaiser-Pendergrast, V., Yang, Y., Lindqvist, J.: Elastic pathing: your speed is enough to track you. In: Proceedings of the 2014 ACM International Joint Conference on Pervasive and Ubiquitous Computing, UbiComp 2014, pp. 975–986. ACM, New York (2014)
14. Gazdag, A., Holczer, T., Buttyán, L., Szalay, Z.: Vehicular can traffic based microtracking for accident reconstruction. In: Jármai, K., Bolló, B. (eds.) VAE 2018. LNME, pp. 457–465. Springer, Cham (2018). https://doi.org/10.1007/978-3-319-75677-6_39
15. Hoppe, T., Kuhlmann, S., Kiltz, S., Dittmann, J.: IT-forensic automotive investigations on the example of route reconstruction on automotive system and communication data. In: Ortmeier, F., Daniel, P. (eds.) SAFECOMP 2012. LNCS, vol. 7612, pp. 125–136. Springer, Heidelberg (2012). https://doi.org/10.1007/978-3-642-33678-2_11

16. Le-Khac, N.A., Jacobs, D., Nijhoff, J., Bertens, K., Choo, K.K.R.: Smart vehicle forensics: challenges and case study. Future Gener. Comput. Syst. **109**, 500–510 (2018)

17. Li, Z., Pei, Q., Markwood, I., Liu, Y., Pan, M., Li, H.: Location privacy violation via GPS-agnostic smart phone car tracking. IEEE Trans. Veh. Technol. **67**, 5042–5053 (2018)

18. Mansor, H., Markantonakis, K., Akram, R.N., Mayes, K., Gurulian, I.: Log your car: the non-invasive vehicle forensics. In: 2016 IEEE Trustcom/BigDataSE/ISPA, pp. 974–982 (August 2016)

19. Matuschek, J.P.: Finding points within a distance of a latitude/longitude using bounding coordinates. http://janmatuschek.de/LatitudeLongitudeBounding Coordinates. Accessed 03 Apr 2020

20. Narain, S., Vo-Huu, T.D., Block, K., Noubir, G.: Inferring user routes and locations using zero-permission mobile sensors. In: 2016 IEEE Symposium on Security and Privacy (SP), pp. 397–413 (May 2016)

21. Nilsson, D.K., Larson, U.E.: Combining physical and digital evidence in vehicle environments. In: 2008 Third International Workshop on Systematic Approaches to Digital Forensic Engineering, pp. 10–14 (May 2008)

22. Paleti, R., Eluru, N., Bhat, C.R.: Examining the influence of aggressive driving behavior on driver injury severity in traffic crashes. Accid. Anal. Prev. **42**(6), 1839–1854 (2010)

23. Reif, K. (ed.): Bosch Autoelektrik und Autoelektronik. Vieweg+Teubner Verlag (2011). https://doi.org/10.1007/978-3-8348-9902-6

24. Sivasankaran, S.K., Balasubramanian, V.: Data mining based analysis of hit-and-run crashes in metropolitan city. In: Bagnara, S., Tartaglia, R., Albolino, S., Alexander, T., Fujita, Y. (eds.) IEA 2018. AISC, vol. 823, pp. 113–122. Springer, Cham (2019). https://doi.org/10.1007/978-3-319-96074-6_12

25. Uphoff, M., Wander, M., Weis, T., Waltereit, M.: SecureCloud: an encrypted, scalable storage for cloud forensics. In: 2018 IEEE TrustCom/BigDataSE, pp. 1934–1941 (August 2018)

26. Van Ly, M., Martin, S., Trivedi, M.M.: Driver classification and driving style recognition using inertial sensors. In: 2013 IEEE Intelligent Vehicles Symposium (IV), pp. 1040–1045 (June 2013)

27. Waltereit, M., Weis, T.: An approach to exonerate innocent suspects in hit-and-run accidents via route reconstruction. In: 2019 IEEE International Conference on Pervasive Computing and Communications Workshops (PerCom Workshops), pp. 447–448 (2019)

28. Waltereit, M., Uphoff, M., Weis, T.: Herleitung von Fahrtstrecken aus Distanz- und Kurvenbewegungsdaten. Mobilität in Zeiten der Veränderung, pp. 253–264. Springer, Wiesbaden (2019). https://doi.org/10.1007/978-3-658-26107-8_19

29. Waltereit, M., Uphoff, M., Weis, T.: Route derivation using distances and turn directions. In: Proceedings of the ACM Workshop on Automotive Cybersecurity, AutoSec 2019, pp. 35–40. ACM, New York (2019)

30. Waltereit, M., Zdankin, P., Matkovic, V., Uphoff, M., Weis, T.: Online driving behavior scoring using wheel speeds. In: Proceedings of the 6th International Conference on Vehicle Technology and Intelligent Transport Systems, VEHITS, vol. 1, pp. 417–424. INSTICC, SciTePress (2020)

31. Wei, X., Rizzoni, G.: Objective metrics of fuel economy, performance and driveability - a review. In: SAE Technical Paper. SAE International (March 2004)

An Intelligence Criminal Tracker for Industrial Espionage

Applying Digital Data Acquired Onsite to Target Criminals

Jieun Dokko[1,2(✉)], Michael Shin[1], and Soo Young Park[2]

[1] Texas Tech University, Lubbock, Texas 79409, USA
{Jieun.dokko, Michael.Shin}@ttu.edu,
maggie8482@gmail.com
[2] National Digital Forensic Center, Supreme Prosecutors' Office,
Seoul, South Korea
{dkje8482, hilda01}@spo.go.kr

Abstract. The investigation of industrial espionage basically requires significant levels of expertise and a full data recovery on an entire device. In practice, an investigator cannot conduct an in-depth examination of every device, thereby inevitably collecting all the devices seemingly relevant to the crime. Such excessive collection leads to not only legal concerns about the data privacy but also a massive examination backlog in a lab. To alleviate the challenge, a field triage model enabling an accurate data processing and acquisition is proposed.

Keywords: Digital forensic field triage · Industrial espionage · Real-time data acquisition · Data reduction · Crime specific analysis · Intelligence analysis

1 Introduction

The volume and variety of data in many devices is very challenging to onsite triage investigations. Moreover, data security and privacy concerns oblige investigators to scrutinize every device to only acquire files pertinent to the allegation [6]. To improve the accuracy and speed for the investigation, we propose a filed triage, typical for industrial espionage. It primarily aims to acquire the minimum amount of relevant data from a device by performing on low latency analysis with interesting data related to the crime, and secondly aims to develop a reliable profile by putting together the findings from data processing.

2 Related Works

The authors in [1] propose a digital forensic investigation and verification model for industrial espionage (DEIV-IE). The model defines twelve crime features derived from the investigative line of questioning, a set of evidence file groups being examined for the crime features, and the analysis techniques quite often used to solve the crime in a laboratory. It presents a method for mapping the features, file groups and techniques

S. Goel et al. (Eds.): ICDF2C 2020, LNICST 351, pp. 224–230, 2021.
https://doi.org/10.1007/978-3-030-68734-2_12

and effectively detecting evidence data typical for the crime. The authors in [2] propose "selective imaging" which provides selective acquisition by locating key files, data processing, reviewing findings, and acquiring relevant files while missing their sources, thereby lacking verifiability in some cases. The authors in [3] aim to locate relevant data with improvement in retrieval and correlation analysis in Child Sexual Abuse cases by using existing several NLP techniques and semantic web technologies. The authors in [4] propose the digital forensic framework (D4I) compatible with cyber-attacks by mapping windows artifact categorization of SANS to the seven steps of cyber-attacks in CKC model, although it needs manual determinations.

3 Intelligence Criminal Tracker (ICT)

The ICT is a crime-targeted triage model for industrial espionage. It aims to acquire relevant data (minimal acquisition) by adjusting data acquisition according to its prior data processing results. The processing focuses on discovery of criminals based on the eleven hypotheses about criminal patterns shown in Table 1 and the corresponding forensic techniques borrowed from [1]. With the data processing intelligence, it also generates an ordered list of potential criminals and alleged criminal activities by tracing back the origins of data of the activities.

Table 1. The crime specific hypotheses applied to the ICT

No	Hypothesis
H1	Criminal activities occurring from four months before a suspect's resignation
H2	A suspect using the computer and accessing target files recently
H3	A suspect using the Internet to communicate with an accomplice
H4	Stolen files being commonly MS doc, text, csv, pdf, graphic (over 10 KB), video, and XML in order, albeit being dependent on the business of a victim
H5	Stolen files being likely compressed, archived, and encrypted during exfiltration
H6	Communicating or file sharing with accomplices using email IM, cloud service
H7	Searching crime relating information just before or after the crime occurred
H8	The use of portable storage devices involved in data exfiltration
H9	Unusual, suspicious activities as compared to prior usage
H10	Alternative ways of exfiltration e.g., a MS doc converting to a JPG
H11	A company monitoring employees' activities e.g., data loss prevention (DLP)

4 Investigation Methodology

As shown in Fig. 1, the ICT locates key files of the crime based on the mapping between the predefined eleven hypotheses and corresponding interesting data. In data processing, it performs the four tasks of extracting, ranking, grouping, and profiling to examine identifiers of criminals. Then, it conducts evidence acquisition, and generates a final report. To achieve more accurate findings, we form a methodology for data processing depicted in Table 2. All the tasks use the adjacent date(s) of suspected employee(s) resignation as a default filtering option which was populated as common periods of these types of crime.

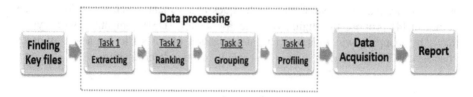

Fig. 1. Investigation methodology of the ICT

Table 2. A methodology for the data processing

No	Method in each step
1	Develop the hypotheses about criminal features of industrial espionages
2	Decide what actions a criminal might have taken based on the hypotheses
3	Identify the specific linked activities in a system to be analyzed
4	Examine the files to prove the alleged linked activities in a system from key files
5	Extract the identifiers creating or relating to the activities and count them
6	Rank the identifiers by its frequency of occurrences in the outputs of the ranking tests
7	Group the ranked identifiers to find a criminal who may use several identifiers
8	Create a profile describing the top ranked criminal-candidate's behaviors temporally by tracing back the data identifiers in the ranked group examined from

4.1 Extracting

The steps from No 1 to 5 in Table 2 depict how to extract alleged identifiers in the crime. The ICT examines files storing the identifiers possibly relating to potential criminal activities [8], and extracts the ten types of identifiers as follows: a) OS user account, b) user name registered in app installation, c) volume label and machine name, d) last modifier, e) account of email and instant message, f) login ID of web-site, g) password of email, instant message, and web-site, h) user name, friendly name or alias used for email, instant message, and web-site or services and, i) phone number linked to any account. Next the ICT decides the scope of potential stolen files and lists them for the ranking task. They are initially defined as the files recently created, accessed or modified, uploaded, downloaded, backed-up, copied and deleted by a user and can be updated.

4.2 Ranking

The ICT assesses a suspect-candidate rate and an accomplice-candidate rate on detected identifiers by the different measures. It sets the eight suspect testing conditions (SC#)

and three accomplice testing conditions (AC#) described in Table 3. The ranking is conducted separately under each condition in sequence.

Table 3. The test conditions for the ranking of criminal-candidates

No	Description of an identifier getting one score per each action under the condition
SC1	Recently or within the alleged crime time, using a file in the stolen file list
SC2	Using an encrypted file or a compressed file containing a stolen file in the list
SC3	Sending an email or IM attaching a file in H4 and H5, attaching a file in the list, having a clickable link in its contents, uploading a file in the list to a server
SC4	Searching Internet for info e.g., the crime, or a new job before or after the crime
SC5	Recently using an external media, additionally having a file in the list stored in it
SC6	Showing suspicious activities e.g., using an unusual account, URL, server, USB, unusual data backups, downloading, installing, running an anti-forensic app
SC7	Converting a file, screen capturing, recording, printing a file in the list
SC8	Having a behavior being monitored, leading to an alert notification
AC1	An correspondent account to an email or IM account detected as a potential suspect
AC2	Receiving an email or IM with an attachment(s) from an alleged local account, additionally the attachment falling in the list
AC3	Sharing a web service with a local account

Under one condition, an identifier accumulates one score whenever the identifier itself is returned as the output from the testing, and according to the score they achieved, all identifiers are ranked under the condition. As a final point, the ranks of identifiers achieved from all the conditions are summed, and prioritized by the sum from small to large sequentially, formulated as below.

$$Identifier.Condition1.RankNum = Rank.DescendingOrder\,(Count$$
$$(identifier1.ScoreOfoccurrence)\ldots Count\,(identifierN.ScoreOfoccurrence)) \tag{1}$$

$$Identifier.RankNum = Rank.AscendingOrder\,(Sum$$
$$(identifier1.allConditions.RankNum)\ldots Sum\,(identifierN.allConditions.RankNum)) \tag{2}$$

Upon the completion, the ICT creates a list of the identifiers achieving at least one score. The list contains the rank number of an identifier with the total scores, the frequency of the occurrence, and the associated sources of each occurrence detected as shown in Fig. 2. The file an identifier is extracted from, is associated to the identifier, so each identifier can be traceable by looking at the file. The source reference on the file is classified into two types: file attributes in the file system or a file header, and entry attributes in the records of Registry [5], Windows artifacts [7], email, IM and the like, and referred to respectively.

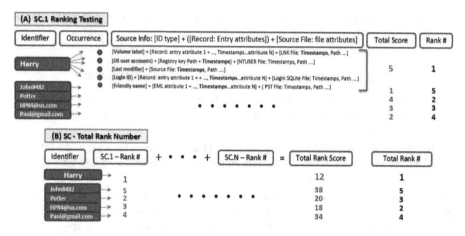

Fig. 2. (A) Ranking under a condition and, (B) Ranking under all conditions of the alleged identifiers

4.3   Grouping

The ICT works by grouping the ranked identifiers by three criteria: commonness, resemblance and connection, to find a criminal who may use several distinct identifiers. The rules for grouping are described below. Identifiers in the rules are not case-sensitive.

Commonness. Check if an identifier includes a white space. If yes, split the identifier by the white space. Next, from the beginning of it, divide an identifier or a segment split by a white space into 'letter string, 'number string, and 'the others'. Discard any segment that is less than three characters. If any segment is a substring of another segment, group the identifiers of each segment into one.

Resemblance. Check if the two identifiers contain the same characters the number of which is more than a half of the characters of them, except for the common components of identifiers like "@domain", or "country code". If yes, extract the same characters in the order from each identifier and determine if they are in the same order. If yes, group the identifiers into one. For instance, "h@rry" is added to the group of "harry" because the number of the same characters extracted in the order from "h@rry" and "harry" which is "hrry" is more than half of the characters of them both.

Connections. If various identifiers in multiple sources are created from a single activity, group them into one, except for common user accounts e.g., administrator, guest, and user. For instance, "Harry" from the Skype subfolder of NTUSER.DAT, and the Skype id of "potter8482@gmail.com" are grouped into one. In addition, if there are different types of paired personal identifiers in the same source, e.g., user ID and password for a website, classify each pair into each single group.

Identifiers in a group sorted above can be put into one of the existing groups by applying the aforementioned algorithms of the commonness and resemblance. Finally, the ICT lists the ranked groups of identifiers, and the formulation is as below.

$$Group A = [identifier1.GroupA,\ identifier3.GroupA\ldots identifierN.GroupA] \quad (3)$$

$$RankScore.GroupA = Sum\ (RankNum.identifier1.GroupA, \\ RankNum.identifier3.GroupA\ldots RankNum.identifierN.GroupA) \quad (4)$$

$$Groups.RankNum = Rank.AscendingOrder \\ (RankScore.GroupA,\ RankScore.GroupB\ldots RankScore.GroupN \quad (5)$$

4.4   Profiling

The ICT traces the activities gaining a score in ranking tests, of all identifiers belonging to the first ranked group and generates timelines describing the activities of the prime suspect and accomplice candidates. As shown in Fig. 3, the descriptive timeline is arranged with identifiers, and their source information as 'Linking time', 'Rank condition #', 'Identifier', 'ID Type', 'Activity', 'Entry attributes' and 'File attributes' in order. But each artifact has a different set of attributes like various timestamps, paths, and counts. The ICT classifies various attributes into several types based on the similarity between theirs roles, and decides time attributes comparable to one another for sorting. The 'Linking time' as a comparable timestamp, is decided on for the time when events observed in the records of artifacts occurred, thereby the timeline ordered by the linking time can reflect the order of a user's activities related to the events. The linking time order may not be exact, due to different mechanism timestamp updates between artifacts, but effectively close.

Linking Time	RC	Identifier	I.D. type	Activity	Entry attributes (name, path, time, count, other..)	File attributes: [type] name, path, time
3/23/2020 16:01	SC7	Harry	OS account	Rename a S-file	Price.xlsx, C:\Users\Harry\PR\..., Happy.jpg...	[Journal] $Usnjrnl, C:\$Extend\$Usnjrnl...
3/23/2020 17:04	SC3	HP84@sn.com	Outlook ID	Send an email	State (Send), subject, body, attachment (Happy.jpg)	[Email] HPmailbox.pst, path, timestamps, size,....
3/23/2020 18:19	SC1	Potter	Last modifier	Modify a file	.... Blank	[S-file] price.xlsx, C:\Users\Harry\PR\....
3/23/2020 18:20	SC2	Harry	OS account	Archive a file	.... Blank	[S-file] PR.zip, C:\Users\Harry\Desktop\PR.zip.....
3/23/2020 21:11	SC5	Potter	Volume label	Use an USB	Price.xlsx F:\project\PR.zip\Price.xlsx, timestamps...	[LNK] price.xlsx.lnk, path, timestamps, size,.........
3/24/2020 09:01	SC3	HP84@gmail.com	Google Drive	Use a G-drive	Price.jpg, C:\Users\Harry\Google drive\ Happy.jpg...	[IE] WebCacheVC1.dat, path, timestamps ...
3/24/2020 12:01	SC4	Harry	OS account	Internet search	http://...search%20disk%20wiping/....	[IE] WebCacheVC1.dat, path, timestamps ...
3/24/2020 16:23	SC5	HarryCD	Volume label	Burn a CD	Price.xlsx, E:\PR.zip\Price.x'sx, timestamps, HarryCD	[Jumplist] 1b4dd57f29cb1962, path times...
3/24/2020 23:01	SC6	Harry	OS account	Download a file	http://download.eraser.com/eraser.exe,...	[IE] WebCacheVC1.dat, path, timestamps...
3/24/2020 23:19	SC6	Harry	OS account	Execute a file	PROGRAM FILES\ERASER\ERASER.EXE..., 2...	[Prefech] ERASER.EXE-BE552234.pf, time...

Fig. 3. Illustration of the descriptive timeline to events regarding a user's certain activities

5   Data Acquisition and Reporting

After processing, the ICT generates a forensic image of the pertinent files referred to during data processing and a final report (detailing the outputs of each task, acquisition information, and a descriptive timeline of the criminal's activities).

6   Conclusions

The ICT is designed to acquire only relevant data with precision from devices on site, reflecting the investigative thinking process with digital forensic techniques through the four processing tasks. It helps improve the decision-making for taking relevant devices to a lab, so that pointless analysis in a lab can be avoided. The approach can be useful for deriving typical criminal behaviors in other crimes and suggesting a crime-based triage model as an adaptive strategy for criminal activities differed and complicated over time. Currently, the tool only works on industrial espionage related to insider threats, thus further studies are needed to focus on developing new hypotheses, criminal patterns for espionage related to cyber-attacks, and corresponding forensic techniques built in it.

References

1. Dokko, J., Shin, M.: A digital forensic investigation and verification model for industrial espionage. In: Breitinger, F., Baggili, I. (eds.) ICDF2C 2018. LNICST, vol. 259, pp. 128–146. Springer, Cham (2019). https://doi.org/10.1007/978-3-030-05487-8_7
2. Quick, D., Choo, K.-K.R.: Big forensic data reduction: digital forensic images and electronic evidence. Cluster Comput. 19(2), 723–740 (2016)
3. Amato, F., Castiglione, A., Cozzolino, G., Narducci, F.: A semantic-based methodology for digital forensics analysis. J. Parallel Distrib. Comput. 138, 172–177 (2020)
4. Dimitriadis, A., Ivezic, N., Kulvatunyou, B., Mavridis, I.: D4I-Digital forensics framework for reviewing and investigating cyber attacks. Array 5, 100015 (2020)
5. Roussev, V., Quates, C., Martell, R.: Real-time digital forensics and triage. Digit. Invest. 10 (2), 158–167 (2013)
6. Korea, S.: Criminal Procedure Act, December 2017. http://www.law.go.kr
7. Singh, B., Singh, U.: Program execution analysis in windows: a study of data sources, their format and comparison of forensic capability. Comput. Secur. 74, 94–114 (2018)
8. Rowe, N.C.: Finding and rating personal names on drives for forensic needs. In: Matoušek, P., Schmiedecker, M. (eds.) ICDF2C 2017. LNICST, vol. 216, pp. 49–63. Springer, Cham (2018). https://doi.org/10.1007/978-3-319-73697-6_4

Retracing the Flow of the Stream: Investigating Kodi Streaming Services

Samuel Todd Bromley[1], John Sheppard[2,3], Mark Scanlon[3],
and Nhien-An Le-Khac[3(✉)]

[1] Royal Canadian Mounted Police, Calgary, AB, Canada
stbromley@gmail.com
[2] Waterford Institute of Technology, Waterford, Ireland
jsheppard@wit.ie
[3] Forensics and Security Research Group, University College Dublin, Dublin, Ireland
{mark.scanlon,an.lekhac}@ucd.ie

Abstract. Kodi is of one of the world's largest open-source streaming platforms for viewing video content. Easily installed Kodi add-ons facilitate access to online pirated videos and streaming content by facilitating the user to search and view copyrighted videos with a basic level of technical knowledge. In some countries, there have been paid child sexual abuse organizations publishing/streaming child abuse material to an international paying clientele. Open source software used for viewing videos from the Internet, such as Kodi, is being exploited by criminals to conduct their activities. In this paper, we describe a new method to quickly locate Kodi artifacts and gather information for a successful prosecution. We also evaluate our approach on different platforms; Windows, Android and Linux. Our experiments show the file location, artifacts and a history of viewed content including their locations from the Internet. Our approach will serve as a resource to forensic investigators to examine Kodi or similar streaming platforms.

Keywords: Kodi · Video streaming · Log file analysis · Forensics

1 Introduction

The rise in illegal streaming services saw the September 2019 shutdown of the Xtream-codes IPTV service. This service was run from Greece and operated through servers in Italy, the Netherlands, France, Germany and Bulgaria. It has been reported that the operation involved over two hundred servers and one hundred and fifty PayPal accounts used by the criminals. It is estimated that there were 5,000 re-sellers of the service to over 50 million subscribers [2].

One of the most popular streaming applications is Kodi. Kodi is an open source media center developed by non-profit technology consortium XBMC. It is compatible with Windows, Linux, OSX and Android. It is used for streaming

© ICST Institute for Computer Sciences, Social Informatics and Telecommunications Engineering 2021
Published by Springer Nature Switzerland AG 2021. All Rights Reserved
S. Goel et al. (Eds.): ICDF2C 2020, LNICST 351, pp. 231–236, 2021.
https://doi.org/10.1007/978-3-030-68734-2_13

music and video from a user's private library on their own network or from public sources over the Internet. It is highly customizable through the use of add-ons. Add-ons, written by third-party developers, are easily installed through the Kodi interface by specifying a repository or "repo" URL to connect to.

In this paper, we aim to answer the following research questions: 1) How should a forensic investigation of Kodi be conducted? 2) What can be recovered from a Kodi system? 3) Where are the Kodi forensic artifacts located? The contribution of this work can be summarized as follows:

- Introducing a framework for conducting IPTV investigations based on Kodi.
- Detailing the Kodi ecosystem where evidence can be found for investigation of digital piracy or streaming of illegal content.

2   Related Work

IPTV Forensics - Users purchase IPTV subscriptions from commercial sellers, which grants access to the sellers' private server's live television feeds using IPTV set top boxes or software. Alternatively, users can download software to access less reliable free streams. The cybercrime aspect of IPTV and cloud investigations are examined in [11]. A case study was conducted, focusing on the cloud based development and distribution networks of the most popular Kodi Add-ons of 2018. Acestreams are an example IPTV service using streaming mesh networks [6]. Acestreams employ the use of BitTorrent technology to distribute live television, the principle being, that one user's upstream data pipe, is used to supply video content to another user's downstream pipe to view video [9].

Android Set Top Box Forensics - Android set top boxes are by far the most popular method of using Kodi. These low cost devices are sold online and are pre-configured to run Kodi and other streaming software. Android-based forensic investigations have primarily focused on mobile phone and tablet versions of Android and applications installed on these devices [10,12]. An overview of Android forensics and the Android file system can be found in [7] and [4]. These provide a framework for Kodi artifacts on the Android operating system. Given the growth of Android powered Smart TVs, Kodi can be expected to become more common place.

3   Findings and Analysis for Kodi on Windows

Media Library - The Kodi media library is a feature of Kodi that allows the cataloging and sharing of downloaded movies and videos that are located on the computer. This feature is used for personal video collections. The media library tracks which videos have been previously played, allowing the user to watch videos without repetition. This is an excellent source of information for investigators. All previously played videos are stored in the media library artifacts, including those from external media. This log of previously viewed media could inform the investigator of hidden portable media that may not have been seized.

Add-Ons - The true benefits of Kodi are the user created add-ons. User created Add-ons allow the user to view copyrighted material hosted for free on the Internet. These add-ons allow the Kodi user to easily navigate, search and stream copyrighted materials. The MPAA and the ACE sub group are actively attempting to have these add-ons eliminated. As soon as one is taken down legally another typically pops up.

Artifacts - The minimum number of pages detected within the databases is eight when no files have been indexed. The file metadata records have all been observed to start from page 8 of the database on-wards. In general, data within the pages are stored little-endian (least significant byte first), however big-endian values have been noted as existing within individual records.

The SQLite database "Addons27.db" is located in `C:\Users\X\AppData\ Roaming\Kodi\userdata\Database\Addons27.db`. This table contains artifacts related to add-ons including associated repositories. These add-on artifacts identify the name of installed add-ons, whether the add-on is still in use, installation date of the installed add-ons, date add-on updated, date add-on last used, and the origin of the add-on.

Repositories - Repository.exodusredux is the Repository that was manually installed in .zip form. "b6a50484-93a0-4afb-a01c-8d17e059feda" is the serial number of the original installer file. This indicates that the file was an original, non-updated, file loaded from the Kodi installer [5]. In the "Addons27.db" SQLite database there is a table called "repo". The 'repo' table provides the following artifacts; name of repository installed, checksum for installed repository, last update check date, and the version of the repository.

Kodi Log Files - Kodi activity is recorded in two log files. One is a current log file active since the latest reboot, the other is an inactive log file from the previous reboot. In the Windows environment, Kodi saves a log file in the following location: `C:\Users\X\AppData\ Roaming\Kodi\kodi.txt`. This file contains all actions by the user for that session. From a forensic point of view, interesting artifacts include: date and time Kodi last used, searches performed, user account, last viewed file, source of last viewed file, and when was Kodi last shut down. As Kodi overwrites its oldest log file on starting the application information will be lost if the investigator executes the Kodi program in a non-forensically sound manner.

4   Examining Kodi Installed on Android and Linux

Android - Our experiments were conducted using a Samsung S9+ Android mobile device running the Android 9.0 OS, as the test Android system to locate the Android artifacts. The artifacts and databases are located in similar locations in the Android operating system as they are in other operating systems.

In the Kodi userData folder (hidden by default), all the same database Kodi artifacts are present which can be logically extracted.

Linux (Ubuntu) - The Kodi file structure once again is the same. The default Kodi installation with that version of Ubuntu is Kodi version 15.2 (Isengard) in the hidden folder ".kodi". The folder and databases structure is identical with the minor difference that in this version of Kodi, the artifacts are called "MyVideos93.db" and "Addons19.db". The 2 numerical digits at the end of the database name are the result of the Kodi version. The information contained is identical. The database is stored ".kodi" folder. Although the SQLite database names are slightly different, the contents are the same.

Linux (OSMC) - The last device investigated was a Raspberry Pi 3 running Open Source Media Center (OSMC). OSMC is a dedicated Kodi Linux operating system. The SD card used was first sanitized and OSMC_TGT_rbp2_20180316 was installed through OSMC's qt_host_installer application. The Pi was configured for a wired network and debugging was enabled on the device. A selection video add-ons were again installed and experiments were conducted as before. Once this was completed, the SD card was removed from the Raspberry Pi and a raw image was created using the command-line tool, *dd*. The image was analyzed using Autopsy and FTK Imager for dual tool verification. The purpose of the analysis was to investigate the filesystem layout, the structure of the add-ons, the location of Kodi logs and the identification of Kodi artifacts.

5   Discussion

Kodi Home Folder - The Kodi directory is the most important directory of a Kodi investigation. This location contains the following directories:

- add-ons - a list of repository add-ons and video add-ons associated with the device under examination
- media - media files
- system - system customization, empty by default
- temp - log files
- userdata - databases, settings files and customization files

The add-ons folder contains a set of sub folders classed as repositories, video plugins, movie and TV metadata scrapers, language resources, and scripts. It also contains a packages folder that contains zipped versions of these files with timestamps of when they were downloaded.

Kodi Add-Ons - Investigation of these add-ons reveals a common core file structure comprising of .xml, python, .txt and image files. These add-on directories typically contain the following files and reveal the following information:

- The file *add-on.xml* comprises of several metadata fields that describe the add-on to the user and system. Other fields reference any required dependencies, credits and version information. It also includes the update URL.
- The file *add-on.py* is the Python code for that add-on.
- The *resources* sub directory stores add-on files that do not need to be stored in the root directory, such as software libraries, translations, and images.
- The file *License.txt* contains the text of the add-on's software license [8].

Kodi Userdata - The userdata folder contains the following folders:

- add-on data - contains configuration data for the add-ons installed in the .kodi/add-ons directory
- database - containing databases that are required for locating Music and Video Libraries and any downloaded or scraped music or video information
- keymaps - contains files for any customized keymapping
- library - custom libraries
- peripheral data
- playlists - where the playlists are stored
- thumbnails - cached thumbnails

Kodi Databases - The database files can be found in the userdata/Database location. The following databases are present in SQLite format. Different versions of Kodi use different numbers appended to the end of the SQLite databases. In each instance the number XX is determined by the current Kodi version in use.

- AddonsXX.db - Database file containing information on all Kodi add-ons
- ADSPXX.db-Database file containing information for Audio Digital Signal Processing add-ons
- EPGXX.db - Database file containing information on Electronic Programme Guide (EPG) for Live-TV
- MyMusicXX.db - Database file containing Music information
- MyVideosXX.db - Database file containing Movie, TV Show and Music Videos information
- Textures13.db - Database file containing information on all Kodi thumbnails, fanart and posters.
- TVXX.db - Database file containing information on Live-TV channels
- ViewModesXX.db - Database file containing information on the use and frequency of the Kodi device.

Kodi Logs - In the event of a Kodi machine being investigated, care should be taken around the Kodi logs. If the machine is switched off, the machine should first be imaged using appropriate controls. This will prevent the log from before the last reboot from being overwritten. This will inform an investigator with information such as when an add-on was installed on the device or recent activity that has occurred on the device.

6   Conclusion and Future Work

This paper has compared the Kodi filesystem, logs, add-ons, databases and other artifacts across a range of devices. It examined Kodi as a software application on a Windows 10 and Ubuntu machine, the Kodi Android app, Kodi as a stand-alone operating system, and OSMC. The primary sources where evidence could be collected were highlighted through the Kodi folder. The structure of the Kodi filesystem has been presented. Future work in this area requires the investigation of the relationships with these add-ons and the cyberlockers providing the illegal streams. In addition, much remains to be done with automated stream content analysis using computer vision to automatically detect illegal content [1,3]. As techniques are created to monetize such illicit services by cybercriminals, the need for the investigation of these machines will increase.

References

1. Anda, F., Le-Khac, N.A., Scanlon, M.: DeepUAge: improving underage age estimation accuracy to aid CSEM investigation. Forensic Sci. Int.: Digit. Invest. **32**, 300921 (2020)
2. Bouma, L.: Police Shutdown an Illegal IPTV service with 50 million subscribers, September 2019. https://www.cordcuttersnews.com/police-shutdown-an-illegal-iptv-service-with-50-million-subscribers/
3. Du, X., et al.: SoK: exploring the state of the art and the future potential of artificial intelligence in digital forensic investigation. In: Proceedings of the 15th International Conference on Availability, Reliability and Security. ACM (2020)
4. Faheem, M., Le-Khac, N.A., Kechadi, T.: Smartphone forensic analysis a case study for obtaining root access of an android samsung S3 device and analyse the image without an expensive commercial tool. J. Inf. Secur. **5**, 83–90 (2014)
5. Foundation, X.: addons/addon.h file reference, kodi documentation. https://codedocs.xyz/enen92/xbmc/addons_2_addon_8h.html
6. Hei, X., Liu, Y., Ross, K.W.: IPTV over P2P streaming networks: the mesh-pull approach. Commun. Mag. **46**(2), 86–92 (2008)
7. Hoog, A.: Android Forensics: Investigation, Analysis and Mobile Security for Google Android, 1st edn. Syngress Publishing (2011)
8. KodiWiki: Kodi addon structure (2019). https://kodi.wiki/view/Add-on_structure
9. Scanlon, M., Hannaway, A., Kechadi, M.T.: A week in the life of the most popular BitTorrent swarms. In: Proceedings of the 5th Annual Symposium on Information Assurance (ASIA 2010), Albany, New York, USA, pp. 32–36, June 2010
10. Sgaras, C., Kechadi, M.-T., Le-Khac, N.-A.: Forensics acquisition and analysis of instant messaging and VoIP applications. In: Garain, U., Shafait, F. (eds.) IWCF 2012/2014. LNCS, vol. 8915, pp. 188–199. Springer, Cham (2015). https://doi.org/10.1007/978-3-319-20125-2_16
11. Sheppard, J.: Cloud investigations of illegal IPTV networks. In: Proceedings of the 17th IEEE International Conference On Trust, Security And Privacy In Computing and Communications, pp. 1942–1947. IEEE, August 2018
12. Walnycky, D., Baggili, I., Marrington, A., Moore, J., Breitinger, F.: Network and device forensic analysis of android social-messaging applications. Digit. Invest. **14**(S1), S77–S84 (2015)

Cybersecurity Methodology
for Specialized Behavior Analysis

Edgar Padilla[1]($^{(\boxtimes)}$), Jaime C. Acosta[2], and Christopher D. Kiekintveld[1]

[1] The University of Texas at El Paso, El Paso, TX 79968, USA
e-padilla@live.com
[2] CCDC Army Research Laboratory, Adelphi, MD 20783, USA

Abstract. Analyzing attacker behavior and generating realistic models to accurately capture the realities of cybersecurity threats is a very challenging task for researchers. Psychological personality and profiling studies provide a broad understanding of personality traits, but lack a level of interactive immersion that enables observers to collect concrete cybersecurity-relevant behavioral data. Participant's intricate actions and interactions with real computer systems are seldom captured in any cybersecurity studies. Our work focuses on capturing human actions and decisions to provide an empirical basis for these types of models. We provide a practical methodology that helps bridge the gap between theory and practice by facilitating construction, experimentation, and data collection for repeatable and scalable human experimentation with realistic cybersecurity scenarios. While our methodology is platform agnostic, we describe state of the art technologies that may be used to satisfy the objectives of each of the stages of the methodology.

Keywords: Cybersecurity · Attacker profiling · Methodology

1 Introduction

Prevailing literature on cybersecurity behavioral analysis is limited to basic psychological profiles. Although there is an abundance of work related to behavioral analysis and personality profiling in psychology, these works mainly focus on profiling attackers using the results of surveys taken by non-technical participants [1]. Most of these studies originate from speculative actions and responses to questions. Participants are typically drawn from Amazon Mechanical Turk (AMT), in which the target population does not possess technical or cybersecurity training and qualifications [1–3]. The resulting datasets and models built from these studies fail to capture interactions of attackers and defenders with real systems and networks.

Presently, cybersecurity datasets that enable analysis and model generation are incomplete or unavailable. This is in part due to the sensitive nature of forensic data resulting in non-releasable information associated with real attacks [4].

© ICST Institute for Computer Sciences, Social Informatics and Telecommunications Engineering 2021
Published by Springer Nature Switzerland AG 2021. All Rights Reserved
S. Goel et al. (Eds.): ICDF2C 2020, LNICST 351, pp. 237–243, 2021.
https://doi.org/10.1007/978-3-030-68734-2_14

After compromise, organizations do not commonly publish details about incidents risking it could lead to loss of revenue [5]. If released, datasets are altered e.g., removed network packet payloads and anonymization. This may result in loss of valuable information for researchers [6]. Frequently these datasets do not contain ground truth such as tools and configurations employed. Furthermore, participants' technical proficiency, psychological characteristics, and demographic information is often not documented or made available.

Our approach combines solutions to the shortcomings presented in psychology and computer forensics when compiling experimental data. In summary, our work described here brings forth the following objectives:

1. Guidelines for valid and experimental datasets that are aimed at bridging the gap between technical experiments and psychological profiling by enabling the generation of an effective dataset.
2. A mechanism that incorporates elevating participants' technical skills, which can be expensive and difficult to recruit otherwise.
3. While the methodology is platform agnostic, we provide a set of state-of-the-art tools and frameworks that can be used to implement a system to meet the research objectives.

2   Related Work

An abundant number of psychological studies pursue to profile cybersecurity attackers based on high-level traits. These profiles include motivation, personality traits, and propensity to commit a crime among others. These studies are not technical in nature but directed towards technical participants [5,7]. Most models developed from these studies are built from answers to hypothetical questions in an attempt to characterize participants [1]. Nonetheless, hypothetical answers may not capture participant actions when interacting with real computer systems. Our methodology aims on capturing these key missing interactions.

In McClain et al., an experimental procedure is presented similar to our research method where participants are trained and raised to a proficiency level before conducting a technical experiment. These experiments generate datasets that capture detailed interactions between participants and computer systems including keystrokes, network traffic, and process trees [8]. Nonetheless, their approach does not scale well. A preliminary implementation of this methodology allows a large number of remote participants using a web browser. Similarly, Acosta et al. also developed a novel data collection system, ECEL, and platform for hosting exercises focused on penetration testing and other cybersecurity analyst tasks [9]. Our approach is similar to [8,10], however we refrain from educating participants with live instructors. This approach may lead to inconsistent teaching across the sample population.

3   Methodology Design

We developed a methodology that improves upon prevailing mechanisms for collecting human behavioral information such as AMT. Existing methods do not capture interactions between cybersecurity experts and information systems. We propose bridging this gap by targeting participants with minimal technical background. These participants are trained to fulfill the particular needs of an experiment. A well-tuned experimental setup and trained participants, we believe, can compensate for the need of experienced and expensive ones. This novel cybersecurity methodology consists of five stages: Questionnaires, Theoretical Education, Practical Education, Experimentation, and Model Creation/Validation (See Fig. 1).

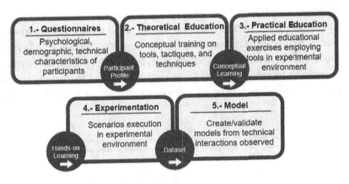

Fig. 1. Five-stage methodology for training, experimenting, and collecting technical cybersecurity data.

3.1   Questionnaires

A fundamental stage in our methodology is to collect participants' ground truth. With these questionnaires, researchers can inquire about psychological, demographic, and similar characteristics. This facilitates capturing participant inherent features to build robust participants' profiles [1]. This is not intended to inquire about any hypothetical actions an attacker or defender might carry out.

3.2   Theoretical Education

Education is a critical stage in our methodology. During this stage, researchers can recruit participants with basic cybersecurity knowledge and then train them on specific concepts, tasks, and tools employed during an experiment. Even though we work with novice participants, they can provide powerful insights into human behavior such as propensity towards certain actions. This involves their cognitive processes of selection across multiple alternatives including spontaneous actions and reactions [11]. Our methodology does not serve the purpose of gathering data from domain experts, but instead looks at human behavior such as decision making on scenarios with high technical complexity. We elevate the participants' skill level required for a technical study as opposed to simplifying an experiment and considerably diminishing its impact and relevance of its findings. This allows researchers to abstain from formulating assumptions where participants are asked hypothetical or abstract questions and consequently obtain hypothetical and high level answers that are later unrealistically mapped to higher complexities in real-world scenarios. Instead, we gather information from informed beginners connected to the cybersecurity domain such Computer Science students and IT professionals, and turn them into qualified participants.

3.3   Practical Education

Our methodology emphasizes an educational model where practical instruction is a cornerstone for learning cybersecurity. Practical education ought to be directed toward aiding participants to improve understanding of concepts and tools. Complementing integration of theoretical concepts and development of practical experience to reinforce learning in preparation for an experiment. This stage promotes practical teaching of cybersecurity at an operational level [12].

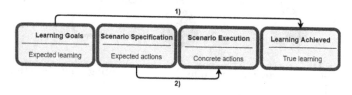

Fig. 2. Relationship between 1) theoretical and 2) practical learning effectiveness with respect to their anticipated outcomes.

We adapted Millar and Abrahams [10] stages of teaching and learning effectiveness for cybersecurity tasks and scenarios into four stages: Learning Goals, Scenario Specification, Scenario Execution, and Learning Achieved (See Fig. 2). The *Learning Goals* stage aims to clearly define the scope of the learning plan. Artifact design ought to be driven by type of expected audience, technical complexity, and experiment's goals. Interactive content, videos, and supplemental lesson notes can be options for effective learning artifacts. Next, the *Scenario Specification* stage defines the desirable tactics and techniques participants should follow during an experiment. Scenario configurations are meticulously defined and act as the authoritative source of content for the practical education section of this paper. Practical exercises must be designed to complement theoretical education to achieve a comprehensive grasp of concepts. *Scenario Execution* is concerned with the actual actions performed by participants during an experiment. These actions are the result of the quality of educational methods, particularly practical education leading up to this stage. Also, actions are influenced by the experiment's design and complexity, as well as the performance metrics known to participants. Finally, *Learning Achieved* is the credible learning attained. We measure practical education effectiveness contrasting intended activities (Scenario Specification) and actual activities performed by participants (Scenario Execution). Similarly, we compare Learning Goals with Learning Achieved to assess effectiveness of theoretical learning [13]. For our experimentation methodology, we are primarily interested in the relationship between Scenario Specification and Scenario Execution. Learning efforts are centered on short term goals addressing technical requirements allowing participants to competently progress through the experimental scenarios. Theoretical lessons and practical activities must be constantly evaluated employing small focus groups to measure their effectiveness where revisions must trigger an increase in learning performance [13].

3.4 Implementation and Experimentation

At present time, availability of valid, complete, and labeled cybersecurity data constraint research efforts. This unmet data demand raises the need for experimental frameworks and testbeds that accurately emulate cybersecurity scenarios. Nonetheless, sophisticated testbeds are complex and expensive to build. For this reason, during the scenario design time, deciding on implementation options such as emulation versus simulation is of the utmost importance. On the one hand, simulations only reproduce external visible behavior from a model. This is more efficient and inexpensive, but fails to capture low level interactions. On the other hand, emulation do reproduce low level interactions. Emulation increases system development and complexity, in addition to greater computational resources. Nonetheless, emulation allows a more comprehensive experimental settings where forensic level interactions can be recorded and analyzed. Sandia National Laboratory developed a cyber-physical testbed that combines simulation and emulation in an attempt to alleviate implementation costs [14].

Our methodology lays novel groundwork for an experimental framework. We propose tools for accessibility, portability, and scalability of a framework. Complex technical studies may require human subjects to be physically present for training and participation [10]. Similar to AMT, a web-based tool, we propose Apache Guacamole to increase accessibility to participants. Moreover, we propose the Common Open Research Emulator (CORE) as the center of our experimental environment. CORE facilitates the creation of network scenarios and supports connecting emulated networks seamlessly to real ones [15].

3.5 Model Creation/Validation

The final stage in this methodology is to create and validate new or existing models from the experimental data collected. The goal of decision-making models is to reasonably predict actions from cybersecurity actors. Performance metrics must be defined to evaluate the validity of models [16]. Models are not expected to always be correct, but as complexity increases, must yield reasonable answers to our questions. [17]. This stage is open to any research area, such as psychology and mathematics, to create and validate their own models.

4   Conclusions and Future Work

A central issue for developing realistic models is data availability revolving around the human aspects of decision-making in a valid cybersecurity context.

Existing data does not provide context for researchers to account for cybersecurity actor's intentions, technical skills, psychological traits, and demographics. Additionally, predominant research methods do not capture realistic interactions among cybersecurity actors. Similarly to the scarcity of valid data, cybersecurity professionals are difficult to find and expensive to recruit when conducting technical studies.

We have defined a five-stage methodology that works around inadequate sources of qualified cybersecurity participants. Our methodology elevates the skills of novice technical students and professionals to an acceptable proficiency turning them into more suitable participants. This leveling enables participants to complete realistic exercises using tools and techniques that mimic those used by field professionals.

Moreover, we recommend tools and software, laying the groundwork for an experimental framework and testbed. We believe it is well-suited for experiments that observe decision-making phenomena, not skill level, associated with humans in technical environments.

Future work involves validating this methodology with a larger pool of participants in a formal setting. We also plan to perform a study and collect associated data to determine what human factors influence decision making, at the reconnaissance phase, when scanning a computer network. An in-depth analysis will involve extrapolation of salient features and patterns in the data.

Acknowledgement. This research was sponsored by the U.S. Army Combat Capabilities Development Command Army Research Laboratory and was accomplished under Cooperative Agreement Number W911NF-13-2-0045 (ARL Cyber Security CRA). The views and conclusions contained in this document are those of the authors and should not be interpreted as representing the official policies, either expressed or implied, of the Combat Capabilities Development Command Army Research Laboratory or the U.S. Government. The U.S. Government is authorized to reproduce and distribute reprints for Government purposes notwithstanding any copyright notation here on.

References

1. Gaia, J., et al.: Psychological profiling of hacking potential. In: Proceedings of the 53rd Hawaii International Conference on System Sciences (2020)
2. Basak, A., et al.: An initial study of targeted personality models in the FlipIt game. In: Bushnell, L., Poovendran, R., Başar, T. (eds.) GameSec 2018. LNCS, vol. 11199, pp. 623–636. Springer, Cham (2018). https://doi.org/10.1007/978-3-030-01554-1_36
3. Gutierrez, M., et al.: Evaluating Models of Human Behavior in an Adversarial Multi-Armed Bandit Problem (2019)
4. Abbott, R.G., et al.: Log analysis of cyber security training exercises. Proc. Manufact. **3**, 5088–5094 (2015)

5. Crossler, R.E., et al.: Future directions for behavioral information security research. Comput. Secur. **32**, 90–101 (2013)
6. Shiravi, A., et al.: Toward developing a systematic approach to generate benchmark datasets for intrusion detection. Comput. Secur. **31**(3), 357–374 (2012)
7. Seebruck, R.: A typology of hackers: classifying cyber malfeasance using a weighted arc circumplex model. Digit. Invest. **14**, 36–45 (2015)
8. McClain, J., et al.: Human performance factors in cyber security forensic analysis. Proc. Manufact. **3**, 5301–5307 (2015)
9. Acosta, J.C., et al.: A platform for evaluator-centric cybersecurity training and data acquisition. In: MILCOM 2017–2017 IEEE Military Communications Conference (MILCOM). IEEE (2017)
10. Abrahams, I., Millar, R.: Does practical work really work? a study of the effectiveness of practical work as a teaching and learning method in school science. Int. J. Sci. Educ. **30**(14), 1945–1969 (2008)
11. Karat, J., Dayton, T.: Practical education for improving software usability. In: Proceedings of the SIGCHI Conference on Human Factors in Computing Systems (1995)
12. Wang, H., et al.: Construction of practical education system for innovative applied talents cultivation under the industry-education integration. In: Proceedings of the 5th International Conference on Frontiers of Educational Technologies (2019)
13. Millar, R., Abrahams, I.: Practical work: making it more effective. School Sci. Rev. **91**(334), 59–64 (2009)
14. Hahn, A., et al.: Cyber-physical security testbeds: architecture, application, and evaluation for smart grid. IEEE Trans. Smart Grid **4**(2), 847–855 (2013)
15. Networks and Communication Systems Branch. Common Open Research Emulator (CORE) — Networks and Communication Systems Branch. https://www.nrl.navy.mil/itd/ncs/products/core. Accessed 15 April 2020
16. Law, A.M.: How to build valid and credible simulation models. In: 2008 Winter Simulation Conference. IEEE (2008)
17. Sargent, R.G.: Verification and validation of simulation models. In: Proceedings of the 2010 Winter Simulation Conference. IEEE (2010)

Neural Representation Learning Based Binary Code Authorship Attribution

Zhongmin Wang, Zhen Feng, and Zhenzhou Tian[(✉)]

Xi'an University of Posts and Telecommunications, Xi'an, China
{zmwang,tianzhenzhou}@xupt.edu.cn

Abstract. Authorship attribution on binary code is of great value in applications such as malware analysis, software forensics, and code theft detection. Inspired by the recent great successes of neural network and representation learning in various program analysis tasks, this study proposes NMPI to achieve fine-grained program authorship attribution by analyzing the binary codes of individual functions from the perspective of sequence and structural. To evaluate the NMPI, the study constructs a large dataset consisting of 268796 functions collected from Google CodeJam. The extensive experimental evaluation shows that NMPI can achieve 91% accuracy for the function-level binary code authorship attribution task.

Keywords: Authorship attribution · Binary code · Neural network · Representation learning

1 Introduction

The authorship attribution has extracted a set of features from the code to represent the programmer's code style to identify the anonymous programmer. In recent years, relatively few works have been conducted on authorship attribution, which mainly falls into two categories: authorship attribution on source code [1, 2, 6] and authorship attribution on binary code [4]. The former is often difficult to obtain source code in actual situations. The latter, the accuracy of these methods, much depends on the quality of manually-crafted feature extraction strategies. In this paper, we attempt to adopt some of the most popular representation learning algorithms to achieve fast and accurate fine-grained programmer identification on function level.

Supported by National Natural Science Foundation of China (61702414), the Natural Science Basic Research Program of Shaanxi (2018JQ6078), the Science and Technology of Xi'an (2019218114GXRC017CG018-GXYD17. 16) and the International Science and Technology Cooperation Program of the Science and Technology Department of Shaanxi Province, China (Grant No. 2019KW-008) and Science and Technology Project in Shaanxi Province of China (Program No. 2019ZDLGY07-08.).

S. Goel et al. (Eds.): ICDF2C 2020, LNICST 351, pp. 244–249, 2021.
https://doi.org/10.1007/978-3-030-68734-2_15

Our contributions are summarized as follows:

- We propose to reveal fine-grained programmer code style details for individual functions by designing a lightweight function abstraction strategy and adapting typical sequence-oriented and structure-oriented model NMPI (**N**eural **M**odeling based **P**rogrammer **I**dentification).
- We use clustering to treat programmer with similar coding styles as a class, which alleviates the impact on results when there are too many programmer.
- We evaluated NMPI performance of revealing the programmers on a large dataset consisted of 268796 unique functions that we constructed via Google Code Jam. The experimental results show that the recognition rate of NMPI for 50 programmers is over 91%.

The rest of our work is structured as follows. Section 2 describes the model. Section 3 reports the experimental results. Section 4 concludes the paper.

2 The Approach

Our approach overall architecture is as follows (See Fig. 1). After disassembling the binary code to extract the function information, it is sent to our model NMPI to identify the programmers.

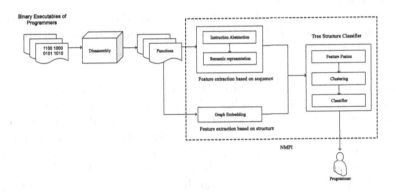

Fig. 1. The figure shows the overall framework for identifying programmer.

2.1 Feature Extraction Based on Structure

Deepwalk [7] is the most common graph embedding algorithm. We will use Deepwalk to extract the structure information of the binary code (See Fig. 2). Convert the control flow graph of function to a directed graph $G = (B, E)$. Get multiple paths by random walking. One of the paths is expressed as $path = \{B_1, B_3, B_7, B_9, ..., B_L\}$. Treat this obtained path use word2vec to learn, and get the structural representation vector VB_i^{T} of the basic block. The basic block node vector under each function is passed through the average pooling layer to obtain the structure-based feature V_f^T of the function f.

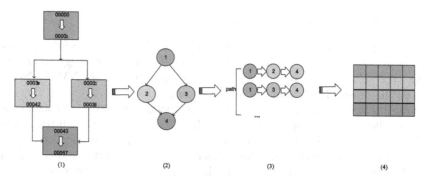

Fig. 2. The figure shows the extract structure features of binary code using Deepwalk.

2.2   Feature Extraction Based on Sequence

Instruction Abstraction. Firstly, we need to represent a function as $f = \{B_1, B_2, B_3, ..., B_n\}$, where n denotes the number of basic blocks within the function. We formulated the following rules for instruction abstraction. Firstly, the mnemonics remain unchanged. Secondly, all registers in the operands remain unchanged. Thirdly, all base memory addresses in the operands are substituted with the symbol MEM. Finally, all immediate values in the operands are substituted the symbol IMM.

As an example, with the above abstraction rules, the instruction "*add eax*, 6" will become "*add eax, IMM*", the instruction *mov ebx*, $[0 \times 3435422]$ will become "*mov ebx, MEM*".

Semantic Representation. Given a set of abstracted assembly instruction sequences, it is promising to utilize skip-gram [5] to learn the embedding for each instruction. LSTM [3] is known to learn the sequential dependency. In this work, we employ Long Short-term Memory (LSTM) to address the vanishing and exploding gradient issue (See Fig. 3). Each instruction in the input sequence embedded in vector space. Afterwards, the model reads the input instruction sequence through LSTM units to obtain the basic block vector $VB_i^S = O(H(i - 1) \times ins_i)$. Finally, each basic block node vector under the function sends a pooled average layer to obtain the function's sequence-based features.

2.3   Tree Structure Classifier

Tree structure classifier framework is divided into three parts (See Fig. 4).

Feature Fusion. We obtain the sequence-based and structure-based features of the function through the above two feature extraction methods. In order to consider the programmer's coding style from multiple perspectives, we fuse the two features. For example, a function extracts sequence-based features as V_f^S , structure-based features as V_f^T. We get the feature expression of the function $V_f = V_f^S \oplus V_f^T$ through feature fusion. The dimension of V_f depends on the dimension of V_f^S and V_f^T. Finally, the sequence V_f^S and structural features V_f^T of the function V_f are included.

Clustering. Firstly, we use $L_a = \{V_{f1}, V_{f2}, V_{f3}, ..., V_{fn}\}$ to represent all the feature vectors of a label a in the training set. These vectors form a matrix $R^{n \times k}$, where n is the number of functions under label a in the training set. Through average pooling layer get the matrix $V_a^{1 \times k}$ into a representative vector label a.

Secondly, we use K-means to cluster the representative vectors. The number of clusters is set to 2 categories, and the reason will be discussed in Section IV. Construct two classifiers based on A and B categories. When we input the code snippet, we first determine which category it belongs to, and then input it into the classifier under the corresponding category for classification. This avoids adverse effects on the results when there are too many labels.

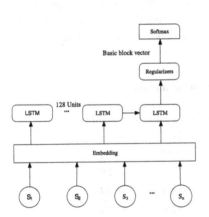

Fig. 3. LSTM model structure

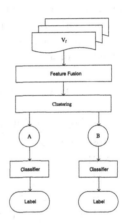

Fig. 4. Overview of tree structure classifier framework implementation

3   Experimental Evaluation

3.1   Dataset

To evaluate the performance of NMPI, we follow the google code jam used in previous authorship attribution work as the data set, collect C++ code written by 191 programmers from Google Code Jam, it consists of 13112 programs and 268796 functions.

3.2 Evaluation

The Results of NMPI's Use of Different Classifiers to Authorship Attribution. We use DNN, SVM, and Random forest for comparison experiments, and the results are shown in Table 1. We observe that DNN has the highest accuracy. The reason for the DNN network can adjust its structure according to the task and perform automatic learning.

Table 1. Experimental result.

Classifier	Top-1	Top-5	Precision	Recall
DNN	91.8%	96%	91.3%	91.6%
SVM	87.9%	94.3%	87.1%	87.3%
Random forest	84.5%	92.3%	84.4%	84.6%

Comparision with Other Programmer Identification Techniques. Rosenblum et al. [8] achieved 70% accuracy among 50 programmers and 51% accuracy among 191 programmers. We compare the results of NMPI programmer identification with Rosenblum as in Table 2. The result showing that we have improved accuracy.

Table 2. Comparison with existing methods.

The Approach	Number of Programmer	Accuracy	Classifier
Rosenblum [8]	50	70%	SVM
NMPI	50	86%	SVM
NMPI	50	91%	DNN
Rosenblum [8]	191	51%	SVM
NMPI	191	87%	DNN

Determination of the Number of Clusters. We set the number of clusters to 2, 3, 4, and 5. The results are shown in Fig. 5. It can be seen that when the number of classifiers is two, the classification effect is the best.

Classification Results for Different Features and Determination of Sample Size. We respectively used independent features for classification and combined features for classification. The result is shown in Fig. 6. The results show that our fusion feature classification results are much higher than the individual feature classification results. Then, we explore the relationship between sample size and accuracy, as in Fig. 6. We can find that when the sample size is 50, the accuracy rate is close to 90%.

Tree Structure Classifier Vs Simple Classifier. We set up two classifiers, one is a tree structure classifier, and the other is a simple classifier. We compare the accuracy of the two classifiers to verify our opinion, as in Fig. 7. The results show that when we use the tree structure classifier, as the number of programmers increases, the accuracy rate decreases slowly, improving the accuracy rate of 5% under the same number of programmers.

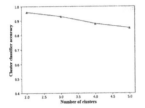 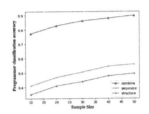 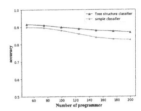

Fig. 5. Number of clusters   **Fig. 6.** Sample size and feature type   **Fig. 7.** Comparative analysis on accuracy

4   Conclusion

In this paper, we designed a model NMPI, extract features based on sequence and structure, and use SVM, DNN, Random Forest to classify. We compare the accuracy of classification of single features and classification of combined features. Observed the relationship between the number of samples per label and accuracy. Our experiment prove that DNN as classifier can better capture the characteristics of the author.

References

1. Burrows, S., Uitdenbogerd, A.L., Turpin, A.: Application of information retrieval techniques for source code authorship attribution. In: Zhou, X., Yokota, H., Deng, K., Liu, Q. (eds.) DASFAA 2009. LNCS, vol. 5463, pp. 699–713. Springer, Heidelberg (2009). https://doi.org/10.1007/978-3-642-00887-0_61
2. Burrows, S., Uitdenbogerd, A.L., Turpin, A.: Comparing techniques for authorship attribution of source code. Softw. Pract. Experience **44**(1), 1–32 (2014)
3. Hochreiter, S., Schmidhuber, J.: Long short-term memory. Neural Comput. **9**(8), 1735–1780 (1997)
4. Meng, X., Miller, B.P.: Binary code multi-author identification in multi-toolchain scenarios (2018)
5. Mikolov, T., Chen, K., Corrado, G.S., Dean, J.: Efficient estimation of word representations in vector space (2013)
6. Pellin, B.N.: Using classification techniques to determine source code authorship. Department of Computer Science, University of Wisconsin, White Paper (2000)
7. Perozzi, B., Alrfou, R., Skiena, S.: Deepwalk: online learning of social representations. In: Proceedings of the 20th ACM SIGKDD International Conference on Knowledge Discovery and Data Mining, pp. 701–710 (2014)
8. Rosenblum, N., Zhu, X., Miller, B.P.: Who wrote this code? identifying the authors of program binaries. In: Atluri, V., Diaz, C. (eds.) ESORICS 2011. LNCS, vol. 6879, pp. 172–189. Springer, Heidelberg (2011). https://doi.org/10.1007/978-3-642-23822-2_10

Author Index

Printed in the United States
By Bookmasters